THE PRICE OF GOD'S MIRACLE WORKING POWER

A. A. ALLEN

CONTENTS

FOREWORD i
THE PRICE OF GOD'S MIRACLE WORKING POWER 1
"THE DISCIPLE IS NOT ABOVE HIS MASTER, NOR THE SERVANT ABOVE HIS LORD" 21
"THE DISCIPLE IS NOT ABOVE HIS MASTER: BUT EVERYONE THAT IS PERFECT SHALL BE AS HIS MASTER" 29
"BE YE THEREFORE PERFECT, EVEN AS YOUR FATHER IN HEAVEN IS PERFECT" 42
CHRIST OUR EXAMPLE 59
SELF DENIAL 67
THE CROSS 78
"I MUST DECREASE" (John 3:30) 84
"HE MUST INCREASE" (John 3:30). 93
IDLE WORDS AND FOOLISH TALKING 98
PRESENT YOUR BODY 108
A PARTAKER OF HIS DIVINE NATURE 113
PERSONAL THINGS 118
DEATH CERTIFICATE 132
PROPHECY FROM THE 1950's 133

FOREWORD

According to his death certificate Evangelist Asa Alonzo Allen died from acute alcoholism. This would cause many to banish him from Christian memory and forget all the good and mighty works he performed in the Name of Jesus. Is alcoholism a sin? Yes it is. But don't discount what he accomplished just because he had a blemished end. Not everyone mentioned in the Hall of Faith in Hebrews 11 was perfect and spotless. They were humans just as you and I with issues and struggles. Let's not forget the many lives changed and families touched by the ministry of this mighty man of God.

All have sinned and come short of the Glory of God but not all have allowed themselves to be used so mightily of God as Evangelist A. A. Allen.

In addition to being a miracle worker AA Allen was also prophetic and a prophecy he gave in the 1950's is included that may have some relevance to the 9/11 attack on the United States.

Chapter One
THE PRICE OF GOD'S MIRACLE WORKING POWER

How long had I been here in this closet? Days or just hours? Surely it seemed days since at my own request I had heard my wife lock that closet door from the outside! What would she think about me shutting myself away for so long? Had it really been days or just hours? Was I really getting anywhere with God? Would God answer? Would God satisfy that hunger of my soul or would I have to admit defeat again as so often I had done? No! I'd stay right here on my knees until God answered, or I would die in the attempt! Hadn't God's word said, "They that wait upon the Lord shall renew their strength, they shall mount up-up-UP-with wings-with wings as eagles; they shall run and not be weary; they shall ---."

Had my wife opened the door? No, it was still closed! But the light, where was the light coming from? It was then that I began to realize that the light that was filling my prayer closet was God's glory! It wasn't the closet door that had opened, but rather the door of heaven instead!

The presence of God was so real and powerful that I felt I would die right there on my knees. It seemed that if God came any closer, I could not stand it! Yet I wanted it and was determined to have it. Little wonder that Paul under like circumstance, "fell to the earth". Acts 9:4. No wonder John, "fell at his feet as dead". Rev. 1:17.

Was this the answer? Was God going to speak to me? Would God at last, after these many years, satisfy my longing heart? I seemed to lose consciousness of everything but the mighty presence of God. I trembled, I tried to see Him and then was afraid that I would, for suddenly I realized that should I see Him, I would die. Just His glorious presence was enough!

Then like a whirlwind, I heard His voice. It was God! He was speaking to me! This was the glorious answer that I had sought so diligently and for which I had waited so long. Yes, this was what I had been waiting for since my conversion at the age of twenty-three. Yes, this was what my longing soul had cried for ever since God called me to the ministry.

That call to the ministry had come with such force and was so definite that nothing could ever make me doubt it. From the time of my conversion God had made it so real to me even though my past life had not been spent in such a way as to provide any preparation for this work.

From the time of my conversion, I realized my need of much study if ever I were to fulfill the call of God upon my life. Therefore, I spent many hours reading the Bible, and seeking to understand its message and meaning. To my simple untaught soul, God seemed to mean exactly what he said -- and seemed to say it directly to me through His Word -- "As ye go, preach, saying, The kingdom of heaven is at hand. HEAL THE SICK, cleanse the lepers, raise the dead, cast out devils: freely ye have received, freely give." Matt. 10:7. All this seemed included in a call to the ministry, yet I DID NOT SEE IT BEING DONE! I was myself powerless to carry out these commands of Christ. Yet I knew that it COULD BE DONE, for Christ would not give a command which could not be carried out!

Before my conversion, I knew so little about God and his word, that I could not even quote John 3:16, nor name the four gospels. In the Methodist church where I was converted and of which I became a member, I was not taught to expect to be baptized with the Holy Ghost as the first disciples were on the day of Pentecost, nor to expect the signs mentioned in Mark 16:17,18 to follow me as a believer in the Lord. I was taught to believe on the Lord Jesus

Christ for salvation, and was gloriously saved, and set free from condemnation for sin. Then as I searched the Scriptures, asking God to lead me to those readings from which I would receive the greatest benefit, the Lord began to reveal to me the truths of the baptism of the Holy Ghost, the signs following, the gifts of the spirit, and the supernatural things of God.

It was not long until God led me into a Pentecostal church, where I began to see in a small measure the blessings of God, and a few of the manifestations of the Spirit. It was in these meetings that I became convinced that I needed the Baptism with the Spirit, and there I began to pray and earnestly seek God for that experience.

Thirty days after my conversion, I was gloriously filled with the Holy Ghost, in an Assembly of God camp meeting in Miami, Oklahoma, speaking in other tongues as the Spirit gave utterance.

I had read, "Ye shall receive power after that the Holy Ghost is come upon you." Acts 1:8. I fully expected that with the infilling of the Holy Ghost, I would immediately have power to heal the sick, and to perform miracles. It did not take me long to realize that more was required than the baptism with the Holy Ghost, in order to consistently see these results. The baptism with the Spirit provides access to this power, but the gifts of the Spirit provide the channels through which this power operates. I began immediately to pray and seek the gifts of the Spirit. I felt I must have power to heal the sick, for I knew that God never called anyone to preach the Gospel without commissioning him also to heal the sick.

The power of the Holy Ghost may be readily likened to the power of electricity. When one is filled with the Spirit, it is as though he has had his house wired, and established connection with the "power house". Many people use electricity for years just to provide light! They never take advantage of the great possibilities that are available through using the appliances which electricity will operate. The gifts of the Spirit may be likened to the appliances. As new gifts are added more work can be done, with greater ease. The power has not changed, but it is made more effective. God never intended to STOP when he had filled his people with the Spirit. This is just the beginning. "Covet earnestly the best gifts." I Cor. 12:31. This, I found, is the path to greater accomplishment for God.

Two years after my conversion, I was happily married, and began my ministry.

For more than a year, my wife and I continued preaching this glorious gospel of salvation, the baptism with the Spirit, the second coming of

Christ, and DIVINE HEALING. In every revival meeting, I always planned at least two nights in each week to be set aside for preaching divine healing, and prayer for the sick. During this time, we saw a large number of miraculous healings, for God honored the preaching of His word. But I knew that God's plan included greater things for me, and I believed that there would be a time in the future when they would be a reality in my life.

Many times, my wife and I would search the scriptures together, becoming more convinced as we did so that God's promises concerning the signs following, the gifts of the Spirit, healings, and miracles were meant for us, today. It was also plain to see that we did not possess that power in the fullness that God had promised. We knew there must be a scriptural reason why we were so lacking in power. Since God cannot lie, the fault had to be WITHIN OURSELVES!

It was while Pastoring my first church, an Assembly of God church in Colorado, that I definitely made up my mind that I MUST hear from heaven, and know the reason that my ministry was not confirmed by signs and wonders.

I felt sure that if I would fast and pray, God would in some way speak to me, and reveal to me what stood between me and the miracle-working power of God in my ministry. I was so hungry for the power of God in my own life that I felt I could not stand in my pulpit, nor even preach again, until I had heard from God, and told my wife that this was my plan.

It was then that I had the greatest battle of my life. Satan was determined that I should NOT fast and pray until God answered. Many times he whipped me or tricked me out of that prayer closet. Satan knew that if I ever actually contacted God, there would be much damage to his kingdom, and he meant to do all in his power to hinder me from making that contact.

Day after day, I went into the prayer closet, determined to stay until God had spoke to me. Again and again, I came out without the answer.

Again and again my wife would say to me, "I thought you said this was the time you were going to stay until you got the answer." Then she would smile in her own sweet way, remembering that "the spirit indeed is willing, BUT THE FLESH IS WEAK!"

Again and again I answered her, "Honey, I really meant to pray it through this time, but --!" It seemed there was always a reason why I couldn't stay in that closet until the answer came. I always justified myself by saying I would pray it through tomorrow. Things would be more favorable then.

The Lord encouraged my heard by calling to my attention how Daniel held on in fasting and prayer, and wrested the answer from the hands of Satan, although it took three weeks to do so. (See Daniel 10:1 and 12)

The next day found me on my knees in the closet again. I had told my wife I would never come out until I heard from God. I REALLY THOUGHT I MEANT IT.

But a few hours later, when I began to smell the odor of food that my wife was preparing for herself and our small son, I was soon out of the closet and in the kitchen, inquiring, "What smells so delicious, dear?"

A few moments later, while I was at the table, God spoke to my heart. I had only taken one bite of food, and I stopped. God had spoken to me. I knew that until I wanted to hear from God MORE THAN ANYTHING ELSE IN THE WORLD, more than food, more than the gratification of the flesh, GOD WOULD NEVER GIVE ME THE ANSWER TO THE QUESTION THAT WAS IN MY HEART!

I arose quickly from the table, and said to my wife, "Honey, I mean business with God this time! I'm going back into that closet, and I want you to lock me inside. I am going to stay there until I hear from God."

"Oh," she replied, "you'll be knocking for me to open the door in an hour or so." She knew that so many times I had said THIS was the time I would stay until I had the answer, she was beginning to wonder if I really could subdue the flesh long enough to defeat the devil. Nevertheless, I heard her lock the door from the outside. Before she left, she said, "I'll let you out any time you knock."

I answered, "I'll not knock until I have the answer that I have wanted so long." At last I had definitely made up my mind to stay there till I heard from God, no matter what the cost!

Hour after hour, I battled with the devil and the flesh in that closet! Many were the times I almost gave up. It seemed to me that days were slipping by, and my progress was so slow! Many times I was tempted to give it all up, and try to be satisfied without the answer -- to go on just as I had been doing. But deep in my soul I knew I could never be satisfied to do that. I had tried it, and found that it was not enough.

No! I would stay right here on my knees until God answered, or I would die in the attempt!

Then the glory of God began to fill the closet. I thought for a moment that my wife had opened the door, as the closet door began to grow light. But my wife had not opened the door of the closet -- JESUS HAD OPENED THE DOOR OF HEAVEN, and the closet was flooded with light, the light of the glory of God!

I do not know how long I had stayed in the closet before this happened, but it doesn't matter. I do not care to know. I only know I prayed UNTIL!

The presence of God was so real, so wonderful, and so powerful that I felt I would die right there on my knees. It seemed that if God came any closer, I could not stand it! Yet I wanted it, and was determined to have it.

Was this my answer? Was God going to speak to me? Would God, at last, after these many years, satisfy my longing heart? How long had I been here? I didn't know! I seemed to lose consciousness of everything but the mighty presence of God. I tried to see Him, and then was afraid that I would, for suddenly I realized that should I seem Him, I would die. (Exodus 33:20.) Just His glorious presence was enough!

If only He would speak to me now! If He would just answer my one question, "Lord, why can't I heal the sick? Why can't I work miracles in Your name? Why do signs not follow my ministry as they did that of Peter, John and Paul?"

Then like a whirlwind, I heard His voice! It was God! He was speaking to me! This was the glorious answer for which I had waited so long!

In His presence I felt like one of the small pebbles at the foot of the towering Rockies. I felt I was unworthy even to hear His voice. But He wasn't speaking to me because I was worthy. He was speaking to me because I was needy. Centuries ago, He had promised to supply that need. This was the fulfillment of that promise.

It seemed that faster than any human could possibly speak faster than I could follow mentally, God was talking to me. My heart cried out, "Speak a little more slowly. I want to remember it all!"

It seemed God was speaking to me so fast, and of so many things I could never remember it all. Yet I knew I could never forget! God was giving me a list of the things which stood between me and the power of God. After each new requirement was added to the list in my mind, there followed a brief explanation, or sermonette, explaining that requirement and its importance.

Some of the things God spoke to me sounded like scriptures. I knew some of them were, but those first three -- could they be from the Bible?

If I had known there were so many things to remember, I would have brought a pencil and paper! I hadn't expected that God would speak in such a definite way, and give me such a long list. I had never dreamed that I was falling so far short of the glory of God. I hadn't realized there were so many things in my life that generated doubt and hindered my faith.

While God continued to speak to me, I began to feel in my pockets for a pencil. At last I located a short one, but the lead was broken. Quickly I sharpened it with my teeth. I searched for a piece of paper. I couldn't find any. Suddenly I remembered the cardboard box filled with winter clothes which I was using for an altar. I would write on the box.

Now I was ready!

I asked the Lord to please start all over again at the beginning, and let me write the things down one at a time -- to speak slowly enough so that I could get it all on paper.

Once more God started at the first, and spoke to me one after another the many things He had already mentioned. As God spoke to me, I wrote them down.

When the last requirement was written down on the list, God spoke once again, and said, "This is the answer. When you have placed on the altar of consecration and obedience the last thing on your list, YE SHALL NOT ONLY HEAL THE SICK, BUT IN MY NAME SHALL YE CAST OUT DEVILS. YE SHALL SEE MIGHTY MIRACLES AS IN MY NAME YE PREACH THE WORD, FOR BEHOLD, I GIVE YOU POWER OVER ALL THE POWER OF THE ENEMY."

God revealed to me at the same time that the things that were hindrances to my ministry, and had prevented God from working with me, confirming the Word with signs following, were the very same things which were hindering so many thousands of others.

Now it began to grow darker in the closet. I felt His mighty power begin to lift. For a few more moments, His presence lingered, and then I was alone.

Alone, yet not alone.

I trembled under the mighty lingering presence of God. I fumbled at the bottom of the cardboard box on which I had been writing. In the dark, I tore the part on which I had written from the box. In my hand I held the list. At last, here was the price I must pay for the power of God in my life and ministry. THE PRICE TAG

FOR THE MIRACLE-WORKING POWER OF GOD!

Frantically, I pounded on the locked door. Again and again I pounded. At last, I heard my wife coming. She opened the door. The moment she saw me, she knew I had been with God. Her first words were, "You've got the answer!"

"Yes, honey. God has paid me a visit from heaven, and here is the answer."

In my hand was the old brown piece of cardboard, with the answer that had cost so many hours of fasting and prayer and waiting, and -- yes -- believing!

My wife and I sat down at the table with the list before us, and as I told her the story, we both wept, as together we went down the list.

There were thirteen items on the list when I came out of the closet, but I erased the last two before showing the list to my wife, because those two were so personal that even my wife shall never know what they were. She has never asked, for she realizes that these things MUST remain between me and God.

The remaining eleven things make up the contents of this book. There is one entire chapter devoted to each of these eleven requirements. If you, too, have longed for the manifestation of the mighty power of God in your own life and ministry, I trust that these thoughts shall inspire you, and that God may speak to you, as he did me, and lead you on to new victory and greater usefulness because of this book.

Since God spoke to me that day in the closet, many pages have been torn from the calendar. In fact, many calendars have been replaced by new ones. As the time has passed, one by one, I have marked the requirements from my list. The list grew smaller and smaller, as I shouted the victory over Satan, and marked off one after another!

Finally, I was down to the last two. Satan said to me, "You've marked off eleven items, but here are two you'll never mark off. I've got you whipped."

But by the grace of God, I told the devil he was a liar. If God said I could mark them all off, He would help me to do it!

Yet, it seemed I would never be able to mark off the last two.

Never will I forget the day I looked over my list, and found, praise God, there was only one thing left! If I could mark that off, I could claim the promise that God had made to me.

I had to claim that promise! Millions were sick and afflicted, beyond the help of medical science. Some one MUST bring deliverance to them. God had called me to take deliverance to the people. GOD HAS CALLED EVERY MINISTER OF THE GOSPEL TO DO THE SAME! (Ezek. 34:1-4.)

Many have been the times when God has poured out His Spirit in my meetings in a measure, as I have traveled across the states. However, I knew that when I marked the last item from my list, I would see such miracles as I had never seen before. In the meantime, I would patiently strive toward victory, trusting God to help me until victory came. Trusting that when that victory was mine, God would be glorified, and others, too, would be encouraged to seek God for his power.

At this writing, I am conducting a "BACK TO GOD HEALING REVIVAL" at Calvary Temple in Oakland, California. Many say it is the greatest REVIVAL in the history of Oakland. Hundreds say that they have never witnessed such a dynamic moving of the power of God. The meeting is now in its fifth great week. From the growing interest and increasing attendance the meeting could, no doubt, continue indefinitely.

Night after night, the waves of Divine Glory so sweep over the congregation that many testify of being healed while sitting in their seats. Again and again as we have felt the mighty power of God settling over the meeting, people have risen to their feet to testify of instant healings, some of which are visibly miraculous, such as outward tumors disappearing, the crippled made whole.

I have felt goiters disappear at the touch of my hand in Jesus' name!

The shouts of victory are many as the blind see. One woman testified, "It was like coming out of the dark into the sunlight."

We prayed for a woman with throat trouble. After a few moments, she was seen hurrying to the ladies rest room. After returning to the auditorium, she testified that after prayer, something came loose out of her throat and came up into her mouth. she had hurried to the rest room to dispose of it. It was some kind of foreign growth (doubtless cancer) -- whitish orange in color.

Ruptures as large as a person's fist have disappeared overnight. Cancer, deafness, tumors, goiters, sugar diabetes, every known disease and many unknown, disappear, as in the name of Jesus, we lay hands upon the sick. Genuine healings are proven in many cases by doctors' statements and x-rays.

We stand in holy awe, and marvel at the miracle working power of God, as it has moved night after night from the very beginning of this meeting. Hundreds have been delivered from the power of the enemy -- saved, healed, or filled with the Spirit.

In this meeting, it has been impossible to have what is generally termed a "healing line". At least ninety percent of those upon whom we have laid hands are prostrated under the mighty power of God immediately. Some dance a few steps, or weave drunkenly under the power of the Spirit before falling. (See Jer. 23:9). Under these circumstances, it is impossible to have people march on after prayer.

This is the mighty power of God moving upon the people. It is the same power that caused John to "fall at his feet as dead". (Rev. 1:17.)

Many say that the most outstanding thing about this meeting is that such a large percentage of the sick are receiving such miraculous deliverance. It would be a conservative estimate to say that at least ninety percent, or even more of those prayed for have been marvelously healed.

Tonight's service was designated "Holy Ghost Night." Calvary Temple was packed to the doors, with people sitting on the altar benches.

(This is being written at 2:00 am after a great Holy Ghost service.) Eternity alone will reveal the number of people who were filled or refilled with the Spirit. We had announced that in this service, hands would be laid upon seekers for the infilling of the Spirit, according to Acts 8:17. After the sermon, all who had not already been filled during the service came down the outside aisle in a line. With only a few exceptions, everyone we touched in the name of Jesus fell prostrate. What an unusual sight to stand on the platform afterwards, and look upon the many "slain of the Lord" in every available altar space, and even down the aisles! Sweeter yet, the sound of the heavenly music of voices raised in united praise to God, as the Spirit filled obedient believers, and they began to speak in new tongues and magnify God. (Mark 16:17; Acts 10:46)

I do not claim to possess a single gift of the Spirit, nor to have power to impart any gift to others, yet all the gifts of the Spirit are in operation, night after night.

Many are exercising the gifts of the Spirit WITHOUT IMPOSITION OF HANDS OR PROPHETIC UTTERANCE!

God is confirming His Word WITH SIGNS FOLLOWING!

Why have I seen such a change in the results of my ministry? You ask WHY? Have you not guessed?

THE LAST ITEM OF THE LIST GOD GAVE TO ME in the closet of prayer HAS BEEN MARKED OFF THE LIST AT LAST! Hallelujah! Many times, I almost gave up hope of ever being able to mark that last one off, but at last it is gone! By God's grace, GONE FOREVER!

With the marking off of the last requirement on my list, has come the fulfillment of God's promise. THE SICK ARE HEALED. DEVILS ARE CAST OUT. MIGHTY MIRACLES ARE SEEN IN THE NAME OF JESUS, AS HIS WORD IS PREACHED!

The chapters which follow give the requirements which God gave to me, and are dedicated to all those who are hungry for the MIRACLE WORKING POWER OF GOD.

Chapter 2
"THE DISCIPLE IS NOT ABOVE HIS MASTER, NOR THE SERVANT ABOVE HIS LORD"

What strange words! Why should God speak thus to me?

Somehow, I knew that I had read those words somewhere, but where? (I later discovered that this was quoted from the Bible -- Matt. 10:24.) But this was the voice of God, speaking directly to ME. This was the same voice which had spoken to Phillip (Acts 8:30), saying, "Go near, and join thyself to this chariot." It was the voice which Peter had heard (Acts 10:15), saying, "What God hath cleansed that call not thou common." The voice which God's Word tells us may still be heard today. "As the Holy Ghost saith, today if ye will hear his voice harden not your hearts, as in the provocation, in the day of temptation in the wilderness." Heb. 3:7,8. Now I was hearing the voice of God. All others who might share in the message of these words were for the moment blotted out of my thinking. I had asked God for a solution to my problem, and God was giving the answer.

First of all, I must know that NEVER could there be any possibility of being above my Master, Jesus.

You say, "What is so strange about that? Surely no one would expect to be above HIM!

But wait! You may find that you too, just as I had, have been seeking and expecting that very thing. I had read His promise, "He that believeth on me, the works that I do shall he do also; and greater works than these shall he do; because I go unto my Father." John 14:12. Although it seemed hardly reasonable that anyone could really do a greater miracle than those done by Jesus, yet this seemed to be what the scripture said. Many times I had wondered about the meaning of this scripture. The thought that the disciple could do a greater miracle than his Lord seemed to be a direct contradiction of the spirit of the scripture. Now I could see that this promise, like all God's promises, is true when rightly understood. "Greater works shall he do," in the sense that Jesus was only one, limited by time and transportation difficulties to a small area and a few people. Those who believe on Him are many. They are scattered over the face of the entire earth. Many of His modern disciples have circled the globe, preaching to thousands at one time by means of electrical amplification systems, and to vast unseen audiences through radio and television, bringing deliverance to greater multitudes than did Jesus. Where Jesus reached hundreds, His followers are reaching thousands. The works of power which are done today are THE SAME WORKS which He did -- greater in quantity, but not in quality. EVERY BELIEVER has promised to him the same power which Jesus used -- miracles after the same pattern which they saw their Master do, first in the flesh and later through the written record found in the four gospels. What mighty things would have been accomplished had all the followers of Jesus made use of this power!

The words quoted at the beginning of this chapter were part of the message of Christ to twelve believers who were sent out to do the very things which I knew God had called me to do --"Heal the sick, cleanse the lepers, raise the dead, cast out devils: freely ye have received, freely give." Matt. 10:8. With these wonderful promises of power were included warnings of persecution -- "Ye shall be brought before governors and kings for my sake." Verse 18. "Brother shall deliver up brother to death, and the father the child: and the children shall rise up against their parents, and cause them to be put to death." Verse 21. No deliverance from this persecution was promised to the followers of Christ, although they were to have power to do the things which

He did. Christ Himself was persecuted. If His disciples could do the works He did, and in addition be delivered from persecution, then indeed would the disciple be above his master.

"Yea, and all that will live godly in Christ Jesus shall suffer persecution." II Tim. 3:12.

Persecution is one of the universal results of manifested power.

Jesus was not persecuted while He remained in the carpenter shop at Nazareth, but the moment He started to do mighty things, He was called "Prince of devils," and attempts began to be made to destroy his life. (See Luke 4:29.) Persecutions continued for three and one-half years, until at last He was crucified, for no other reason than because He had power which the powerless religious leaders of his day feared. Peter was a "good fellow" so long as he was a mere fisherman, but when he healed the lame man, they threw him in jail. Acts 3:7; 4:3. So long as Stephen was just a "member" in the First Church at Jerusalem he got along nicely, but the moment he "did great wonders and miracles among the people" (Acts 6:8), he was called into judgment and stoned. Paul never had to flee at night for his life, because of his religion, until after he had met God in a supernatural way.

Even so, you will not meet with much opposition and persecution so long as you are just, as the world would say, a "normal Christian," but when you begin to accept God's promises for your life, and to do the UNUSUAL, persecution will come!

Personally, I met with very little opposition until I made up my mind to have all God had promised me as a minister.

This opposition may appear to come from people, but it is really directed by Satan, the commanding general of the opposing army, and using all the methods of warfare from direct frontal attack to "fifth column activities" among our own people.

Again and again, Jesus pointed out to His disciples the price of following in His steps, recommending that they count the cost, and offering them the opportunity of turning back if the price seemed too great, in proportion to the value of the blessing to be received. Our master "for the joy that was set before him endured the cross, despising the shame, and is set down at the right hand of the throne of God." Heb. 12:2.

If we suffer we shall also reign with him." II Tim. 2:12. To the disciple who seeks to share in His power and glory, it must FIRST OF ALL be pointed out that he, being not greater than his master, must follow the same path of suffering, faithfulness and consecration which his Master followed, if he is to reach the goal, if he would know the abundant life -- the powerful life -- in this world, and share in heaven's glory.

If the Son of God must suffer rejection, persecution, cruel scourgings, and crucifixion, at the hands of those to whom He came to minister, His disciple is not above suffering in order that he may carry the gospel of deliverance to those in bondage.

If Christ Himself must reject all earthly ambitions -- even refusing the opportunity to rule the world, when that opportunity was presented aside from the principals of godliness (see Matt. 4:8¬10) -- then surely His disciple, if he is to know real power, must have an eye single to the purpose of God, rejecting all offers but His, no matter how attractive they may be. His cry must be, like his Master, "Lo I come to do thy will, O God." Heb. 10:7. Like Paul, he must be able to say, "I count all things but loss for the excellency of the knowledge of Christ." Phil 3:8.

If the Son of God must spend long hours of the night, when the rest of the world was sleeping, alone on the mountain top with His Father, in order that He might be able to cast out even those demons of whom He said, "This kind goeth not out but by prayer and fasting" (Matt. 17:21), surely His disciple also must spend hours in fasting and prayer, waiting upon God -- learning to think and act in unison with God -- before he can expect to cast out such demons.

"Men ought always to pray and not to faint," Luke 18:1. Persistent, habitual prayer was one of the outstanding characteristics of the life of Christ. When Judas desired to find Jesus in order to betray Him to the priests, he knew that he would find Him in the garden of prayer. Prayer to our Lord was more important than teaching and healing, for He refused to allow Himself to be swept off His feet by the multitudes who "came together to hear, and to be healed by Him" (Luke 5:15,16), but withdrew Himself from the crowd which demanded His attention into the wilderness, and prayed. Prayer was more important to Him than the working of miracles, for miracles do not generate themselves. Prayer is the cause -- miracles the result. Prayer to Jesus was more important than rest and sleep, for we find that "in the morning rising up a great while before day, he went out and departed into a solitary place, and there prayed." Mark 1:35. And again, "He went out into a mountain to pray and he continued all night in prayer to God." Luke 6:12.

If the disciple could attain the same results which Jesus did WITHOUT PAYING THE SAME PRICE WHICH JESUS PAID, then it would have to be confessed that the disciple had become greater than his master. The "student" would have learned a better, more efficient method than that taught to him by his "teacher." In the world, this often happens. Many a musician has advanced beyond the one who gave him his training. Many an artist has far excelled the one who taught him to draw and paint. And many a scientist has learned for himself things which his science teachers never knew. But the student of Jesus Christ CANNOT become greater than his teacher. He cannot learn anything which Jesus did not know. He cannot find a short cut to power with God. If he should try it, he will only meet with disappointment and sorrow. His life will be shipwrecked and his ministry useless.

For the disciple (student) of Christ, "It is enough for the disciple that he be as his master (teacher)." Matt. 10:25.

Before I could fully comprehend all which God has spoken to me, suddenly He was speaking to me again, the words which form the second step of the revelation which God gave to me as I waited before Him in fasting and prayer.

Chapter 3
"THE DISCIPLE IS NOT ABOVE HIS MASTER: BUT EVERYONE THAT IS PERFECT SHALL BE AS HIS MASTER"

My spirit which had been humbled and almost crushed by the words of the first message was suddenly lifted up in a blaze of glory, as I realized that although I could never be above my Master, God had said I should be AS MY MASTER! (This I also found to be a quotation from scripture -- Luke 6:40.)

This is not a promise (as some have thought) which awaits the coming of Christ for its fulfillment. It is meant for the followers of Christ HERE AND NOW! This promise was spoken to me directly, for my own instruction and edification, but since it is a direct quotation of scripture, it does not apply to me alone, but to EVERY ONE WHO WILL BELIEVE IT! It is to YOU! You can heal the sick! You can see miracles! You can exercise the gifts of the Spirit! (I Cor. 12:8-11) YOU CAN DO THE WORKS HE DID! God has said that you could, and HE CANNOT LIE!

"God is not a man, that he should lie; neither the son of man, that he should repent: hath he said, and shall he not do it? or hath he spoken, and shall he not make it good? Num. 23:19.

"My covenant will I not break, nor alter the thing that is gone out of my lips." Ps. 89:34.

Then, "Every one that is PERFECT" (that will meet the requirements, I COULD BE AS MY MASTER!

But some will say, "That is impossible, for He was God, as well as human. And we are only human."

These are unmindful of the plain statements of scripture, "Verily he took not on him the nature of angels: but he took on him the seed of Abraham. Wherefore IN ALL THINGS it behooved him to be made LIKE UNTO HIS BRETHREN." Heb. 2:16,17.

"But made himself of no reputation, and took upon him the FORM OF A SERVANT, and was made in the LIKENESS OF MEN: And being found IN FASHION AS A MAN, he humbled himself." Phil. 2:7,8.

"The MAN Christ Jesus." I Tim. 2:5.

One night, when Jesus and his disciples were in a small boat, there came a great storm at sea, which caused the disciples to be very fearful for their lives. Jesus rebuked the winds and the sea, and immediately there was a great calm. The men who were with him in the boat marveled, saying, "What manner of MAN is this?" Matt. 8:27.

Their question is still the cry of many today, when they observe some of His disciples, who by faith are claiming His promises, and going forth healing the sick, raising the dead, and ministering the word (as Jesus himself said they should -- Mark 16:17,18) with the supernatural confirmation of signs following. Many seem to think that these are some peculiar and different species, or manner, of men. They are not. They are simply common, ordinary men, full of the Holy Ghost, and yielded to God for his work -- men who have discovered that they can be AS THEIR MASTER, and have dedicated their lives to reaching that goal.

When the people at Lystra saw that Paul's command could bring healing to a man lame from his mother's womb, they said, "The gods are come down to us in the likeness of men." Being untaught heathen they of course did not know that men could have such power. But many Christian people seem to be just as unaware of the power which God has made available for his people. When these poor heathen people would have offered sacrifices unto Paul and Barnabas as Gods, they refused to permit this, saying. "We also are men of like passions with you, and preach unto you that ye should turn -- unto the living God." See Acts 14:8-15.

Jesus truly was God, as well as man. Yet it was not in His nature of deity that He walked upon earth and performed miracles. The often neglected question is not "What manner of God is this?" We as His disciples, need to ask as did those disciples of old, "What manner of MAN is this?"

Jesus, by His own statement, was a member of the eternal triune Godhead, composed of the Father (Jehovah), the Son (Jesus Christ), and the Holy Ghost. He existed before the world was made, and shared in the work of creation. (John 1:1-3.) He was not only WITH God and LIKE God, HE WAS GOD! All the attributes of deity were His. With the Father, He was omnipotent, omniscient, omnipresent, and eternal. All these are His today, as He is glorified on the right hand of God in heaven. At the close of His earthly ministry of healing the sick and working miracles, when He was ready to be offered as a sacrifice for our sins, he prayed, "I have glorified thee on the earth. I have finished the work which thou gavest me to do. And now O Father, glorify thou me with thine own self WITH THE GLORY WHICH I

HAD WITH THEE BEFORE THE WORLD WAS." John 17:4,5.

The glory which was His before the world was!

The glory which is His today!

But the glory which was LAID ASIDE when he took on human flesh. Coming as a helpless babe, born of a woman, circumcised like any other Jewish boy, increasing in wisdom and stature during childhood and growth (Luke 2:52), weeping, hungering, thirsting, weary, sleeping and waking -- partaking in every weakness and limitation of human flesh and blood. (Forasmuch then as the children are partakers of flesh and blood, he also HIMSELF LIKEWISE TOOK PART OF THE SAME. Heb. 2:14.) He was "IN ALL POINTS tempted like as we are, yet without sin." Heb. 4:15.

He was "in the beginning with God. All things were made by Him; and without him was not anything made that was made." John 1:2,3. Yet for all this, Jesus USED NO POWER when He was here on earth in the flesh WHICH IS NOT AVAILABLE TODAY to every believer! Such a statement would be blasphemy HAD NOT JESUS HIMSELF made it plain, again and again, that this was His plan.

"Everyone that is perfect SHALL BE AS HIS MASTER." Luke 6:40.

"As thou hast send me into the world, EVEN SO have I also sent them into the world." John 17:18.

"The works that I do SHALL HE DO ALSO." John 14:12.

Although He was Omnipotent God, yet in His earthly life and ministry He declared "The son can do nothing of himself." "I can of mine own self do nothing." John 5:19,30. "The words that I speak unto you I speak NOT OF MYSELF: But the Father that dwelleth in me, he doeth the works." John 14:10.

The answer to the disciples' question, "What manner of MAN is this?" is found not in the powers of deity which He used before He "was made flesh and dwelt among us," nor in the power which is His today in the heavenlies today. The answer can be found only in His earthly (human) life. He lived that life AS AN EXAMPLE to those whom He left in the world to finish the work which he had started while He was here. "Leaving us an EXAMPLE, that YE should follow his steps." I Pet. 2:21. He was our teacher (master) and we, His disciples (every one that is perfect), SHALL BE AS our master! Had He used power which was not available to us, it would be impossible for us to follow His example. But He left to us the promise that we would receive THE SAME

POWER and from the SAME SOURCE, that was His!

"Behold I send the promise of my Father upon you: but tarry ye in the city of Jerusalem, until ye be endued with POWER FROM ON HIGH." Luke 24:49.

"Ye shall receive POWER after that the Holy Ghost is come upon you." Acts 1:8.

These signs shall follow them that believe: IN MY NAME they shall cast out devils; they shall speak with new tongues -- they shall lay hands on the sick and they shall recover." Mark 16:17,

18.

"Behold, I give unto you POWER -- over all the power of the enemy." Luke 10:19.

"He that believeth on me, THE WORKS THAT I DO SHALL HE DO ALSO." John 14:12.

"Though he was rich (in heavenly glory and divine power) yet for your sakes he became poor, THAT YE THROUGH HIS POVERTY MIGHT BE RICH." II Cor. 8:9 He folded it all away as a garment, and laid aside His great wealth of power, and came into the world as a babe, in the form of a servant, of no reputation, lived among men as one of them. (Phil. 2:7.) Tradition has invented miracles in his childhood, but the Word of God plainly declares that "This BEGINNING of miracles did Jesus in Cana of Galilee," (where He turned water into wine). John 2:11. He DID NO MIRACLE nor manifested any superhuman power, BEFORE THE HOLY SPIRIT DESCENDED UPON HIM! (Matt. 3:16,17; John 1:33.) It was when "God anointed Jesus of Nazareth with the HOLY GHOST AND WITH POWER" that he "went about doing good, and healing all that were oppressed of the devil; FOR GOD WAS WITH HIM." Acts 10:38. This is the secret of His success AS A MAN.

What manner of man?

A man ANOINTED WITH THE HOLY GHOST AND WITH POWER. And God was WITH HIM!

Yet -- don't forget this -- a man who was EVERY INCH A MAN! A man who faced -- and conquered -- EVERY TEMPTATION known to humanity! A man who (though as God, He had been omnipresent) could only be in one place at a time. Although as God He had neither slumbered nor slept (Ps. 121:4), as man, He suffered weariness (John 4:6) and required sleep (Matt. 8:24). He must go from place to place upon hot, weary, dusty feet -- His rate of travel limited to the speed of walking, His feet which had trod the immaculate golden streets of heaven soiled and bruised by the dust and stones of the unpaved and filthy Oriental streets and paths of Palestine. How He welcomed the cleansing coolness of the customary foot bath before meals --when some unselfish person thought to minister to Him in this way! He suffered hunger and thirst, loneliness, weariness, and pain. He of whom it had been said, "Every beast of the forest is mine, and the cattle upon a thousand hills. The world is mine and the fullness thereof" (Ps. 50:10,12), claimed no part of it for Himself AS A MAN, but became even more poor than the foxes and birds, for He had not so much as a place to lay His head. (Luke 9:58).

All this He did WILLINGLY for us, that we might share the riches of His glory.

When Satan tempted Him in the wilderness (Matt. 4:3,4), the first temptation was that He should act in the creative power of the ETERNAL SON OF GOD, in order that His human hunger might be satisfied. Had He done this, He would have failed in being "in all points like unto his brethren." It was important to the plan of Satan that this point should, if possible, be spoiled. But Jesus did not fall into this temptation. In His reply is no assumption of deity. He answered firmly AS A MAN! "MAN shall not live by bread alone, but by every word that proceedeth out of the mouth of God."

He loved to refer to Himself as the "SON OF MAN."

Since it is so apparent by the scripture that Jesus took upon Himself our own nature and limitations, in order that He might be made a proper example for us, it behooves us to study that example carefully, considering the question, "What manner of persons OUGHT YE TO BE in all holy conversation and godliness." II Pet. 3:11.

He was a man of power. He spoke as one having authority (Mark 1:22). The people were astonished at this, for the religious leaders of their day knew nothing of this power, but taught traditions and theories and theological explanations. Jesus cut across all the lines drawn by their fine points of doctrine, and DROVE OUT BY HIS WORDS OF AUTHORITY demons, sickness and infirmity. When he spoke THINGS HAPPENED! He spoke as one having authority BECAUSE HE HAD AUTHORITY! The traditional religious leaders did not speak as He spoke because they had never been given authority over the power of the enemy. How many "religious" leaders today speak as the scribes and Pharisees! Those who are LIKE their master speak with authority -- the authority which was Christ's while He was here to use it, because He had received it from the Father (John 5:27). He came in the Father's name (John 5:43), and His legal AGENT, to work the works of His Father. ("I must work the works of him that sent me." John 9:4.) While He was on earth He chose disciples (first twelve, Luke 9:1, then seventy others, Luke 10:1,19) which He appointed as "deputies," giving them the same power of attorney which He used. ("Lord, even the devils are subject unto us THROUGH THY NAME." Luke 10:17.) Thus were they trained under His direct supervision to be ready to carry forward "all that Jesus BEGAN both to do and to teach" (Acts 1:1), when the time should come for Him to return to the Father.

Having now returned to the Father, and being on the right hand of God exalted, He has not planned that the work which He began through such suffering and sacrifice should cease to be carried forward. Before He went away, He left command and authority for the continuation of His work. Those who believe on Him are made His agents, and are commanded to do IN HIS NAME (by His authority, as by the power of attorney) all the things which He Himself would do if He were present in the body! "IN MY NAME shall they cast out devils; they shall speak with new tongues; they shall take up serpents (not as tempting God, but should it so happen by accident, as it did to Paul, Acts 28:3-5) and if they drink any deadly thing it shall not hurt them; they shall lay hands on the sick, and they shall recover." Mark 16:17,18. "And whatsoever ye shall ask IN MY NAME, that will I do, that the Father may be glorified in the Son." John 14:13.

The gifts which He placed in the church, for the perfecting of the saints, for the work of the ministry, for the edifying (up building) of the body of Christ (His church), Eph. 4:8-12, cover all the great and mighty things which Jesus did when He was here in the flesh (see I Cor. 12:7-11).

Never once did He teach, either by inference or by direct statement, that this power would be gone from the world when He went away. Rather, in his last commission to those He left behind, He declared, "All power is given unto me in heaven and in earth. GO YE THEREFORE (because this power is HIS, and through Him OURS, Luke 24:49, Acts 1:8) and teach ALL NATIONS -- teaching them to OBSERVE (obey -- Webster's definition) ALL THINGS (Heal the sick, cleanse the lepers, raise the dead, cast out devils, freely ye have received, freely give. Matt. 10:8.) whatsoever I have commanded you: and lo, I am with you alway, even unto the end of the world. Amen." Matt. 28:18-20.

These disciples, anointed with the Holy Ghost (Acts 2:4), "went forth and preached everywhere, the Lord was working WITH THEM, and confirming the word with SIGNS FOLLOWING."

Mark 16:20.

So long as men are anointed with the Holy Ghost, and God is with them, as it was with Jesus (Acts 10:38) and the early disciples (Mark 16:20) and as Jesus said it should be "even unto the end of the world" (Matt. 28:20), the works Jesus did will continue to be done!

The disciple should not be above his master, but he SHALL BE AS HIS MASTER!

But if we are to be like Him in POWER, we must also be like Him in holiness, in consecration, in meekness, in compassion. We must be like Him in prayer and in fellowship with the Father. We must be like Him in faith. We must be like Him in fasting and self denial. If it were possible for the servant to be like Him in power without paying the price He paid, then the servant would be above his Lord.

There is a price to be paid for all that God offers to mankind. In a sense, it is all free, but there is a price of obedience and preparedness. Even our free salvation is ours only when we have heeded the admonition of God to repent and believe upon the Lord Jesus Christ. The "gift of the Holy Ghost" is ours only when we obey Him. Acts 5:32. Power with God LIKE JESUS HAD is for those -- ALL THOSE -- who meet the condition, "every one that is PERFECT shall be as his master." Luke 6:40.

Chapter 4
"BE YE THEREFORE PERFECT, EVEN AS YOUR FATHER IN HEAVEN IS PERFECT"

These words seemed even more startling than the ones which God had already spoken. Surely this was too much! Could any mortal ever hope to be perfect? Yet surely God would not ask me to do something which He knew I could not do! And without doubt, this was the voice of God. I had asked bread of my heavenly Father, and I knew that He would not give me a stone. How thrilling to my soul when I learned that this, too, was a quotation from scripture! I found it in Matt. 5:48. It was Christ's own command, not only to me but to all who would be the "children of your Father which is in heaven" (verse 45). Perfection is the GOAL set by Christ for every Christian. Not every Christian has reached that goal. No Christian has a right to boast that he has attained it. Even the great Apostle Paul declared, "Not as though I had already attained, either were already perfect, but I follow after" (Phil 3:12). No Christian worthy of the name will be satisfied to be less than perfect. No Christian should make excuse for his own imperfections, but should recognize them as failure to keep the command of Christ, and strive earnestly to overcome them. PERFECTION IS THE GOAL!

For the benefit of those who may have been taught that no person except Christ was ever perfect, let us note that GOD HIMSELF ascribes perfection to a number of men. They did not claim perfection for themselves, but God declared that they were perfect.

First of all, Job, the hero of the oldest written book of the Bible was a perfect man. His friends didn't think he was perfect; they accused him of hypocrisy (see Job 8:6,13.) Satan did not think he was perfect; he accused him of serving God only because of the material blessings which God had given him. Job himself was willing to admit that he was imperfect, for he declared, "I abhor myself, and repent in dust and ashes," Job 42:6. But when Satan accused him before the Lord, God himself declared, "Hast thou considered my servant Job, that there is none like him in the earth, a PERFECT AND AN UPRIGHT MAN?" Job 1:8. And then for the benefit of all who might read this scripture, God added his definition of human perfection -- "one that feareth God and escheweth (shunneth, avoideth) evil."

Many object to the teaching of possible perfection on the grounds that they have never seen a perfect man. In Job's day, God declared that there was only one. Again, in Noah's day there was only one. Yet God declares that Noah was PERFECT! "Noah was a just man and PERFECT in his generations, and Noah walked with God." Gen. 6:9.

Some declare that if one should become perfect, he would immediately be translated, as was Enoch, carelessly disregarding the fact that the scripture declares that Enoch 'walked with God" for at least three hundred years before he "was not", Gen 5:22, and that "BEFORE his translation he had this testimony, that he pleased God." Heb. 11:5.

All these Old Testament saints were perfect, before even the law was given. No divinity, nor superhuman perfection is attributed to any one of them. They were MEN, subject to like passions as we are, but they knew and feared God, kept his commands, and carefully avoided the overflowing evils of the idolatrous people among whom they lived, in some of the most outstandingly evil ages in history.

Was perfection possible under the law?

Moses, speaking God's message to the entire congregation of Israel, declared "Thou shalt be PERFECT with the Lord thy God." Deut. 18:13.

Man is sometimes more critical than God. When Mirian and Aaron complained against

Moses, God took his part, speaking to them out of the pillar of cloud and saying, "My servant Moses --is FAITHFUL in all mine house!" Numbers 12:7. While this does not use the word "perfect", surely it meets the definition given in Job 1:8.

David was not persuaded that perfection was impossible, for he declared, in one of his inspired Psalms, "I will behave myself wisely IN A PERFECT WAY. I will walk within my house with a PERFECT HEART." Ps. 101:2.

All these, and no doubt many others (such as Daniel, Joseph, Abraham, Elijah, and Elisha, etc.) lived lives of holiness (perfection) in the days before many of our advantages were given. It was to his New Testament church that God gave the complete scriptures. "ALL scripture is given by inspiration of God, and is profitable -- that the man of God may be PERFECT, thoroughly furnished unto all good works. II Tim. 3:16,17.

It was not until our own dispensation that Christ was preached, "Whom we preach, warning every man, and teaching every man in all wisdom; that we may present every man PERFECT in Christ Jesus." Col. 2:28.

It was to his New Testament Church that Christ gave apostles, prophets, evangelists, pastors and teachers "FOR THE PERFECTING OF

THE SAINTS, for the work of the ministry, for the EDIFYING OF THE BODY OF CHRIST." Eph. 4:11,12.

Unto them, the glorious outpouring of the Holy Spirit, our constantly abiding Comforter, teacher and guide, (John 14:26) had not been given. But to us he is given -- to every one who will obey God (Acts 5:32).

How much easier it should be for us, with all these advantages, to be perfect than for those who lived before these things were given!

God says to us, "Ye are the temple of the living God: as God hath said, I will dwell in them and walk in them . . . . Wherefore come ye out from among them, and be ye separate, saith the Lord, and touch not the unclean thing, and I will receive you, and will be a Father unto you and ye shall be my sons and daughters, saith the Lord Almighty. Having therefore these promises, dearly beloved, let us cleanse ourselves from ALL filthiness of the flesh and spirit, PERFECTING HOLINESS in the fear of God." II Cor. 6:16-7:1.

These promises are ours! We CAN cleanse ourselves from ALL FILTHINESS! We can PERFECT HOLINESS in the fear of God! Like Job, we can fear God and shun evil, and be perfect in the sight of God.

This is not a "new thing". The doctrine of entire sanctification has been taught by many outstanding servants of Christ throughout the church age, and is accepted as sound doctrine by a number of major denominations. Since this is only a small book, space prevents quoting from the statements of fundamental truths of many groups. I will quote here from only one, that found in the Constitution of the General Council of the Assemblies of God. (Minutes and Constitution, with Bylaws, Revised (1949 edition), Page 38, Section 9.)

Entire Sanctification

The Scriptures teach a life of holiness without which no man shall see the Lord. By the power of the Holy Ghost we are able to obey the command, "Be ye holy, for I am Holy." Entire sanctification is the will of God for all believers, and should be earnestly pursued by walking in obedience to God's Word. Heb. 12:14; I Peter 1:15, 16; I Thess. 5:23, 24; I John 2:6."

Call it what you will -- perfection, holiness, entire sanctification -- it is not only possible, it is not only our privilege, it is God's COMMAND.

"Be ye holy in ALL MANNER OF CONVERSATION." I Peter 1:15.

"Be ye therefore perfect." Matt. 5:48.

You say, "I know a lot of Christians, even preachers, who say you can't be perfect, and there is no use to try."

We know them, too. They are not healing the sick nor casting out demons! Sin is the devil's bridgehead in your life. Let him hold the bridgehead, if you will. But it will rob you of power!

Jesus did not allow the devil to maintain a bridgehead in his life, for he declared just before he was crucified, "The prince of this world (Satan) cometh, and hath NOTHING in me." John 14:30. He had power to accomplish the work he came into the world to do because Satan had NOTHING -- not even one little bridgehead of pet sin or self-indulgence -- in Him.

We, his followers, are admonished to keep the coasts of our lives free of "bridgeheads" too. "Neither give PLACE to the devil." Eph. 4:27. It is his business to make you think that you can't expect to keep your life entirely free of his hideouts and landing strips. If he can get you to leave him a place to work from, he can sabotage every effort you make for God, and rob you of the power you have longed for. The work God has given you to do will go undone. The sick will not be healed, the captives not set free. Should you attempt to cast out demons, they will laugh in your face, saying, "You let us remain in your own life, and then would cast us out of others!" Demons know the power of Christ, and they know and fear the power of a Christ filled Christian. But they have no fear of one who is not holy.

Seven sons of one Sceva, a Jew and chief of the priests, decided that they could say the same words which Paul used, adjuring the demons in Jesus name to come out of those who were possessed, without being careful to have the background of holiness and consecration which Paul had. (See Acts 19:13-15). The evil spirit answered and said, "Jesus I know, and Paul I know; but WHO ARE YE?! Then the man in whom the evil spirit was, leaped on them, and overcame them, so that they fled naked and wounded. They didn't think holiness was necessary, but they found to their sorrow that it CAN NOT BE OVERLOOKED, if one is to exercise the miracle working power of God! The reaction is not so immediate and violent in every case, for these "vagabond Jews" had tried it before, and only once did this happen. But never once did they succeed in casting out a demon. Demons flee only before the power of Christ, or of a Christ-filled life. There is no way to have power with God without holiness -- for Jesus himself said, "Every one that is PERFECT shall be AS HIS MASTER." Luke 6:40.

There is much that could be said about perfection. An entire book could easily be written in defense of the possibility of obeying the command of God, "Be ye holy, for I am holy." I Peter

1:16. However, enough has been said to open the eyes of the person who is hungry for truth, and eager to have the power which Jesus promised to his followers, THE MIRACLE WORKING POWER OF GOD.

But it will take more than knowing that holiness is possible. You want to know how you can attain it.

Not every Christian has reached the goal. Not every follower of Christ has the power which he promised. The twelve chosen disciples, even after having healed many that were sick and cast out many demons in Jesus' name, met a demon one day who refused to go at their command. Matt. 17:15. When Jesus had cast out the demon, the disciples asked him why they could not do it. He gave as the reason their UNBELIEF, and lack of fasting and prayer. These twelve chosen men were at times found to lack in the manifestation of the fruits of the Spirit, and to show evidence of such works of the flesh as pride (Mark 10:37), jealousy (Mark 10:41), anger (Matt. 26:51). They slept when they should have prayed (Matt. 26:40), and deserted him in times of trial (vs. 56). They failed to discern the plan of God, and rebuked Jesus because he told them that he would be killed, so that Jesus said to one of them, "Get thee behind me, Satan: -- Thou savourest not the things that be of God, but those that be of men." Matt. 16:23. These men had not reached perfection, but they earnestly desired to be perfect, and worked diligently to attain the promises of God, and God honored them, and was not ashamed to be called their God.

Do not be discouraged because you have not attained unto perfection. There is an ultimate perfection which will only be reached when we see Jesus face to face at his coming. There is a growth in grace, growing toward perfection, which must continue so long as we remain in the flesh. Our perfection may be likened to the fruit on a tree. From the time the bud appears, the apple on the inside, though very tiny, can be perfect. It has not taken on the size, color, nor flavor which it will eventually have, but nevertheless in its present state it is perfect. As it is nourished, and fed, and protected from frost and disease -- as the sun and the rain touch it, and the heat and the cold, it grows into a perfect little green apple, and finally the large, beautiful, rich, full-ripe fruit.

It was this "unripe fruit" perfection which Paul referred to in Phil. 3:15 -- "Let US (including himself) therefore, as many as be PERFECT be thus minded." Three verses before, he had said, "Not as though I had already attained, either were ALREADY PERFECT." (vs. 12.) Here he was speaking of the ultimate perfection of the full ripe fruit, the perfection which will only be complete with the resurrection of the dead. Paul was not unmindful of the perfection which had already been attained, but with the true Christian spirit, he was not satisfied to remain in that state, but, though he didn't claim to be perfect, declared, "I follow after." "This one thing I do, forgetting those things which are behind, and reaching forward to those things which are before, I PRESS TOWARD THE MARK." (vs. 12,13,14.)

There is no stopping place short of ultimate perfection. Although the immature Christian may be perfect in God's sight, HE WILL CEASE TO BE PERFECT WHEN HE IS WILLING TO STOP GROWING! When the little green apple stops growing, it will soon wither and fall from the tree. Perfection must be attained, and constantly striven for.

Growth must be maintained through FOOD "Desire the sincere milk of the word (the Bible) that ye may grow thereby." I Peter 2:2. A good appetite for the word of God is very necessary if we are to "grow in grace and in the knowledge of our Lord and Savior." 2 Pet. 2:2.

A real love for the Word of God is a part of our perfection NOW, and means much toward our ultimate perfection when Jesus comes. "All scripture is given by inspiration of God and is profitable for doctrine, for reproof, for correction, for instruction in righteousness: that the man of God MAY BE PERFECT." 2 Tim. 3:16,17.

Many have plenty of time to read comic strips, magazine, novels -- everything else but the Word of God. But they are just too busy to study their Bibles! No wonder they do not grow! No wonder they have no power to heal the sick and cast out demons. No wonder they are not perfect, and do not expect to be. They are not feeding their souls the right food. "Grow in grace and in the KNOWLEDGE of our Lord and Savior." 2 Pet. 2:3. This knowledge comes through study of God's word. Read it a great deal. And read it as God's revelation to you. Believe it as you read it. It is the word of Him who cannot lie. He means EXACTLY WHAT HE SAYS!

Ample protection is provided for those who abide in Christ. Whatever our temptations may be, we need not sin for "God is faithful, who will not suffer you to be tempted above that ye are able, but with temptation also make a way of escape that ye may be able to bear it." I Cor. 10:13.

"He that hath begun a good work in you will perform it until the day of Jesus Christ." Phil 1:6.

The Lord is faithful, who shall establish you and KEEP YOU FROM EVIL." 2 Thes. 3:3.

"Now unto him that is able to keep you from falling and to present you FAULTLESS before the presence of his glory." Jude 24.

Hallelujah! It is possible to be kept by God, and to live on a higher plane than sin.

We are not ignorant of the devices of Satan. He can quote scripture, too. How quickly he comes to comfort the imperfect Christian, by quoting the last half of Matt. 26:41 -- "The spirit indeed is willing, but the flesh is weak." This portion should never be quoted without the first part of the verse -- "Watch and pray, that ye ENTER NOT INTO TEMPTATION!" Thus may we overcome the weakness of the flesh.

Walk in the Spirit, and ye shall not fulfill the lust of the flesh." Gal. 5:16. (You may be sure Satan will not add this passage to his quotation.) "Now the works of the flesh are manifest -- of the which I tell you -- that they which do such things SHALL NOT INHERIT THE KINGDOM OF GOD." Gal. 5:19-21.

"For to be CARNALLY (fleshly) MINDED is death." Rom. 8:6.

Hide behind the weakness of the flesh if you like, but do not overlook what God says will be the result! Do not accept Satan's suggestion, even when he quotes scripture. "RESIST THE DEVIL AND HE WILL FLEE FROM YOU!" James 4:7.

You can be perfect! God says you can. Only Satan says you cannot.

God has provided food for you in his word, protection for you through his spirit, and a mighty agency for your perfecting in his Church. In order that the church might serve to this end, "He gave some, apostles; and some, prophets: and some, evangelists; and some, pastors and teachers; for the PERFECTING of the saints --." Eph. 4:11,12.

Do not think that you shall attain the perfection which God desires for you if you fail to heed his warning, "Not forsaking the assembling of yourselves together, as the manner of some is." Heb.

10:25. Find a good church home, where God's word is taught and BELIEVED, where the power of God is present and welcome, where God is confirming his word with signs following, and where God's people "Speak the things which become SOUND DOCTRINE." Titus 2:1. Then make it a practice to be present whenever God and his people meet. Only thus can you be perfected by the ministry gifts which God has placed in the church. Every service in your Spirit filled church is planned of God to contribute something to your perfection.

Patience also has a part. "Let patience have her perfect work that ye may be PERFECT AND ENTIRE wanting nothing." Jas. 1:4.

The tongue also plays an important part, for "If any man offend not in word, the same is a PERFECT man and able also to bridle the whole body." James 3:2.

"And above all these things put on charity, which is the bond of perfectness." Col. 3:14.

Christ is sufficiently interested in pointing out the way, that if you desire to find the way of perfectness, he will place his finger on your pet sins, and show you what is keeping you from the goal. A young man once fell at the feet of Jesus and asked the question, "What must I do?" Although this young man was inquiring the way of salvation, Jesus pointed out to him the way to perfection. "If thou wilt be PERFECT, go ----." Matt. 19:21. He laid his finger upon the young man's pet sin. Like so many others the young man felt that this was too much. Yet it would have been a small price to pay for perfection here, and eternal life in the world to come. Jesus is just the same today. When you come inquiring how you can be perfect, he will not send you away without an answer.

Perfection and more perfection is always the Christian goal. "I press toward the mark for the prize of the high calling of God in Christ Jesus. Let us therefore, AS MANY AS BE PERFECT, be thus minded: and if in anything ye be otherwise minded, GOD SHALL REVEAL EVEN THIS UNTO YOU." Phil. 3:14,15.

As you read this book, Satan will probably whisper to you many times, as Pharaoh said unto Moses (Ex. 8:25) "Sacrifice in the land." In other words, it isn't necessary to go so far, to separate yourself from the things of the world in order to have power with God. If you insist, he will say, "All right then, only don't go too far." He infers there is danger in going too far.

You can't go too far with God. You may go too far in sin. You may go too far in self righteousness. But if you are walking with Jesus, in the Spirit, you need not fear going too far. No believer has gone as far as God wants him to go until the signs follow his ministry. We have not gone as far as we should go until we can lay hands on the sick and see them recover! No church has gone as far as the Lord meant it should go until all nine gifts of the spirit are in operation in its services. DON'T LET PHARAOH (SATAN) KEEP YOU BACK! Go on! Go all the way. God's grace is sufficient for you. Don't let anything keep you from appropriating the promises of God in your own life, whether you be lay member or minister.

"Let us go on unto PERFECTION!" Heb. 6:1.

Chapter 5
CHRIST OUR EXAMPLE

"For even hereunto were ye called; because Christ also suffered for us, LEAVING US AN

EXAMPLE, that ye should FOLLOW HIS STEPS; who did no sin, neither was guile found in his mouth; who when he was reviled, reviled not again; when he suffered, he threatened not; but committed himself to him that judgeth righteously." I Peter 2:21-23.

This scripture makes it very plain to any honest hearted child of God that Christ is OUR EXAMPLE in WORD and in DEED! We can, then, WALK AS CHRIST WALKED, and we can TALK AS HE TALKED. This is not a condition of one's feet or lips, but of the HEART! "For from within, out of the heart of man, proceed evil thoughts, adulteries, fornications, murders, thefts, covetousness, wickedness, deceit, lasciviousness, an evil eye, blasphemy, pride, foolishness: all these evil things come from within, and defile a man." Mark 7:21-23.

For as he thinketh in his heart, so is he." Prov. 23:7.

Before one can walk as Christ walked, and talk as he talked, he must first begin to THINK AS CHRIST THOUGHT! This is possible only as we "Bring into captivity every thought to the obedience of Christ." II Cor. 10:5. This doesn't just happen. It is an act of determined consecration, requiring purpose and continual application, for the mind loves to wander. It also requires a willing exchange, giving up the former ways of thinking, and accepting as our own the MIND OF CHRIST. "LET this mind be in you which was also in Christ Jesus." Phil. 2:5.

God draws the line on some thinking. It is possible to lead a victorious thought life. Not that Satan can no longer come with evil suggestions. Nowhere in God's word has He declared that man would not be tempted. Even Christ was tempted. But one can refuse to allow his thought to dwell upon evil things. A sane mind is a controlled mind. Evil thoughts can be driven out, by filling the mind with right thoughts. We are instructed as to what these thoughts are. "Finally, brethren, whatsoever things are true, whatsoever things are honest, whatsoever things are just, whatsoever things are pure, whatsoever things are lovely, whatsoever things are of good report; if there be any virtue, and if there be any praise, THINK ON THESE THINGS." Phil. 4:8.

Jesus thought right thoughts. That was the reason that he could walk and talk right, and be a right example for us to follow.

"Christ suffered for us, leaving us an example, that we should follow his steps, WHO DID NO SIN." I Pet. 2;21,22. Christ did not live in habitual sin. He did not make excuses for sin. He resisted the devil, and temptation, although he was "Tempted in all points like as we are, yet without sin." Heb. 4:15. He is our example. And He stands ready to help us to walk as He walked -- in his steps!

"Whosoever abideth in him sinneth not." I John 3:6.

This is contrary to much of the religious teaching today. I am aware of this. I am also aware that multitudes of religious people today, even many who believe in divine healing, find themselves powerless when faced with those who need deliverance from sickness, or demon possession. If you really want power with God, surely this matter is worthy of serious, prayerful thought, regardless of former opinions or religious teaching. There is a reason why some have power and some do not. And it is not because God is a respecter of persons. Power is a direct result of faith, and faith comes by obedience.

"Beloved, if our heart condemn us not, then have we confidence (faith) toward God, and whatsoever we ask, we receive of him, because we keep his commandments, and do those things that are pleasing in his sight." I John 3:21,22.

Hope is available to people without holiness, BUT FAITH IS NOT!

If faith were available to people without holiness, then people who can never see God could have power to ask and receive ANYTHING THEY DESIRE from God, for God's unqualified promise to those who have faith is, "Whatsoever ye shall ask in prayer, BELIEVING YE SHALL RECEIVE." Matt. 21:22. And God has also said, "Follow peace . . . and holiness, WITHOUT WHICH NO MAN SHALL SEE THE LORD." Heb. 12:14.

Although many religious teachers declare that everyone sins all the time; that it is impossible to live above sin; that as long as one is in this world he must partake of a certain number of sins of this life; that one must sin every day, and repent every night;--God's word still calmly, simply states the command of God, "BE YE HOLY, FOR I AM HOLY." I Peter 1:16.

Paul writing to the Corinthians, declared, "Awake to righteousness and SIN NOT, for some have not the knowledge of God. I speak this to your shame." I Cor. 15:34.

People who are finding excuse for their habitual sin, according to this verse, have not the knowledge of God. This is a SHAME! It is evidence that many professed Christians are spiritually ASLEEP! They are not led by the spirit of God nor by the word of God, for the work of the spirit is to reprove the world of sin and of righteousness, (John 16:8), and the word hidden in the heart will prevent sinning against God. (Ps. 119:11.)

You can't have power when you are asleep. WAKE UP! Quit making excuses for sin. Walk in the steps of him who DID NO SIN!

"Neither was guile found in his mouth." I Peter 2:22.

Jesus healed by HIS WORD. (See Matt. 8:16.) "His word was with power." Luke 4:32. The follower of Christ is assured that his words may also be words of power. (Matt. 21:21.) But if our words are to be words of power, we must talk as he talked. Guile (cunning craftiness, deceit) must not be found in our mouths.

Jesus WALKED IN THE SPIRIT. We who are his followers are also exhorted to walk in the spirit. (Gal. 5:16.) In verses 19 to 21 are listed the works of the flesh, which are not present in the lives of those who walk in the Spirit. There are some who harbor some of these works of the flesh in their lives, making very little if any effort to overcome, who yet feel that God should honor their word and their prayer, and give them miracle working power. Yet verse 21 tells us that they which do such things shall not only fail to have power, but "SHALL NOT INHERIT THE KINGDOM OF GOD." How could one who is not even fit for the kingdom of God expect to have power to work the works of Christ?

By studying this list of "works of the flesh" with a dictionary, you will find that God has listed uncleanness, lustfulness, immoderate desire, covetousness, hatred, discord, quarreling, contention, jealousy, violent anger, rage, riotous feasting, "and such like".

Those who do such things are NOT walking in his steps who DID NO SIN, NEITHER WAS GUILE FOUND IN HIS MOUTH.

Paul exhorts us to "Put off the old man (or, works of the flesh -- see context) with his deeds," and "put on the NEW MAN, which is renewed in knowledge after the image of him that created him." Col. 3:9-10.

Listed below are some of the characteristics of the person who is carnal, and is not walking in the spirit. This list, though incomplete, may open up new channels of thought for many.

PRIDE; important, independent spirit, stiffness, or precisiveness.

LOVE OF PRAISE; love to be noticed; love of supremacy; drawing attention to one's self, as in conversation.

ARGUING; talkative spirit; stubborn, unteachable spirit; selfwill; unyielding; headstrong disposition; driving, commanding spirit; criticizing spirit; peevishness; fretfulness; love to be coaxed and humored.

Speaking of faults and failures of others rather than of virtues of those more talented and appreciated than yourself.

Lustful stirrings, unholy actions, undue affection and familiarity toward the opposite sex. Wandering eyes.

Dishonest, deceitful disposition; evading or covering the truth; leaving a better impression of yourself than is true; exaggeration, or straining the truth. >p>Selfishness; love for money; love for ease; laziness.

Formality; spiritual deadness; lack of concern for souls; dryness and indifference.

LACK OF POWER WITH GOD!

Get on your knees before God, and let him talk to you about these things, and give you a list of your own. You may find that there will be many other things which are now present in your life, which God will show you MUST BE CHANGED.

A good check up on the things which we do, say, and think is to ask yourself the question, "Would Jesus do this?" If He would you are following his steps. If He would not, you are missing the mark. You cannot have power with God. You may even fail to reach heaven.

Such a life of holiness is not impossible. God has commanded it, and "He that hath begun a good work in you will perform it --" Phil. 1:6.

"Is anything too hard for the Lord?" Gen. 18:14. God said to Paul, "My grace is sufficient for

thee". His grace is sufficient for you as well.

IF YOU REALLY WANT HOLINESS it is not beyond your reach.

And without it you will never share in GOD'S MIRACLE WORKING POWER!

Chapter 6
SELF DENIAL

"If any man will come after me, let him DENY HIMSELF, and take up his cross daily, and follow me." Luke 9:23.

The path that Jesus walked is a way of self denial.

You are reading this book because you desire to "come after him." Then DENY YOURSELF!

Someone once said, "No man spake as this man! Few have learned to deny self.

While we read in the scripture of Jesus, "Rising up A GREAT WHILE BEFORE DAY, he went out, and departed into a solitary place and there prayed". (Mark 1:35) How many of those who would do the works he did, find little or no time for prayer. How few of them can bear solitude. Yes, often they pray beautifully in a crowd, or when others may be listening. But the lonely hours of the night spent in solitary prayer bring no glory to SELF. Self would rather turn a little, to find a more comfortable spot on his comfortable bed, and drift softly back to sleep. Self says, "I must have my rest." Self will raise his hand smilingly, when asked who will pray an hour during the night or early morning. Self will rejoice that he has been seen taking this sacrificial hour, and how well his neighbors will think of him. But self will turn off the alarm when it sounds, and go back to sleep. Self says, "It does no good to pray anyway, when you don't feel like it." Jesus said, "Let him DENY HIMSELF." This is sacrifice -- real sacrifice to God. And God honors sacrifice.

In one of my early meetings, in southern Missouri, good crowds had been attending for a week, but not one soul had responded to the altar call. My wife and I decided that this MUST be changed, and agreed between ourselves that we would pray all night for souls to be saved in that meeting. Already we were weary in body, for the hour was late, and the service had been a hard one. Soon weariness began to creep down upon us, and even to stay awake seemed almost impossible. Again and again one must waken the other. There was no shouting, no excitement --nothing to keep us awake but the knowledge that in this little community which God had given to us as our responsibility, souls were lost, and we must see them saved. And we had promised God to pray it through. As the sun crept over the eastern horizon, we knew that we had kept our vow, and that something was going to happen that night. We could hardly wait for the time of the service. And that night, victory came. One after another responded to the call, until nineteen souls had found salvation, and were shouting the praises of God in a little country schoolhouse, under the ministry of a preacher who had only been preaching three weeks. As we went home rejoicing from that service, we knew that God had taught us a lesson -- it pays to DENY SELF the rest he may think is rightly his. It pays to pray it through, whether self is stimulated by any good feelings, or urge to pray, or not.

SELF says, "Pray if you feel like it." SELF DENIAL says, "PRAY ANYWAY."

There are times when prayer is a delight -- when it is a time of refreshing to the weary soul. But there are times when prayer is meeting the enemy face to face upon the battleground of the world, to drag by force from his grasp the things which by God's promise are rightly ours, but which Satan will keep us from having, if he can possibly do so. There are times when we must wrestle in prayer, as did Jacob, when he cried, "I will not let thee go, except thou bless me." Gen. 32:26. There are times when the answer is slow in coming, and we must hold on patiently as did Daniel, for three full weeks (Dan. 10:2). There are times when this wrestling may leave the body weary, and the nerves overwrought, as in the case of

Elijah when he had prayed down the fire and the rain (See I Kings 18, and 19:4). At times like that, prayer requires self denial. But it pays. Only the person who BELIEVES in the power of prayer will deny himself the rest which his body demands, in order to pray. And God's promise is "Whatsoever ye shall ask in prayer, BELIEVING, ye shall receive." Matt. 21:22.

Real prayer -- determined, prevailing prayer -- is the greatest outlet of power on earth.

The early church prayed ten days and then -- the miracle of Pentecost.

Moses spent forty days in the mountain talking with God, and his face shone so that he wore a veil.

Muller prayed, and secured one million dollars, making possible the care of 2,000 orphans.

Jesus went upon the mountain to pray, and returned to cast out demons which go forth only by prayer and fasting. (Mark 9:29.) He did not say to the sorrowing father, "This kind goeth not out but by prayer and fasting. Wait while I go away to fast and pray." He had already fasted and prayed! Self denial, fasting and prayer, was a part of his daily life. It was his habit of life. He prayed first, and when the need arose, he was already "prayed through", and ready to meet the need.

How many think they are denying self, when their self denial is only for selfish ends, to make their voice to be heard on high. (See Isa. 58:3-7.)

Fasting is an important part of self denial. The desire for food -- the richest, the tastiest, and the best -- is one of the strongest desires of self. It was for food that Esau sold his birthright. It was to physical hunger -- the desire for food -- that Satan directed the first of the series of temptations to Christ when he was in the wilderness. Paul, that great apostle of power, declared that he was "in fastings often". (II Cor. 11:27.)

Food itself is not sinful. But if it is given undue importance, it becomes a god, and when it becomes a god, it becomes a SIN.

Paul warned his church at Philippi of some whom they might be tempted to follow, "they are the enemies of the cross of Christ: whose end is destruction, whose GOD IS THEIR BELLY, and whose glory is their shame, WHO MIND EARTHLY THINGS." Phil. 3:18,19.

Many who desire the miracle working power of God in their lives today are hindered by the fact that they still would rather miss God's best for them than to miss a good meal.

How hard it was for me to remain on my knees in my closet of prayer when the good smell of food cooking began to filter in through the cracks around the door! And it was not until I resolutely turned my back upon the delicious stew, and went back to my closet without my dinner, that I heard the voice of God. It was only then that I proved to God that he meant more to me than food -- that my belly was not my God.

Fasting itself has no power to accomplish miracles, unless it is done rightly. The Israelites of Isaiah's time cried out, "Wherefore have we fasted, and thou seest not?" (Isa. 58:3). God's reply, through his prophet, was, "Behold, in the day of your fast ye find pleasure, and exact all your labors. Behold ye fast for strife and debate, and to smite with the fist of wickedness: ye shall not fast as ye do this day, to make your voice to be heard on high." (v. 3,4.) If our fasting is to help any about making our voice to be heard on high, it must be accompanied by a real heart searching, and seeking after God. It must include an enlarged vision of our responsibility to be our brother's keeper. Fasting must be done unselfishly, if it is to be done effectively. "Is not this the fast that I have chosen? to loose the bands of wickedness, to undo the heavy burdens, and to let the oppressed go free, and that ye break every yoke? Is it not to deal thy bread to the hungry, and that thou bring the poor that are cast out to thy house? when thou seest the naked that thou cover him; and that thou hide not thyself from thine own flesh?" (V. 6:7). When fasting is done God's way, he has given the promise, "Then shall thy light break forth as the morning, and thine health shall spring forth speedily; and thy righteousness shall go before thee; the glory of the Lord shall be thy reward. THEN SHALT THOU CALL, AND THE LORD SHALL ANSWER: thou shalt cry and he shall say, Here I am." V. 8,9.

Jesus fasted, and expected that those who followed him would fast, but pointed out to his followers that not every fast was acceptable with God (See Matt. 6:16-18). Those who fasted boastfully were branded by him as HYPOCRITES. He declared that they received ALL of their reward in the admiration of those around them, who looked only upon the outward appearance. The fasting which he recommended was to be done privately -- a secret transaction between the individual and God. If possible, even the immediate family were not to be informed that a fast was in progress. When fasting is done this way, God will hear from heaven, and will reward you openly, by answering your prayer.

How much better to have people say, "That man has power with God. The sick are healed, the lame walk, the dumb speak, and the blind see when he prays," than to have them say,

"That man is sure a pious man. He fasts three days of the week. He has completed a twenty one day fast, and is even now in the tenth day of a forty day fast."

Some fine people have been misled into wasted time and sacrifice, which brought no good to anyone because they became puffed up and did their fasting with a spirit of boastfulness. It is Satan's business to spoil all that we try to do for God. Let us be watchful in this matter, or else he will make useless one of our most effective weapons, the weapon of self denial through fasting.

True fasting is a matter of giving God first place over all the demands of the self life. It goes deep into the personal life. Paul recommended that while husband and wife are each to consider his or her body the personal property of the other, and to be subject one to the other, seeking to please each other in every way possible, that it is wise that the Christian husband and wife set aside by agreement times when personal gratification is to be ruled out, in order that God may be FIRST, that he may occupy all their thoughts, that one or the other, or both together, may give themselves to fasting and prayer. God does not condemn marriage, nor the rightful relationship of husband and wife. But even this, which is rightfully yours, may, like our food, be set aside for a time of seeking God, with great profit.

The closer we walk to God, the greater will be the power in our lives. This closeness can be achieved in one way -- "Draw nigh to God and he will draw nigh to you." James 4:8.

Self denial will many times take you out of the company which you would find most enjoyable. No doubt, the company you keep is good company. But if you are to have power with God, you must have fellowship with God. Fellowship with god's people is wonderful, and is needed by every Christian, especially those who are young in the Lord. But there is another fellowship which is even more necessary. "Truly our fellowship is with the Father, and with his Son Jesus Christ" I John 1:3.

Those who have power with God, and are bringing deliverance to the sick and suffering, and winning souls to Christ, are spending much time alone with God before they spend time with the people.

These things cannot be done in a moment. Power is the result of WAITING UPON THE LORD. Self says hurry. But self must be denied again. Pentecost followed ten days of waiting upon the lord. Daniel's vision of the last days followed 23 days of waiting. Because Moses had not learned to wait upon the Lord to know His method as well as His will, he had to wait forty years in exile before he was ready to do the work of deliverance which God had given him to do.

"Rest in the Lord, and wait patiently for him." Ps. 37:7.

Waiting is almost a lost art. Everything is done in a hurry. So many things require only the pushing of a button, but there is no button to push -- no magic formula -- no "royal road" -- to power with God. The man who has waited upon God commands the demon to depart, and the tormented one is free. The man who hasn't time to "waste" in waiting speaks the same words, seems to do the same things, but nothing happens. Waiting upon God is not wasted time, although it many times may seem to you as well as to others that you are doing nothing. Waiting on God includes fasting, prayer, and just plain waiting. When we pray, we talk to God. but when you have prayed until there seems to be nothing more to say, then you need to wait for an answer. Let God speak to you.

Self is restless and impatient, always clamoring for action or for attention, or for gratification. Self is mindful of the things that are of this world, the things of the flesh. But "If any man will come after me, let him DENY HIMSELF." Luke 9:23.

Will you come after Him? Will you do the works He did? Then wait in His presence and let Him speak to your soul about the things of self which have not yet been denied. Let His life of self denial be your pattern, and you are well on the way to sharing in His MIRACLE-WORKING POWER.

Chapter 7
THE CROSS

"If any man will come after me, let him deny himself, and TAKE UP HIS CROSS DAILY and Follow me." Luke 9:23.

There will be very little gained by self denial unless you also take up your cross, and follow Jesus.

By the cross I mean that load, or burden, of pain or sorrow or sacrifice which could, if we choose, be laid aside, but which is willingly carried or endured for the sake of others. It is that which in the natural we WOULD lay aside, but spurred on by the realization that there is no other way to bring salvation, deliverance or healing to the lost, the sick and the suffering, we willingly endure OUR CROSS.

"Looking unto Jesus -- who FOR THE JOY THAT WAS SET BEFORE HIM, ENDURED THE CROSS, despising the shame." Heb. 12:2. Jesus didn't have to endure the cross. Even on the night when He was taken, He declared that He could yet, at that late hour pray to the Father, and He would send more than twelve legions of angels, to rescue Jesus from such a fate. (See Matt. 26:53,54.) He went to the cross because he had purposed in His heart to fulfill the scriptures, and to deliver the race of lost and sinful men from the double curse of sin and sickness, by bearing the stripes upon His back, and by being sacrificed, a lamb without spot or blemish, upon THE CROSS.

Moses partook of this spirit, when he turned away from the throne of Egypt to identify himself with his brethren, a race of slaves, that he might through suffering and sacrifice bring deliverance to them all. (See Heb. 11:24,26.)

Paul demonstrated the same determination, when he left his place in the Sanhedrin to join the despised and persecuted sect of Christians, that he might not be disobedient to the heavenly vision, and that he might bring deliverance to the Gentiles. He was following Jesus, BEARING HIS CROSS, when he declared, "I go bound in the spirit unto Jerusalem, not knowing the things that shall befall me there: SAVE THAT THE HOLY GHOST WITNESSETH in every city, saying that BONDS AND AFFLICTIONS ABIDE ME. But none of these things MOVE ME, neither COUNT I MY LIFE DEAR unto myself, so that I might -- testify the gospel of the grace of God." Acts 20:22-24.

When Charles G. Finney left a promising law practice to enter the ministry -- an untried field for which he had no special training -- he took up his cross.

But taking up the cross is not enough. It must be taken up DAILY! It must be taken up willingly, and carried faithfully, without fretting. It is easy to make a consecration -- to take up the cross --during the heat of an inspiring consecration call, but many fail to take it up again the next morning, or the next.

Christ never took a vacation from His cross. The cross even went with Him on His vacation! Although He stepped aside many times to rest, even then the burden was heavy upon Him.

when He sat down by the well in Samaria, weary and hungry, to rest while His disciples went into the city to buy food, He had time and strength to lead a soul to salvation, and to start a movement which later brought about the great revival, which swept most of Samaria into the Kingdom of God. (Acts 8.)

When He was confronted with one of the greatest griefs which came into His life as a man in the flesh, the sudden and violent death of His cousin and dear friend, John the Baptist, He thought to slip away alone for a little time. (See Matt. 14:13,14.) But the people observed His going, and followed Him even then. When He looked upon them, He was filled with compassion, His own grief was forgotten, and

He took up His cross and went forth to heal their sick, and to minister to their needs.

The cross was not an accident which came to Him at the end of life. He was born, and lived and died under the shadow of the cross. He knew it was there all the time, but never once did He shun the cross. Never once did He fail to take up His cross DAILY. There was never a day that He could say, "This day is my own. I will go about my Father's business again tomorrow." Never an experience came into His life which He could say, "This is mine to enjoy. The people must wait until this is over. Then I will meet them and minister to their needs again." Even in His times of sorrow, He could not say, "My own grief is so great. It is no more than right that NOW I should be comforted. Let them minister unto me, now."

It was the night in which He was betrayed, when He knew that the time had come, and that the false disciple who would betray Him sat among those to whom He ministered, that He rose from the table to wash the feet of His disciples, demonstrating the thing which He had said before, "The Son of man came not to be ministered unto but to minister, and to give his life a ransom for many." Mark 10:45.

To the eyes of the world it would seem that it was only on that dark day of Calvary that "he bearing his cross went forth." John 19:16. But

He had been bearing His cross as he went forth among the people, poor, despised, lonely, misunderstood -- willingly, that He might bring with Him many sons unto glory -- going about doing good and healing all that were oppressed of the devil.

The world may not see nor understand your cross and mine. But each of us has his own cross, God appointed, which he can bear or not as he sees fit. This is not sickness which we are helpless to lay aside. It is not those unpleasant circumstances of life which would be ours whether we serve God or not. It is that which we accept willingly, at personal sacrifice to ourselves, in order that we may be obedient to God and a blessing to others. Have you been complimenting yourself on your cross bearing, and is it just a matter of feeling sorry for yourself about the circumstances of your life? Have you willingly taken upon yourself the burdens and griefs and sorrows of others, that you might lift them, and be a blessing -- that you might bring salvation and deliverance to those in need?

You say you want God's miracle working power. Are you willing to pay the price? Are you willing to take up YOUR cross, DAILY, and follow Jesus all the way?

If you follow Christ fully, it will mean following Him to the place where he was filled with the

Spirit, then on to the wilderness -- to the hours of fasting and prayer, to the hours of unappreciated service, through the misunderstandings and persecutions, the nights of watching alone in prayer. It will mean following Him into the garden -- bearing the burden of a lost world -- thinking someone nearby is sharing the load, only to find that all the rest have gone to sleep. Then away to the judgment hall -- false accusations, and unjust decisions. Now away to the whipping post, and the cat-o-nine tails -- the vinegar and the gall. It will allow no drawing back, even from the pain and suffering of the cross.

You may say, "That sounds like losing my life altogether."

Indeed it is. But Jesus said, "Whosoever will save his life shall lose it; but whosoever shall lose his life for my sake and the gospel's, the same shall save it." Mark 8:35.

This is life more abundant -- the life of POWER! The life of real satisfaction. The life of knowing that your living has not been in vain! Surely it is worth every sacrifice to know that we have followed in the steps of the son of God.

Chapter 8
"I MUST DECREASE" (JOHN 3:30)

Under this heading, God began to deal with me about my pride. I had never felt that I was proud. If such a thought were suggested to my mind, either through preaching or by direct accusation, or even by the faithful dealing of the spirit, I, like so many others, excused myself by calling this thing "self respect," "poise," "good breeding," or "high-mindedness." But God called it "SIN." Prov. 21:4

"An high look, and a proud heart . . . is sin." Prov. 21:4.

In the searchlight of His presence, there was no use to try to make explanations. Like John of old, I was made to realize my utter dependence upon God, and how little my own efforts were worth. I was made to realize, as I had never realized before, that even the best of my efforts were so futile, that truly God must take full control of my life, and that, before that could happen, I (my own personality, talents, knowledge, or natural ability) MUST DECREASE in importance in my own opinion.

I have since discovered that the power and success of any man's ministry depends upon the amount, or greatness, of God in his life. The New Testament disciples depended entirely upon "The Lord working with them, and confirming the Word with signs following." Mark 16:20. They claimed no power nor holiness for themselves, although at their work of command, a man lame for forty years -- having to be carried by his friends to a place where he might beg for his living -- was instantly healed, so that he not only walked, but leaped and ran. (See Acts 3:2-8 and 12-16). These were the same men who had once rejoiced, saying, "Lord, even the devils are subject unto US through thy name." Luke 10:17. Now they have decreased in their own sight, and are ready for an increased ministry. Hear them say, "Why look ye so earnestly on us, as though by our own power or holiness we had made this man to walk? . . . His name through faith in his name hath made this man strong." Acts 3:12,16.

It is only as God increases in the life of one of His followers that power can increase, and this can never happen until SELF is decreased.

Oh that God's ministers -- yes, and laity as well -- could realize that it is "Not by MIGHT nor by POWER, but by my Spirit, saith the Lord of hosts." Zech. 4:6. The might and power here spoken of refer to man's might and power -- not to God's. To the natural and not to the supernatural. There are two sources of power. Many great church organizations today boast of their "power," "influence," or "popularity" in their community. Their power and influence are derived from the magnificence of their great church plants, their immense bank accounts, the efficiency of their organization, their numerical strength, and their connection with the "right" people -- those with wealth and influence in this world (though many of them do not so much as pretend ever to have been born again by the power of God, but only have joined the church as they would a social club.) Their fine talent, and soothing (spiritual sleep producing) worship services, their beautiful forms, all help to make them popular -- to give them power in a world of "religious," "respectable" sinners. It is from such as these that Paul has warned us (speaking as he was inspired by the Holy Ghost) that we must separate ourselves. "Having a form of Godliness, buy DENYING THE POWER THEREOF, from such turn away." II Tim. 3:5. These people would be greatly displeased if God should interrupt the controlled orderliness of one of their services by speaking out as He so often did in days gone by through one of His prophets, rebuking sin and calling them to lives of holiness and power. They make no plans, nor leave any room in their services, for the supernatural manifestation of the power of God.

True, there is a certain feeling of security and power, when we have achieved the building of a fine church edifice, have succeeded in bringing our organization to a state of good operating efficiency, have ceased to live in constant fear of not being able to meet our financial obligations, and are reaching the multitudes with the gospel. None of these things are wrong. We can gratefully thank God for them when they come our way. But all these things are nothing -- they are only a lifeless shell -- if the SUPERNATURAL POWER OF THE SPIRIT OF GOD is not there. They are a mere tower of Babel, reaching up toward a sky that is too far away, and doomed to failure and confusion, even though they appear to be enjoying success.

How blessed to have talent, consecrated and used for the glory of God. How good to have knowledge. What a comfort to have proper accommodations. But the one thing that is needful is the POWER OF GOD.

How many fine churches in our cities are finding their auditoriums hard to fill, while men and woman stand in the rain outside some great gospel tent, pitched on the edge of town, trying to find some space to get inside, in order that they may see what God is doing through His ministers who have placed the power of God first in their lives -- who have been willing to decrease that God might increase.

"Might," as Zechariah speaks of it, refers to the might of man, as physical effort, natural ability, talents, forms, ceremonies, rituals, ordinances and programs.

When the supernatural is gone, man will substitute the natural. He will substitute songs about the power of God for the reality, laying more and more stress upon the harmony and musical flourishes, as the real power of God decreases. Thank God for good music, but in itself it IS NOT THE POWER OF GOD! The might and the power of natural man will never fulfill the great commission, and bring deliverance to the multitudes. Although God may use them to some extent, with the anointing of the Spirit upon them, they cannot be used as a SUBSTITUTE FOR THE SPIRIT!

Even beautifully outlined sermons, eloquently preached by men of strong personality and charm, will never get the job done alone. After all, even preaching is not our objective. It is merely a means to an end. If good sermonizing and beautiful preaching could get the job done, it would have been done long ago.

Oh that men would decrease!

Oh that they would realize that without God they are NOTHING!

If preachers could only realize that it is not the beauty and forcefulness of their preaching, altogether, which brings results, but the ANOINTING OF THE SPIRIT upon the sermon, and God in POWER in the man who does the preaching. People need more than to hear a sermon. They need to FEEL SOMETHING while that sermon is being preached. It is the SPIRIT that causes people to FEEL the preaching.

Paul was not, like some of the other disciples, an ignorant and unlearned man. His was the best education available in his time. His speech to the men of Athens, on Mars Hill, is still recognized as one of the best classics of persuasive debate, and of homoletical and literary arrangement. (See Acts 17:22-31.) His background, education, and reputation among his fellows was such that he could declare, "I might also have confidence in the flesh. If any other man thinketh that he hath whereof he might trust in the flesh, I more." Phil. 3:4. But Paul turned it all aside. He was willing to decrease. "But what things were gain to me, those I counted loss for Christ." Phil. 3:7. Although, as we have already seen, Paul was capable of eloquent speech, he wrote to the Corinthians, "My speech and my preaching was NOT with enticing words of man's wisdom, BUT IN DEMONSTRATION OF THE SPIRIT AND OF POWER." I Cor. 2:4. In the next verse he tells us why he had laid aside his natural talents to depend upon the power of God and that alone. "That your faith should not stand in the wisdom of men, but in the power of God."

If the power of God were given its rightful place today, more people's faith would stand in the power of God. Not so many would be trusting in their CHURCH (instead of the lord) for salvation, and not so many would be carried away by some preacher's personality, so that they are of no use to God nor man unless they can work under His leadership.

Paul recognized the importance of the spirit upon his preaching. "Not that we are sufficient of our selves to THINK ANYTHING as of our selves; but our sufficiency is of God; who also hath made us able ministers of the New Testament; NOT OF THE LETTER, BUT OF THE SPIRIT: FOR THE LETTER KILLETH, BUT THE SPIRIT GIVETH LIFE." II Cor. 3:5-6.

People today need LIFE (life cannot come without the Spirit). God will make us able ministers -- able to bring life and deliverance -- of the New Testament as we decrease to the extent that we place man with all his natural ability, all that calls attention to and glorifies man, in the background.

Although Paul was a man of more than usual knowledge, due to his fine education and his richly varied experience, he was willing to cast it all aside, and to declare that he was "DETERMINED not to know ANYTHING among you save CHRIST." I Cor. 2:2.

Knowledge "puffeth up." I Cor. 1:8. Some people are of little use to God because they "know" too much. Paul speaks of some who are puffed up at the church at Corinth. (See I Cor. 4:18.) By this he meant they were "oversize," or needed to decrease, or be deflated. These seemed to be fine speakers, but Paul declared the test of what they were should be, not their speech, but POWER. "For the Kingdom of God is not in word, BUT IN POWER." Verse 20.

How easy it is to see that this is true! And how foolish we make ourselves appear many times, by trying to appear to be what we are not, because of pride!

Pride takes five forms. Pride of FACE. (How much better we DO look than those around about us!) Pride of PLACE. (Don't ask THAT of one in my POSITION!) Pride of RACE. (We come of an excellent family, you know, and must uphold the family honor at any cost.) Pride of PACE. (Everyone should be able to see that we are the most capable and efficient person available. No one else could keep up with us!) And then that last and WORST of all the forms of pride -- pride of GRACE! Proud of our spiritual accomplishments; proud of the length of our fasts; proud of visions and dreams and revelations; proud of the gifts we think we possess; feeling that we must be a special favorite with God; yes, even proud of our humility! Whatever form our pride may have taken, puffing us up like a toy balloon, the first thing that must be done, before we can have real power with God, is "I MUST DECREASE."

"Whosoever exalteth himself shall be abased; but he that humbleth himself shall be exalted." Luke 14:11.

"God resisteth the proud, but giveth grace unto the humble." James 4:6.

How, then, can you hope for God to work with you, confirming the Word with signs following, when God has said He is RESISTING YOU!

Yes, I must decrease. Only the gold must remain. All the dross must be taken away, and all the tin, before God can work with it as he desires to work. And how little there is left, when the dross is gone!

Chapter 9
"HE MUST INCREASE" (JOHN 3:30)

Did you ever drive across the prairie, and note in the distance a mountain? At first sight the mountain seems very small. But as you drive on, and come closer to the mountain, you are astonished to see how rapidly it seems to grow. Really, the mountain isn't growing. It is still the same size as when you first observed it. The difference is that you have drawn closer to the mountain. This is exactly what takes place when God "increases." He is the same God to all men. But to some people, He seems to be a little, shriveled up, impotent God, who can scarcely be expected to do anything that really matters. The reason for this is that these people are living TOO FAR AWAY FROM HIM! This is why we are instructed, "Draw nigh to God." James 4:8.

God is far away from many people because they have allowed so many things to come in between. Some even draw nigh to God with their mouth, while their heart is far from Him. (Matt. 15:8.) Of these He says, "In vain do they worship me." The only way that it is possible to draw near to God, is to begin earnestly, with all your heart to search out those things which come between, and GET RID OF THEM!

Pride certainly will keep God at a distance. "The proud he knoweth AFAR OFF." Psalm 188:6. God cannot work WITH you when He is FAR FROM you. You must come to Him humbly.

Some have excused the lack of power in their lives, by saying, "The day of miracles is past. The church is established now, and it doesn't need miracles any more." Nowhere does the scripture confirm any such thought. "Jesus Christ (is) the SAME, yesterday, today and forever." Heb.

13:8.

Behold, the Lord's hand is not shortened, that it cannot save; neither his ear heavy, that it cannot hear: BUT YOUR INIQUITIES HAVE SEPARATED BETWEEN YOU AND YOUR GOD." Isa. 59:1,2. Don't blame God for your lack of power. Put the blame squarely where it belongs. YOU are too far from God, because there are too many iniquities (sins) in between.

Friends and loved ones may come between. Jesus said, "He that loveth father or mother more than me is not worthy of me: and he that loveth son or daughter more than me is not worthy of me." Matt. 10:37.

The cares of life may come between, as weeds choking out a crop, making it unfruitful. Some give all their thought to the things of this life, as though they would live here forever. God cannot work with such as these. To be near to the heart of God, and to feel the pulse beat of His compassion for the lost, and the suffering, one must have a constant realization of the shortness of life, and the inevitability of eternity.

Some are kept at a distance from God by lack of appreciation. Praise is lacking in their lives. Real appreciation for what God IS and what He has done, will bring forth praise. Praise brings us into the very presence of God. "Enter into his gates with thanksgiving, and into his courts with praise." Ps. 100:4.

Some who read this book, may not know that God desires to be so near to his people, as to send his HOLY SPIRIT to take up his abode not simply near, but WITHIN the child of God. When you have opened your heart and allowed the Spirit of God to fill you, baptize you, taking possession of every part of your body, you will find him much nearer than ever before. He will be a much greater God to you, than you have ever known. Then as he is allowed to continue to dwell in you richly, teaching and guiding you day by day, into a closer relationship with the father, and into a more pure life of holiness, the greatness of God will become more and more apparent. He will increase in your life.

The more you come to know Him, by walking by his side day by day, and the more you feed upon his word, the more he will increase in your sight. All that we know of God, we know by faith. "Faith cometh by hearing, and hearing by the word of God." Rom. 10:17. Feed upon the Word of God. It is strange, but some even hope to have power with God who pay very little heed to the word of God. He will not honor with his presence those who dishonor his word.

It is the Word of God which will help us to cleanse from our lives the SINS which stand between. "Wherewithal shall a young man cleanse his way? By taking heed thereto according to thy word." Psalm 119:9.

In dealing with me about this matter, God made it very plain to me that if these things were allowed to persist in my life, if sin were tolerated and allowed to remain, God would continue to be at a distance from me. He would be so far away, that he would be to me only the little, meaningless God whom so many others profess to serve. The only way that God could increase in my life to the point where he would be working through me in power, was for me to keep everything out from between me and God. The only way he could remain the great "I AM" in my own experience, was for me to continually walk in the light of his word, by the power of his spirit, DECREASING day by day, becoming more and more absorbed in Him who must INCREASE.

He MUST increase! Not could increase. Not might increase. He MUST increase. He must increase in glory, and majesty and power. He must increase in control of my life.

"I am crucified with Christ. Nevertheless I live; YET NOT I, BUT CHRIST LIVETH IN ME." Gal. 2:20.

"Fill me with thy spirit, till all the world may see,

Not me, but Jesus only, shining out through me."

Chapter 10
IDLE WORDS AND FOOLISH TALKING

"Every idle (unprofitable) word that men shall speak, they shall give account thereof in the day of judgment." Matt. 12:36.

Nothing more quickly and thoroughly reveals the lack of real spirituality than does foolish talking, jesting, and IDLE WORDS. There is nothing that will more surely label the shallow Christian as one who has no concern for others, nor any burden for the lost and suffering than his perpetual flow of foolish talking, and nonsensical joking. Although in the eyes of many, this seems to be a small matter, there are few spiritual diseases more devastating, nor more contagious.

God classes foolish talking along with some very unattractive companions, -- "But fornication, and all uncleanness, or covetousness, let it not be once named among you, as becometh saints: neither filthiness, nor FOOLISH TALKING, nor JESTING, which are not convenient: but rather giving of thanks." Eph. 5:3,4.

Jesus himself declared, "--Evil thoughts, adulteries, fornications, murders, thefts, covetousness, wickedness, deceit, lasciviousness, an evil eye, blasphemy, pride, FOOLISHNESS: all these EVIL THINGS come from within, and DEFILE the man." Mark 7:21-23. Foolishness, then will defile a man, the same as fornication! There are many who would never kill nor steal, but will even enter the pulpit, and publicly and unashamed, reveal through their words that they are defiled within. I have never yet found a man whom the Lord is using mightily for the deliverance of the sick and sinful whose mouth is filled with foolishness. They may entertain the people, and get a few hearty laughs in response to their jokes and nonsense, but when it comes to really being able to bring deliverance, or to bring a help and blessing when a real need arises, THEY HAVEN'T GOT THE GOODS! They may even try at times to put off the usual character of lightness for a little while, and to preach or teach about deep things, but to those who hear them there is no ring of sincerity, no real persuasion that they speak as the oracles of God. They are like sounding brass, or a tinkling cymbal.

I do not wish to infer that God's people should go around with a long face all the time, having no joy. God's people are the happiest people in the world. God has commanded, "Rejoice evermore." I Thes. 5:13. God's people are expected to be so happy that they will shout, sing, clap their hands, dance, laugh, and even leap for joy. A few scriptures which show these things are the following:

"Make a JOYFUL NOISE unto the Lord, all ye lands. Serve the Lord with GLADNESS: come before his presence with SINGING." Ps. 100:1,2.

"O CLAP YOUR HANDS, all ye people: SHOUT unto God with the voice of triumph." Ps.

47:1.

"Let them praise his name in the DANCE: let them SING praises unto him with the TIMBREL and HARP." Ps. 149:3.

"David DANCED before the Lord with all his might." II Sam. 6:14.

"Then was our mouth filled with LAUGHTER, and our tongue with SINGING: then said they among the heathen, The Lord hath done great things for us; whereof we are GLAD." Ps. 126:2,3.

"Rejoice in that day, and LEAP FOR JOY." Luke 6:23.

For the Joy of the Lord is thy strength." Neh. 8:10.

The Christian who doesn't have JOY is a weak Christian, a poor representative of the faith he claims, and will probably soon be completely backslidden, and seeking his joy somewhere else.

This joy which brings strength is rejoicing in the Lord. It is not rejoicing in the power of our own strength, nor of our own wit. "But now rejoice ye in your boastings: all such rejoicing is evil." James 3:2.

Many who are guilty of the sin of foolish, excessive, and unprofitable talking will at first be tempted to brand me a fanatic, and to rise to the defense of their pet sin. They will declare that it is a mistake to take things too seriously. For this, they can find no scriptural defense. The rescuing of the lost, and deliverance of the suffering, is a serious matter, requiring the whole heart and mind of the one who is consecrated to the task. Many have reserved the right to talk as much, and in whatever manner, they choose. They would rather have their jokes, foolish jesting and nonsense than to have the power of God in their lives. If this is your case, God will have to go on without YOU.

God has chosen to work through the spoken word of representatives in the world. When Jesus was here, he said to his disciples, "The WORDS that I speak unto you, THEY ARE

SPIRIT, AND THEY ARE LIFE." John 6:63. What are your words?

James compares the speech coming out of our mouths to water coming from a fountain. (James 3:10,11.) He insists that a fountain should give forth the same kind of water all the time -- not sweet water part of the time, and bitter water part of the time. Then he adds, "Who is a wise man and endued with knowledge among you? Let him show out of a good CONVERSATION his works with meekness of wisdom." James 3:13.

"Let no corrupt communication proceed out of your mouth, BUT THAT WHICH IS GOOD TO THE USE OF EDIFYING." Eph. 4:29.

Words which are not good to the use of edifying are IDLE (vain, empty, or unprofitable) words. They are WASTED words. God has given to the believer's WORD an authority and power which makes it precious. Precious things should not be wasted.

Jesus said, "Whosoever (that means you!) shall SAY unto this mountain, be thou removed, and be thou cast into the sea; and shall not doubt in his heart, but shall believe that those things which he SAITH shall come to pass, he shall have WHATSOEVER HE SAITH." Mark 11:23. This gives to US the power to speak with authority, even to the extent of controlling inanimate things. This is the same power which Jesus used when he spoke to the wind and the sea, and the storm was gone. (Mark 4:39.) It is the same power which Moses used when he spoke to the rock in the desert, and water gushed forth. (Num. 20:8.) Joshua used the same power when he commanded the sun and the moon to stand still. (Joshua 10:12, 13.) Jesus demonstrated the use of this power when he spoke to the fig tree, saying, "No man eat fruit of thee hereafter forever." (Mark 11:14.) He told the tree to die, AND it died! It was on this occasion that he expressly delegated this same power and authority to ANY who BELIEVE.

It is to men and women whose words can be with such power -- whose spoken words can bring deliverance from every oppression of Satan -- salvation for the soul and healing for the body --that Jesus warned that IDLE, WASTED, WORDS should be brought into judgment. Words which should have been life and deliverance! Words which should have been bread to starving souls! But words which were nothing but chaff! In the face of a world of dying, starving souls and suffering humanity, withholding the one source of life and deliverance, and offering stones for bread! Sending forth from the fountain which should give forth the PURE WATER OF LIFE a stream of froth and foolishness, which is, if not poisonous, utterly unattractive and unprofitable! What will you say to the judge in that day, when our deeds and WORDS are judged by the standard of the word of God, in which we are exhorted, "If any man SPEAK, let him SPEAK AS THE ORACLES (utterance or speech) OF GOD." I Peter 4:11.

Those who insist upon having their foolishness at any cost, are so like the group of young ladies seen in a vision by a consecrated saint of God, who were too busy making daisy chains to warn the people who were hurrying by that their steps were leading to an awful precipice, where they would quickly fall over, and be dashed to death upon the rocks below. This is far from the spirit of Christ, who HAD COMPASSION UPON THE MULTITUDES.

I do not intent to infer that there is no place for humor in the conversation of the Christian, or even in the preaching of the Word. Many times, our speech or preaching can be humorous, and yet sanctified. Often, a bit of humor, especially when used to illustrate a point, can be very profitable, in arousing the attention and interest of the hearers, and in driving home the message of the gospel, so that souls are aroused and turned to God. So used, it is NOT idle, nor unprofitable.

The reason so many Christians speak so many idle words, is that they speak SO MANY

WORDS! They talk so much that they have no time to think, and no time to listen to the voice of God. Foolish words come so easily. We do not even have to think of them. We can listen to any conversation, anywhere, and come away with a large supply of them which can be produced by repetition. The spirit of the age is an ever increasing spirit of levity, which makes serious thinking difficult for both sinner and saint. It is typified by the oft repeated saying, "Don't take life too seriously. After all you'll never get out of it alive." In such an age it takes real effort and consecration to "Study to be quiet", and to wait before God long enough to have words to speak which are the words of God, and which can have power. But the wise man will do it. "He that hath knowledge, spareth his words." Prov. 17:27. "But the mouth of fools FEEDETH ON FOOLISHNESS." Prov. 15:14.

"In the multitude of words there wanteth not sin." Prov. 10:19.

A fool's voice is known BY MULTITUDE OF WORDS." Eccl. 5:3.

Holiness is necessary for power, as has already been shown in previous chapters of this book. And holiness is not complete until it has also taken possession of the tongue. "But as he which hath called you is holy, so be ye holy IN ALL MANNER OF CONVERSATION." I Pet. 1:15.

I beseech you, brethren, for the sake of the lost and suffering who will never find deliverance UNLESS YOU MAKE YOURSELF READY TO TAKE IT TO THEM, give this matter your prayerful consideration. Consecrate yourself to God afresh. Present to him YOUR BODY, a living sacrifice, AND DO NOT FORGET NOR NEGLECT TO INCLUDE YOUR TONGUE, YOUR LIPS, YOUR VOICE!"

"Let your speech be always with grace, seasoned with salt." Col. 4:6.

"Keep that which is committed to thy trust (the power to speak in God's stead, and bring deliverance), avoiding profane (not holy) and vain (empty, worthless) babblings." I Tim. 6:20.

It is my prayer that all who read this book will put all on the altar, and get in a place where they can carry a burden for the lost and suffering: that they will cast aside ALL those things which hinder the power of God in their lives. God can go on without you. But if YOU go on with God, you must go His way. Put foolishness aside NOW! Get out of the eddy and into the stream of God's power.

The PROMISES are for you, if you will only believe them, meet God's conditions, and PAY THE PRICE.

Chapter 11
PRESENT YOUR BODY

I beseech you therefore, brethren, by the mercies of God, that ye present your bodies a living sacrifice, holy, acceptable unto God, which is your reasonable service." Rom. 12:1.

God has never made it a habit to use things THAT DO NOT BELONG TO HIM. He uses those things which are yielded to him. Things that are CONSECRATED. THINGS THAT ARE SANCTIFIED -- SET APART FOR HIS USE. Do you want God to USE YOU? Then you must PRESENT YOUR BODY. It must be completely yielded and surrendered to God. A body that is not completely yielded and surrendered to God is still more or less domineered by Satan, or by self.

Many no doubt have, at special times, after a fashion, presented their bodies to the Lord for his use in stretching forth the borders of his Kingdom. But it is obvious from the fact that they are not being used, that many of those who have presented themselves have NOT BEEN ACCEPTED.

God has not refused them because laborers are not needed. Christ himself gave us the command to pray that more laborers would be sent forth because "THE HARVEST TRULY IS PLENTEOUS, BUT THE LABORERS ARE FEW." Matt. 9:37.

God has not refused them because of their handicaps, for he has often used those who seemed to have little natural qualification. Peter and John, men greatly used of God, were "unlearned and ignorant men" Acts 4:13. Moses was "slow of speech." "Not many wise men after the flesh, not many noble, are called; BUT GOD HATH CHOSEN the foolish things of the world to confound the wise; and God hath chosen the weak things of the world to confound the things which are mighty; and the base things of the world and things which are despised --." I Cor. 1:27, 28. You think you are handicapped? All are handicapped in some way.

A young man was saved, and desired to give his testimony in a street meeting that others might know the matchless grace of God, but he could not give his testimony because of his stammering. Yet his love for God, and his desire to work for God drove him to his knees, and out again before the people. God heard his cry and helped him. He became a great preacher of the gospel and for many years was annually the chief speaker at a large camp meeting in New York.

To be an acceptable sacrifice, your body need not be strong nor beautiful. David Brainard, great missionary to the American Indians in the early days, was declared to be dying of tuberculosis. He was warned that the only chance for him to live more than a few weeks was complete rest. But he brought what he had and made an acceptable sacrifice. He fell on his face before God, crying, "Give me souls or take my soul!" Then he rose up and went out to many years of fruitful ministry among the people God had laid upon his heart, and won thousands of them to Christ.

The only reason God has refused some is that THEY ARE NOT ACCEPTABLE!

God makes just two requirements for an "acceptable sacrifice".

It must be HOLY. And it must be HIS.

That which is not holy is an abomination to God. A sacrifice brought in and offered to God for his service, which is defiled by the habits and sins of the world is no more acceptable to him than the pig offered upon the sacred altar of the temple at Jerusalem by Antiochuc Epiphanes. IT WILL NOT BE ACCEPTED.

That which is HIS must be his not only on Sunday and on prayer meeting night, but seven days and nights EVERY WEEK. It must be presented with NO STRINGS ATTACHED.

It must be given with the heart cry, "I renounce all authority over this gift, now and forever. It is yours to use, to set aside, or to destroy. Whatever you choose to do with it, it is yours. If it is only a hidden ministry of prayer and personal testimony -- YES, LORD. If it is in my own home town, that is all right. If it takes me far across the sea, to strange lands and unfriendly peoples -- if it is to die for my faith, at the hands of persecutors, or to live under conditions that are worse than death -- still this body is yours. Do with it as you please. Feed it or starve it. Chill it in the far North, or let it suffer with the heat of Africa. Exalt it or humiliate it. It is all yours."

Acceptable consecration is like handing God a blank paper, with your name signed at the bottom, and saying, "Fill it in any way you want. That shall be my contract for the use of my entire life."

This sacrifice is not complete with merely saying yes or no to certain callings or requests of the spirit of God AFTER THEY HAVE BEEN GIVEN. It is the whole hearted determination to do the will of God ALL MY LIFE, no matter what it may be, nor what it may cost. It is the realization that "Ye are not your own."

You may find a small measure of power, and a small measure of blessing, when you have made a small measure of sacrifice. But if you would really experience the free flow of GOD'S MIRACLE WORKING POWER, you MUST present your body, a living sacrifice, HOLY, ACCEPTABLE UNTO GOD.

Chapter 12
A PARTAKER OF HIS DIVINE NATURE

"Whereby are given unto us exceeding great and precious promises that by these you might be PARTAKERS OF DIVINE NATURE." I Pet. 1:4.

God IS power. There is no power for good in this world except that power come from God. Christ himself, when he came into this world in the flesh, declared that he derived his power from God. "I do NOTHING of myself." John 8:28. "The Son CAN do nothing of himself." John

5:19. "I am in the father, and the Father in me. The Words that I speak unto you, I speak not of myself: but the FATHER THAT DWELLETH IN ME, HE DOETH THE WORKS." John

14:10.

After making the emphatic statement of John 14:10, Christ turned to his disciples with a promise -- "Verily, verily, I say unto you, He that believeth on me, THE WORKS THAT I DO SHALL HE DO ALSO; and greater works than these shall he do; because I go unto my Father." John 14:12. But, even as his own work and fruitfulness was conditioned upon his abiding in the Father, our work and fruitfulness was conditioned upon our abiding in him. "Abide in me, and I in you. As the branch cannot bear fruit of itself, except it abide in the vine; no more can ye, except ye abide in me." Jn. 15:4. "Without ME YE can do nothing." Jn. 15:5.

The branch is PARTAKER of the nature of the vine. The same sap flows through it. The texture of the wood is the same. The leaves are the same. The fruit is the same. The bark is the same. IT IS PART OF THE VINE! So long as it remains in the vine, it can do whatever the vine can do. But whenever it is separated -- cut off -- from the vine, it can no longer do what the vine can do. The life giving sap ceases to flow through the branch, and it is no longer partaker of the nature of the vine. For it is the nature of the vine to BRING FORTH FRUIT, and that the severed branch can never do.

Branches can be "cut off", and they can be grafted.

We, as sinners saved by grace, are compared in God's word to the branches of a wild olive tree, grafted in. Having been grafted in, we become PARTAKERS of the "root and fatness" of the olive tree. (Rom. 11:17.) If a graft is WELL MADE, so that nothing comes between and interferes with the flow of the sap into the new limb, it very soon comes to LOOK AND ACT like the other parts of the tree.

What a privilege to be made a partaker of the divine nature of God -- to LOOK in such a way that those who see us will realize that we have been with Jesus, and to ACT so much like him that the works he did WE DO ALSO!

We can only be partakers of this divine nature by his PROMISES, through faith in his promises. We partake of the divine nature in its effectiveness as we exercise the gifts of the spirit, and in its essence as we show forth the fruits of the spirit. It is in the exercising of the gifts of the Spirit that God shows forth through us his MIRACLE WORKING POWER. "Having then gifts differing -- whether prophecy, let us prophecy ACCORDING TO THE PROPORTION OF FAITH." Rom. 12:6. This is the secret of whatever work we are able to do for God. It is done ACCORDING TO THE PROPORTION OF FAITH. We are partakers of the divine nature ACCORDING TO THE PROPORTION OF FAITH. Little faith, the branch is barely alive, the sap barely getting through, a few green leaves making promise that fruit might come. More faith, more of the divine nature, fruitfulness. Much faith, ABUNDANT LIFE, the life giving sap flowing freely to every part of the branch, the weight of the fruit bowing it almost to the ground!

He who is a partaker of the divine nature of Christ will be a partaker of his nature of meekness and humility. The love and compassion of the nature of Christ will be apparent in all the activities and contacts of his daily life. The gentleness and kindness, the goodness, the longsuffering, and peace. The joy in service, the self denial (temperance) -- all these will be a part of the life of the person who is a partaker of the divine nature. These may not have been part of your nature before Christ came to dwell in you, but when you have become a partaker of his nature, these things will replace the former things, which were your OWN CARNAL NATURE.

Then when you are a partaker of his divine nature, there will be a wisdom which comes from following the leading of the Spirit. Not the wisdom which is purely natural, nor a wisdom gained merely from observation, but a spirit led wisdom which is incomprehensible to those who do not understand the leading of the spirit. There will be knowledge which comes to your mind out of the knowledge stored in the mind of God. Things which you need to know, but have no other way of knowing, God himself can and will reveal them unto you. There will be POWER, for God IS power! Miracles and Signs will follow. The sick will be healed, the lame will walk, cancers will vanish at your command. The blind will see, the deaf hear. Secrets of people's hearts will, when necessary, be made manifest. Souls will be stirred from the sleep of spiritual death, and brought as new creatures into the kingdom. Yea, even some whose physical lives are gone, may be brought again from the dead, in the will of God.

God plays no favorites. The same price of power stands to all. And the same power is available to ALL WHO WILL PAY THE PRICE!

To every one who, by faith, will take his "exceeding great and precious promises" for himself, believing with all his heart that GOD MEANT EXACTLY WHAT HE SAID, thus becoming a PARTAKER OF HIS DIVINE NATURE, the door is open to new adventures of faith, beyond your wildest dreams!

Chapter 13
PERSONAL THINGS

These are the eleven POINTS. I trust that God has made them live to you, and used them, as I have told them to you, to bring you closer to himself and into a position to have THE MIRACLE WORKING POWER OF GOD in your own life.

No doubt you have wondered many times, what were those two things which were so personal. This chapter will deal with this matter of "Personal Things". I cannot tell you what they were, for deep in my heart, I feel the Lord would not have me to do so. But as you read this book, read the Bible, and wait before the Lord in prayer, I am sure that you, too, will find some "Personal Things".

I pray that you may have been inspired to PRESS TOWARD THE MARK for the prize of the high calling of God in Jesus Christ." Phil. 3:14. To keep on pressing, until God is working in your life in Miracle Working Power. To strive earnestly for perfection in the sight of God, and to be in his perfect will.

"Let us therefore, as many as be perfect be thus minded; and if in anything ye be otherwise minded, GOD SHALL REVEAL EVEN THIS UNTO YOU." Phil. 3:15.

This is his promise. You need never know what were those things which God pointed out to me as being my OWN, PERSONAL, pet sins, which had to be pointed out by name. But you do need to recognize your own pet sins, which keep you from having the power God wants you to have!

I have found in my travels as an evangelist, as well as in experiences gained in pastorates, that most people have a pet sin which they have pampered and petted, and developed, for years. Paul terms it, "The sin which doth so easily beset us." (Heb. 12:1.), your "besetting sin". He also says it must be LAID ASIDE if we are to gain the prize at the end of the race. "Let us lay aside every weight and the sin which doth so easily beset us, and let us run with patience the race that is set before us."

Many good people, who COULD HAVE BEEN effective Christian workers have become so discouraged by the excess weights which they have failed to lay aside, that they have long ago dropped out of the race, and have become skeptics, even questioning the words of Jesus, concerning "signs following", and the power which God promised to the believer, that he should do the works which Christ did. Many over the land today are even now on the verge of giving up all hope of ever knowing God in the fullness of His power. DO NOT GIVE UP. Get alone with God. Seek him earnestly, whatever the cost may be, until he has revealed to you YOUR PET SIN. Until he has shown you what in your life needs cleansing before you can experience the power of God.

A rich young ruler once came to Jesus, anxious to know what was wrong with his religious experience. He was so anxious that he literally came RUNNING, and FELL DOWN at the master's feet. When he inquired, 'What must I do --?" Jesus replied, "one thing thou lackest --." Christ then put his finger upon the young man's pet sin, and instructed him how to get rid of it. (See Mk. 10:21.) As you seek the Lord, remember that he is always faithful to put his finger on your pet sin, as he did for the rich young ruler. Failure to place that sin upon the altar will cause you, too, to go away GRIEVED, just as he did. When God speaks to you, no matter how small the voice, OBEY! Get rid of that PET SIN and go on with God!

Your pet sin is the sin that you do not want the preacher to preach about.

It is the sin for which you are always ready to make an excuse.

It is the sin which, although you would not admit that it is sin, you prefer to do it when you think no one is going to find out.

It is the sin which leads you captive most easily.

It is the sin which you are always ready to defend.

It is the sin which causes the clouds of doubt and remorse to cross your spiritual sky, whenever you really feel the need to contact God.

It is the sin which you are most unwilling to give up.

It is the sin which you think is so small that God should scarcely be able to see it, yet so large that you are sure you could never live without it.

Yet it is the sin which must be FLUNG (Weymouth) aside or else you must drop out of the race.

And, last, it is the sin you are continually trying to make yourself believe is an infirmity. Be honest with yourself, and call it SIN! Do not call jealousy, watchfulness. If you are covetous, don't call yourself economical. If you are guilty of the sin of pride, don't dress it up as self respect. If you are one of those who constantly exaggerates (stretches the truth), you may as well admit that that which is not the truth is a LIE! Are you bound by a perverse (stubbornly wrong) demon? Be careful, or you will pride yourself in being very firm. If your besetting sin is lust, don't excuse yourself that you are just oversexed by nature. Don't call criticizing, the gift of discernment, nor claim to be a good judge of human nature. Are you fretful, and complaining? Satan will tell you that you are nervous, and in your condition, this fretfulness can't be helped.

Come on, friend. Be honest with yourself and God. Call it exactly what it is. If it is sin, call it sin, and get down before God and ask him to set you free and make you an overcomer.

No doubt many excuse themselves for their many "little" sins by pointing out, "Why everyone does that! Remember, you can't pattern your life after other people's mistakes. How do you know that God has not spoken to them many times about this very thing? Don't be as guilty of disobedience as they.

And what if he didn't speak to them about it? Remember the exhortation of Jesus to Peter when he enquired what would be required of another disciple. "What is that to thee? FOLLOW THOU ME." John 21:22.

Consecration has much to do with personal things. It is the putting off, out of our lives, the hundred and one little things that in themselves may not be sin, but which if they are allowed to remain, take the place that Christ should take. As an example, many professing Christians admit that they do not read their Bible as much as they should. They declare that they are so busy, they just don't have time to read it. Yet these same people have time to read all the daily and Sunday comic strips, many magazines and stories. There is but one conclusion. These comics, magazines, and stories are more important to them than the word of God. They have crowded out Christ from his rightful place in these people's lives. Some of this reading might be of such a nature as to be actually sinful in itself, but much of it is rather harmless, except for the fact that it HAS CROWDED OUT CHRIST. Thousands of those who profess to be believers in the Lord Jesus Christ today would have more power in their lives if the time they spend in listening to the ball games and "soap operas", and "perpetual emotion dramas" were spent listening to the voice of God, alone in the closet of prayer. These are some of the "little foxes that spoil the vines", destroying the tender grapes and robbing God's people of fruitfulness.

How much more powerful would be the lives of many, if the time they spend in front of their television sets (of course, they wouldn't go to a theater!) watching the wrestling matches were spent down upon their knees wrestling against Satan -- against the principalities and powers and the rulers of darkness of this world, and against spiritual wickedness in high places. (Eph. 6:12).

It isn't always the harsh, gross sins that stand between man and God. In fact, the sins which seem to keep most people from the best that God has for them, are the things that "everybody does". I'd go a little slow in saying "everybody". Those who are carrying a burden for this lost, sin sick, Christ-rejecting, hell-bound world, those who are doing the works which Christ promised them they should do, who have the signs following their ministry, and who are bringing deliverance to the needy, have long ago laid those things aside. You may be right in saying, "NEARLY everyone in my church does it." But don't forget that while they are doing these things, they, too, are wondering why they do not have the MIRACLE WORKING POWER OF GOD, and do not exercise the gifts of the spirit. Many of the same crowd wonder if they are ready for the rapture! Many times I have made altar calls after preaching on the coming of the Lord, for those who do not know that they are ready for the coming of Christ. At such times I have been surprised at the great number of people who raised their hands WHO PROFESSED TO

BE SAVED, AND EVEN SPIRIT FILLED, PEOPLE! It is evident that many so called saints today are not even living a sufficiently victorious life to know they are ready for the rapture. These CANNOT HAVE CONSISTENT MIRACLE WORKING POWER! They may have a prayer answered now and then, but the times in which we live, and the condition of the world about us demand more than that. YOU CANNOT PATTERN YOUR LIFE AFTER THIS CROWD. There is one whose life is worthy to be a pattern for ours. That one is JESUS.

Some may be unwilling to accept the teachings of holiness found in this book. I have no apology to make, if you do not. I quote Jesus all the way through the book. If you disagree with him, it is time you had better take stock of yourself, and begin to agree with God. "Can two walk together except they be agreed?" Amos 3:3. If you expect to walk with God, and to have power in your life to work the works of God, IT IS TIME TO AGREE WITH GOD. When you fully agree with God, this will put you in disagreement with some others. It is better to agree with God, even if in doing so one must disagree with others whose opinions he formerly honored and valued. Too many today are living to please others, and self, rather than the Lord.

There comes a time in the life of every person when he is at the fork in the road. Men of God and of Power throughout the ages have come to this fork in the road, and have chosen the way that seemed hard and that brought persecution, suffering and POWER because of God's approval. Others have come to the fork in the road, and have chosen the way that seemed more attractive, and have found that it led to prosperity, popularity, and destruction. Picture Lot of old, as he pondered the best course to take. There was the watered valley, with the prosperous city of Sodom at its center. Surely this was an easier way than to turn to the lonely rough hills. He felt sure he could go among those people in the valley, mind his own affairs, and not partake of their sins. And even at the end, God still accounted him as a "righteous man", but he had no power for God. Not even so much as to be able to rescue his own married daughters from the destruction of Sodom, for he seemed to them as one that mocked. (Gen. 19;14).

This way is still open to those who choose it. But thank God for the better way. It is open too. It is marked by the feet of such men as Moses, who "By faith -- when he was come to years, refused to be called the son of Pharaoh's daughter; choosing rather to suffer affliction with the people of God, than to enjoy the pleasures of sin for a season." Heb. 11;24,25.

And of Joseph, who when he came to this same fork in the road, chose to keep himself pure, although it meant spending years in an Oriental dungeon, with no assurance (except in his soul) that he would ever be released. And of Daniel, who as a slave boy, declined to drink the king's wine, and who later kept his appointment with God, although it meant a trip to the lion's den.

These men said no to Satan that they might say yes to God. Moses weighed the pleasures and treasures of Egypt against the call of God, and decided in favor of the call of God. He knew that the pleasures of sin could only last for a season. He esteemed the reproach of Christ GREATER RICHES! He had a true sense of values. How many today do not. They seem to think the greater riches are those of Egypt -- Hollywood, Broadway, or Wall Street. It is impossible to say yes to God until we have first said no to the things of the world.

Those whose minds are set upon worldly things would quickly have advised Moses that he was making a very unwise choice, giving up so much for so little. But Moses received his reward. He became a FRIEND OF GOD -- one who talked with God face to face. His face shone so with the brightness of the glory of

God, that the people could not even bear to look upon his face. And working hand in hand with God, he led three million people out of bondage into liberty, and saw them miraculously delivered time after time, and kept by the hand of God so that "There was not one feeble person in all their tribes." Ps. 105:37; Truly this is the reward which we seek today -- that we might be enabled to bring salvation and deliverance to the people. And God is giving that reward to many today who have heard his voice and obeyed his call! Who have said no to the world and yes to God!

God, in days gone by, "Sought for a man, that should make up the hedge and stand in the gap before (him) for the land that (He) might not destroy it." Ezek. 22:30-31. God is looking for such men today. God's holiness demands that he send judgment upon a wicked world. Only the presence of the righteous in the world holds back the floods of judgment. Moses stood in the gap for the children of Israel, and their lives were spared. (See Exodus 32:10,11.) Abraham stood in the gap for Lot and his family, when they were in Sodom. And Lot, had he gathered around him a group of righteous people, saved from their sinfulness through his testimony and influence, could have stood in the gap for the entire city of Sodom. (Gen. 18;23, 19:15.)

The generation in which we live is a wicked generation, similar to those among whom Lot lived. It is a sick sin, judgment bound generation. The wrath of God is already pronounced against ALL who partake of the wickedness of the world in such an age as this. But God does not take pleasure in pouring out judgment. Now as in days gone by, he looks for A MAN -- any man, or a woman will do -- who can and will love the people enough to make the sacrifices necessary to stand in the gap -- to hold back the storm of judgment -- to stand with the storm beating upon his back while he raises his voice long and loud, pleading with the people to flee from the wrath to come.

The world is setting the stage for the last great scene of the great story, "The History of Man upon the Earth." Soon the curtain will rise upon that last scene, the terrible tribulation period, when the wrath of God will be poured out without measure upon a wicked world from which the last righteous person has been hastily snatched away. The clouds are gathering, the lightening is flashing, the thunder rolls -- gusts of the wind which precede the storm can be felt with ever increasing frequency and force.

"Lift up your eyes and look on the fields; for they are white already to harvest." John 4:35.

As never before, it is URGENT that the servants of God should place the work of the harvest ahead of everything else -- that they should "WORK, for the night COMETH WHEN NO MAN CAN WORK!" It is a time when ALL THE POWER OF GOD PROVIDED needs to be brought into use to save as much as possible of the precious harvest before the storm breaks. This is a time when YOU AND I need to find the gap in which God would have us stand, and STAND THERE, faithful.

How sad it was when God looked, hopefully, for a man to stand in the gap and he had to continue his statement, "I found NONE. Therefore have I poured out mine indignation upon them. I have consumed them with the fire of My wrath."

God is still looking for MEN TO STAND IN THE GAP! He is still looking for laborers for the harvest. He offers the same wages -- the same rewards -- for those who will come at this last hour, as for those who have borne the heat of the battle. All he asks is a quick response to his call, and faithfulness in carrying it out. Will you say "YES" to this call of God? Will you give him your ALL? Will you accept his BEST -- the MIRACLE WORKING, SOUL SAVING POWER OF GOD, for the deliverance of the lost, the sick and the suffering?

Much has been done for the deliverance of humanity by holy men and women of God, from the time of righteous Abel until now, but, as I look into God's word, and behold the mighty promises of God, and see the miracles which have been wrought on occasions when someone DARED TO BELIEVE, I am persuaded that it REMAINS TO BE SEEN WHAT GOD COULD DO WITH A MAN OR WOMAN WHO WOULD GO ALL THE WAY WITH HIM, and never doubt in their heart! And what immense power would be turned loose against the destroying enemy of mankind -- Satan -- if A GREAT ARMY OF MEN AND WOMEN should all together determine to stand upon God's promises, and believe God for HIS MIRACLE WORKING POWER!

You can be that ONE, or ONE OF THAT GREAT ARMY!

When God looks for a MAN, will you volunteer? WILL YOU BE THAT MAN?

The End

DEATH CERTIFICATE

CERTIFICATION OF VITAL RECORD

STATE OF CALIFORNIA

DEPARTMENT OF HEALTH SERVICES

70-079608 CERTIFICATE OF DEATH 1633

ASA | ALONZO | ALLEN

Male | White | ARKANSAS | Mar. 27, 1911 | 59

USA | 574-24-0795 | Divorced

Minister | 40 | Self | Clergy

1101 Van Ness Ave (Jack Tar Hotel) | Yes

San Francisco | San Francisco | Transient | Transient

303 Deliverance Way | yes | Carl Hatfield, 608 N. Garden Ave, Sierra Vista, Ariz.

Miracle Valley | Cochise | Arizona

Investigation | 6-12-70

Burial | 6-15-70 | Miracle Valley, Ariz.

BRYANT MORTUARY

Acute alcoholism and fatty infiltration of the liver, Alcohol blood level: 0.36%.

Unknown | Yes | Yes

Natural vs accident undetermined | hotel | No | June 11, 1970

1101 Van Ness Room # 418, San Francisco

Ingestion of alcohol

A.A. Allen's

Death Certificate

PROPHECY FROM THE 1950'S
Vision of Poisonous Gas and Nuclear Attack Against The United

Atop the Empire State Building
As I stood atop the Empire State Building, I could see the Statue of Liberty, illuminating the gateway to the new world. Here, spread before me like an animated map, is an area 60 or 80 miles in diameter. I was amazed that the Spirit of the Lord should so move me, there atop the Empire State building. Why should I feel such a surge of His Spirit and power there?

Giant Telescope
Suddenly I heard the voice of the Lord. It was as clear and as distinct as a voice could be. It seemed to come from the very midst of the giant telescope; but when I looked at the telescope, I knew it hadn't come from there, but directly from Heaven. The voice said, 2 CHRONICLES 16:9, "For the eyes of the LORD run to and fro throughout the whole earth, to show himself strong in the behalf of them whose heart is perfect toward him. Herein thou has done foolishly; therefore, from henceforth thou shall have wars." Immediately when I heard the voice of God, I knew this was

a quotation of scripture; but never before had a thing come to me so forcibly by the power of the Spirit.

Automatic Clock

The ticking of the telescope stopped. The man before me had used up his dime's worth. As he stepped away, I knew that I was next. As I stepped to the telescope and dropped in my dime, immediately the ticking started again. This ticking was an automatic clock which would allow me to use the telescope for a limited time only. As I swung the telescope to the north, suddenly the Spirit of God came upon me in a way that I had never thought of before. Seemingly, in the Spirit I was entirely caught away. I knew that the telescope itself had nothing to do with the distance which I was suddenly enabled to see, for I seemed to see things far beyond the range of the telescope, even on a bright, clear day. It was simply that God had chosen this time to reveal these things to me, for as I looked through the telescope, it was not Manhattan Island that I saw, but a far larger view.

North American Continent

That morning much of the view was impaired by fog; but suddenly as the Spirit of the Lord came upon me, the fog seemed to clear until it seemed that I could see for thousands of miles, but that which I was looking upon was not Manhattan Island. It was all of the North American continent spread out before me as a map is spread upon a table. It was not the East River and the Hudson River that I saw on either side, but the Atlantic and the Pacific Oceans; and instead of the Statue of Liberty standing there in the bay on her small island, I saw her standing far out in the Gulf of Mexico. She was between me and the United States.

I suddenly realized that the telescope had nothing to do with what I was seeing but that it was a vision coming directly from God; and to prove this to myself, I took my eyes away from the telescope so that I was no longer looking through the lens, but the same scene remained before me.

Great Cities

There, clear and distinct, lay all the North American continent with all its great cities. To the north lay the Great Lakes. Far to the northeast was New York City. I could see Seattle and Portland far to the northwest. Down the west coast there were San Francisco and Los Angeles. Closer in the foreground lay New Orleans at the center of the Gulf Coast area. I could see the great towering ranges of the Rocky Mountains and trace with my eye the Continental Divide. All this and more I could see spread out before me as a great map upon a table.

Gigantic Hand

As I looked, suddenly from the sky I saw a giant hand reach down. That gigantic hand was reaching out toward the Statue of Liberty. In a moment her gleaming torch was torn from her hand, and in it instead was placed a cup; and I saw protruding from that great cup a giant sword, shining as if a great light had been turned upon its glistening edge. Never before had I seen such a sharp, glistening, dangerous sword. It seemed to threaten all the world. As the great cup was placed in the hand of the Statue of Liberty, I heard these words, "Thus saith the Lord of hosts, drink ye and be drunken and spew and fall and rise no more because of the sword which I will send." As I heard these words, I recognized them as a quotation from Jeremiah 25:27.

I was amazed to hear the Statue of Liberty speak out in reply, "I WILL NOT DRINK!"

Then as the voice of the thunder, I heard again the voice of the Lord saying, "Ye shall certainly drink" (Jeremiah 25:28). Then suddenly the giant hand forced the cup to the lips of the Statue of Liberty, and she became powerless to defend herself. The mighty hand of God forced her to drink every drop from the cup. As she drank the bitter dregs, these were the words that I heard: "Should ye be utterly unpunished? Ye shall not be unpunished, for I will call for a sword upon all the inhabitants of the earth, saith the Lord of hosts" (Jeremiah 27:29).

War, Death, Destruction

When the cup was withdrawn from the lips of the Statute of Liberty, I noticed the sword was missing from the cup, which could mean but one thing. THE CONTENTS OF THE CUP HAD BEEN COMPLETELY CONSUMED! I knew that the sword merely typified war, death, and destruction, which is no doubt on the way.

Then as one drunken on too much wine, I saw the Statue of Liberty become unsteady on her feet and begin to stagger and to lose her balance. I saw her splashing in the gulf, trying to regain her balance. I saw her stagger again and again and fall to her knees. As I saw her desperate attempts to regain her balance and rise to her feet again, my heart was moved as never before with compassion for her struggles; but as she staggered there in the gulf, once again I heard these words: "Drink ye and be drunken and spew and fall and rise no more because of the sword which I will send among you" (Jeremiah 25:37).

As I watched, I wondered if the Statue of Liberty would ever be able to regain her feet, if she would ever stand again; and as I watched, it seemed that with all her power she struggled to rise and finally staggered to her feet again and stood there swaying drunkenly. I felt sure that at any moment she would fall again, possibly never to rise. I seemed overwhelmed with a desire to reach out my hand to keep her head above water, for I knew that if she ever fell again, she would drown there in the gulf.

"Thou shalt not be afraid for the terror by night, nor for the arrow that flyeth by day, nor for the pestilence that walketh in darkness, nor for the destruction that wasteth at noonday" (Psalms 91:5-6).

Black Cloud Rising

Then as I watched, another amazing thing was taking place. Far to the northwest, just out over Alaska, a huge, black cloud was arising. As it rose, it was as black as night. It seemed to be in the shape of a man's head. As it continued to arise, I observed two light spots in the black cloud. It rose further, and a gaping hole appeared. I could see that the black cloud was taking the shape of a skull, for now the huge, white, gaping mouth was plainly visible. Finally, the head was complete. Then the shoulders began to appear; and on either side, long, black arms.

Skeleton Destroys Multitudes

It seemed that what I saw was the entire North American continent, spread out like a map upon a table with this terrible skeleton-formed cloud arising from behind the table. It rose steadily until the form was visible down to the waist. At the waist the skeleton seemed to bend toward the United States, stretching forth a hand toward the east and one toward the west—one toward New York and one toward Seattle. As the awful form stretched forward, I could see that its entire attention seemed to be focused upon the United States, overlooking Canada at least for the time being. As I saw the horrible black cloud in the form of a skeleton bending toward America, bending from the waist over, reaching down toward Chicago and out toward both coasts, I knew its one interest was to destroy the multitudes.

Mortal Agony

As I watched in horror, the great black cloud stopped just above the Great Lakes region and turned its face toward New York City. Then out of the horrible, great gaping mouth began to appear wisps of white vapor which looked like smoke, as a cigarette smoker would blow puffs of smoke from his mouth. These whitish vapors were being blown toward New York City. The smoke began to spread until it had covered all the eastern part of the United States.

Then the skeleton turned to the west and out of the horrible mouth and nostrils came another great puff of white smoke. This time it was blown in the direction of the west coast. In a few moments' time the entire West Coast and Los Angeles area were covered with its vapors.

Then toward the center came a third great puff. As I watched, St. Louis and Kansas City were enveloped in its white vapors. Then on they came toward New Orleans. Then on they swept until they reached the Statue of Liberty where she stood staggering drunkenly in the blue waters of the gulf. As the white vapors began to spread around the head of the statue, she took in but one gasping breath and then began to cough as though to rid her lungs of the horrible vapors she had inhaled. One could readily discern by the coughing that those white vapors had seared her lungs.

What were these white vapors? Could they signify bacteriological warfare or nerve gas that could destroy multitudes of people in a few moments' time?

Then I heard the voice of God as He spoke again: "Behold, the LORD maketh the earth empty and maketh it waste and turneth it upside-down and scattereth abroad the inhabitants thereof. And it shall be, as with the people, so with the priest; as with the servant, so with his master; as with the maid, so with her mistress; as with the buyer, so with the seller; as with the lender, so with the borrower; as with the taker of usury, so with the giver of usury to him. The land shall be utterly emptied and utterly spoiled, for the LORD hath spoken this word. The earth mourneth and fadeth away. The world languisheth and fadeth away. The haughty people of the earth do languish. The earth also is defiled under the inhabitants thereof because they have transgressed the laws, changed the ordinance, broken the everlasting covenant; therefore, hath the curse devoured the earth, and they that dwell therein are desolate; therefore, the inhabitants of the earth are burned and few men left" (Isaiah 24:1-6).

As I watched, the coughing grew worse. It sounded like a person about to cough out his lungs. The Statue of Liberty was moaning and groaning. She was in mortal agony. The pain must have been terrific, as again and again she tried to clear her lungs of those horrible white vapors. I watched her there in the gulf as she staggered, clutching her lungs and her breast with her hands. Then she fell to her knees. In a moment she gave one final cough, made a last desperate effort to rise from her knees, and then fell face forward into the waters of the gulf and lay still as death. Tears ran down my face as I realized that she was dead! Only the lapping of the waves, splashing over her body which was partly under the water and partly out of the water, broke the stillness.

"A fire devoureth before them, and behind them a flame burneth; the land is as the Garden of Eden before them, and behind them a desolate wilderness, yea, and nothing shall escape them" (Joel 2:3).

Screaming of Sirens

Suddenly the silence was shattered by the screaming of sirens. The sirens seemed to scream, "RUN FOR YOUR LIVES!"

Never before had I heard such shrill, screaming sirens. They seemed to be everywhere—to the north, the south, the east, and the west. There seemed to be multitudes of sirens; and as I looked, I saw people everywhere running, but it seemed none of them ran more than a few paces, and then they fell. And even as I had seen the Statue of Liberty struggling to regain her poise and balance and finally falling for the last time to die on her face, I now saw millions of people falling in the streets, on the sidewalks, struggling. I heard their screams for mercy and help. I heard their horrible coughing as though their lungs had been seared with fire. I heard the moanings and groanings of the doomed and the dying. As I watched, a few finally reached shelters, but only a few ever got to the shelters.

Above the moaning and the groaning of the dying multitudes, I heard these words: "A noise shall come even to the ends of the earth, for the Lord hath a controversy with the nations. He will plead with all flesh; he will give them that are wicked to the sword, saith the Lord. Thus saith the Lord of hosts. Behold, evil shall go forth from nation to nation, and a great whirlwind shall be raised up from the coasts of the earth, and the slain of the Lord shall be at that day from one end of the earth even unto the other end of the earth. They shall not be lamented, neither gathered, nor buried; they shall be dung upon the ground" (Jeremiah 25:31-33).

Rocket Missile Attacks

Then suddenly I saw from the Atlantic and from the Pacific and out of the Gulf rocket-like objects that seemed to come up like fish leaping out of the water. High into the air they leaped, each headed in a different direction, but every one toward the United States. On the ground the sirens screamed louder, and up from the ground I saw similar rockets beginning to ascend. To me these appeared to be interceptor rockets although they arose from different points all over the United States; however, none of them seemed to be successful in intercepting the rockets that had risen from the ocean on every side. These rockets finally reached their maximum height, slowly turned over and fell back toward the earth in defeat.

Then suddenly the rockets which had leaped out of the oceans like fish all exploded at once. The explosion was ear-splitting. The next thing which I saw was a huge ball of fire. The only thing I have ever seen which resembled the thing I saw in my vision was the picture of the explosion of the H-bomb somewhere in the South Pacific. In my vision it was so real that I seemed to feel a searing heat from it.

Widespread Desolation

As the vision spread before my eyes and I viewed the widespread desolation brought about by the terrific explosions, I could not help thinking, While the defenders of our nation have quibbled over what means of defense to use and neglected the only true means of defense—faith and dependence upon the true and living God—the thing which she greatly feared has come unto her! How true it has proven in Psalms 127:1: Except the Lord build the house, they labor in vain that build it; except the Lord keep the city, the watchman waketh but in vain.

Then as the noise of battle subsided, to my ears came this quotation: "Blow ye the trumpet in Zion and sound an alarm in my holy mountain; let all the inhabitants of the land tremble, for the day of the Lord cometh, for it is nigh at hand. 2. A day of darkness and of gloominess, a day of clouds and of thick darkness, as the morning spread upon the mountains, a great people and a strong, there hath not been ever the like, neither shall be any more after it, even to the years of many generations. 3. A fire devoureth before them, and behind them a flame burneth; the land is as the Garden of Eden before them, and behind them a desolate wilderness, yea, and nothing shall escape them. 4. The appearance of them is as the appearance of horses; and as horsemen, so shall they run. 5. Like the noise of chariots on the tops of mountains shall they leap, like the noise of a flame of fire that devoureth the stubble, as a strong people set in battle array. 6. Before their face the people shall be much pained; all faces shall gather blackness. 7. They shall run like mighty men; they shall climb the wall like men of war, and they shall march every one on his ways, and they shall not break their ranks. 8. Neither shall one thrust another; they shall walk every one in his path; and when they fall upon the sword, they shall not be wounded. 9. They shall run to and fro in the city; they shall run upon the wall; they shall climb up upon the houses; they shall enter in at the windows like a thief. 10. The earth shall quake before them; the heavens shall tremble; the sun and the moon shall be dark,, and the stars shall withdraw their shining (Joel 2:1-10).

The Silence of Death

Then the voice was still. The earth, too was silent with the silence of death.

Then to my ears came another sound—a sound of distant singing. It was the sweetest music I had ever heard. There was joyful shouting and sounds of happy laughter. Immediately I knew it was the rejoicing of the saints of God. I looked, and there, high in the heavens, above the smoke and poisonous gases, above the noise of the battle, I saw a huge mountain. It seemed to be of solid rock, and I knew at once that this was the Mountain of the Lord. The sounds of music and rejoicing were coming from a cleft high up in the side of the rock mountain.

Hidden in the Cleft

It was the saints of God who were doing the rejoicing. It was God's own people who were singing and dancing and shouting with joy, safe from all the harm which had come upon the earth, for they were hidden away in the cleft of the rock. There in the cleft they were shut in, protected by a great, giant hand which reached out of the heavens and which was none other than the hand of God, shutting them in until the storm be over passed.

The End

Made in United States
Orlando, FL
08 April 2022

16635131R00083

House of Mirrors

Nola Nash

RAMIREZ AND CLARK PUBLISHERS, LLC

Copyright © 2022 by Nola Nash

All rights reserved.

No part of this book may be reproduced in any form or by any electronic or mechanical means, including information storage and retrieval systems, without written permission from the author, except for the use of brief quotations in a book review.

To the staff at Onyx and Alabaster for being fabulous cheerleaders as I worked on this book and for letting me be their "Norm," taking up space for hours nursing a cinnamon orange London fog.
Cheers, y'all!

The best kind of art or writing holds up a mirror to society.
    ~ Liam Cunningham

The Five Bloodiest Hours

Corpses are like scarecrows. They may not fall for the dead at their feet.
Johann Albert Lotz, 1864

Ragged, starved, and exhausted, but they still stood. For now. Still trudged onward. For now. Dressed in gray, blue, or a combination of the two ripped from corpses of fallen foes, it didn't matter. The war had ravaged one and all and was yet to be finished with them. Each had seen men die. Each thought they would be next. Most were right.

November 30, 1864. Franklin, Tennessee.

Those who could flee, did. Those whose loyalty was not bound to the land they stood upon. Others braced for what they dreaded – war on their doorstep. For years they had escaped it. No more. War, and its spectral shadow Death, walked in lock step on an inevitable march toward them. There was no use in shows of bravery or defiance for those who lived in the houses and farms of the sleepy village that was now wide awake. With the rising of the sun, war began again. Only the cover of night with its fear of friendly fire silenced the guns and cannons. Daylight brought the percussive terrors closer as the drums echoed the advancing footsteps of the soldiers. Soldiers whose feet and shoes had long since become one and the same if shoes were to be found at all. Bare soles were cut and bloodied, but it didn't matter. The men couldn't feel the pain for the numbing cold. Emaciated. Frightened. Broken. And still they stood. Still, they trudged onward.

Dogging the heels of Gen. Schofield on his march to Nashville, Confederate soldiers bent to the will of an infuriated Gen. Hood. Lieutenants' arguments fell on the deaf ears of their commander. Was it patriotism or wounded pride after the loss of Spring Hill caused by embarrassing mistakes and miscommunication that fueled Hood's rage? Each man had their opinion and each would carry it to their graves. It was of no consequence what the soldiers in the ranks thought. Their fates were already sealed as they turned their faces north to follow their enemy. Their only hope was to stop Schofield from reaching Nashville and combining his forces with the stronghold there. Fragile, fleeting hope. Bodies moved by force of habit. Stopping was certain death. Marching on was a thin thread of possibility of living another day. Another day closer to victory, to home. Pushing on kept them from thinking about how tenuous the thread was. No thicker or stronger than a strand of a spider's web, but as long as the thread was there, there was hope. There was a reason to keep marching. To keep fighting. Until the shadowy hand of Death severed the thread forever.

One

Why do people build walls around cemeteries? Is it fear that the residents are going to wander out? If teenagers want to get in, they'll find a way. If it was really about keeping anyone in or out, the walls would be higher. A few feet of dry-stacked fieldstones and a rickety iron gate won't accomplish either of those tasks. Maybe the walls aren't for preventing entry or exit at all. Maybe it's more about keeping the uncomfortably uncontrollable inevitability of death away from the living. Keep it in a nice neat box. Away. Forgotten except on birthdays and anniversaries. Remembered often at first, then less and less as life gets in the way of the dead.

Pawpaw would know, Ruby thought. *Would have known.*

There were even walls inside the walls. Families surrounded by borders of stone, some not even more than a few inches high. Others had a foot or two of more dry-stacked stone. People around this place loved those kinds of walls. Some families were surrounded by wispy iron fencing made dappled by lichen. Some families didn't have any walls at all. Did they not feel the need to hide behind their stone walls from the rest of town or separate themselves from the deceased rabble, or did they not have the money to keep up with the Joneses with their fences and monuments?

Sitting on one of those low stone borders, Ruby Baxter pulled absently at the skinny blades of grass on the outside of it. It was no different from the grass on the inside. Just as in need of watering as the grass on the other side. The only difference was the dirt. On the outside of the border, the dirt was hidden beneath a crispy layer of fescue. On the inside of the border, the dirt was freshly turned and piled in a lumpy oblong mound, the only vegetation being the dead remnants of funeral wreaths and sprays laid across the mound by the workers who covered Pawpaw two weeks ago today.

"This place looks like a chess board," Aunt Jill had said as she gazed around the old cemetery and dabbed at her eyes after the graveside service. Ruby nodded but hadn't taken her eyes off the casket being lowered into the ground – her whole world being buried.

Aunt Jill was right, though. Sitting alone, Ruby could see what she meant. Some of the monuments of Franklin's former well-to-do looked like the game pieces, some with tops resembling a castle, others with stone draped like fabric over obelisk points, some with wreaths carved into them, or vases perched on top. All the little normal headstones served as the pawns. Each in their place on a grid of gravesites. Some of the chess pieces were out of play, lying in the grass or propped against the stone wall. Pawns taken out of the game during the May Flood of 2010 when half the town and the entirety of Rest Haven Cemetery were under feet of water. Water that moved stone.

A chime on her watch pulled her out of the chess match and back to reality. If she left now, Ruby had just enough time to make it to the coffee shop inside Onyx and Alabaster over on Public Square before they closed to get a tea before her first tour group of the night arrived. She reached out to touch the mound in front of her, but her hand stopped and hovered an inch above. Touching it was too close to admitting the only true family she had left was underneath the layer of soil and dead lilies. She wasn't ready to face that. Not yet. "I'll see you tomorrow, Pawpaw," she whispered pulling her hand back and brushing half-dead grass off her jeans. Ruby could almost hear him answer, "I'm glad you got to see me, kid," with that crooked grin of his.

"Wait." The mechanical voice of the crossing signal had zero personality and gave Ruby the creeps. "Wait." The tinny word repeated every few seconds. Ruby knew it was for the visually impaired, but was pretty sure it did more good keeping the distracted tourists and gaggles of Brentwood moms from stepping into traffic. The Real Housewives of Williamson County: leggings and ponytails balancing an expensive coffee in one hand while they unfurled the latest in toddler transportation out of their luxury SUVs when they came to shop in the quaint small town while their music executive hubbies made the money that paid for it all. They would be easy to hate if they weren't so freaking nice. "Walk sign is on," the signal finally said with a bit more spunk.

Ruby picked up her pace and trotted across the street toward Main and Onyx and Alabaster, an upscale interior design shop with a funky coffee house in it with the best coffee in town. And that was saying something since there were a total of six coffee shops in a four-block radius. It was beginning to seem like all the people in Franklin did was buy farmhouse chic décor and drink coffee.

"Hey, Rube! Just in time!" Tilly called from behind the counter as she rang up the customer in front of her. With a nod and a smile to the lady, she turned her attention to Ruby. "Usual?"

"Yep."

"Gotcha. One cinnamon orange London Fog comin' up." Tilly paused and cut her eyes up at Ruby. "How many tours you got tonight?"

"Two."

She nodded and went back to the order screen. "One *large* cinnamon orange London Fog."

"Thanks, Til." Ruby paid for her tea and checked her watch. Plenty of time.

Tilly leaned on the counter as the barista behind her started on Ruby's drink. Her fingers tapped her arms while Ruby pretended to be interested in the tattoo of a vine that wrapped from Tilly's wrist up to her shoulder to avoid 'the look.' No stranger to Ruby's avoidance, Tilly leaned a little further across the counter. "Ruby, you know I have to ask."

"You don't *have* to ask. You *insist* on asking."

"I told you I'd ask you until you actually do it."

Three months ago, James Cavanaugh mentioned to Tilly that he was looking for a historical adviser for his restoration company and Tilly seemed to think Ruby was the girl for the job. Ever since, it seemed to be the only topic of conversation Tilly could come up with. "I'm not qualified for that job, Til," Ruby replied with a shrug. "I can't apply for it. Besides, James knows me. If he wanted me for the job, he'd ask."

"Not true. He knows you've been up to your ears in taking care of your grandfather and his company for months. He's not gonna come to you about a job and you know it," Tilly rolled her dark eyes and twirled the hot pink ends of a strand of hair as she dug her heels into the issue. "You have a history degree and no one knows this town like you do. Besides, apparently no one else is any more qualified for the job than you are. They still haven't filled it. You can at least give it a shot," she insisted as the barista handed her the black paper cup. Ruby reached for it, but Tilly pulled it back in a game of caffeinated keep away. "At least apply to shut me up if nothing else."

Knowing she wasn't going to get tea unless she agreed, Ruby sighed and said, "Fine. Just to shut you up."

"Was that so hard?" Tilly laughed relinquishing her cup of energy for the long night ahead.

"Yes. Yes, it was."

Tilly waved off Ruby's sass with a chuckle. "By the way, I met the couple that bought the Bennett House on 4th this morning. Nice folks. Husband does contract law on Music Row. Wife is an interior designer, I think. Just got settled in. Told 'em they should take your tour to get to know the place."

"I'll keep an eye out for them." Ruby raised her cup in salute for the referral as she headed out so Tilly could lock up behind her for the evening. Leave it to Tilly to get the scoop on the new people in town. She was like a bartender; people just talked to her and told her their life stories. Tilly said it was a gift. Ruby thought it was a curse.

Checking her watch, Ruby decided to do a dawdling loop around the square to kill a few more minutes. There was no sense in overdoing it now with two tours ahead of her. Not like that was a ton of exercise or anything. A few blocks of walking and a lot of standing and talking.

Still, there was plenty of time to stroll around a bit. Most of the shops along the side streets were closing up. In large part, all that meant was turning the 'Open' sign to the 'Closed' side even though a lot of merchandise sat on the front porches of the craftsman homes. It wasn't like anyone was going to abscond with the wrought iron flower pots or antique garden signs in the night. It was Franklin, after all. A couple of the owners waved and smiled as she passed. Behind the genuinely warm smiles was a hint of pity at the loss of her grandfather. Ruby tried to ignore the expressions that made the pain of her loss sting even more as she returned their smiles and left them to continue closing up. Nothing stayed open very late in the sleepy little suburb, but particularly the smaller shops on the side streets. Main Street would be busy for a while longer, especially with the handful of restaurants that opened up recently, but they still rolled up the sidewalks at nine.

Once upon a time, the houses on these streets used to actually be residences. There were no cookie cutter houses here. Each one was as unique as the history surrounding it. Craftsman bungalows sat alongside larger Victorians. Stone, brick, and wood siding added texture and color to the streets. Given the relentless sticklers on the historical building commission, the whole town was like a step back in time. Or a movie set. Halloween looked like a Disney movie, and Christmastime looked like the Hallmark Channel set designers had taken over. Now, houses that were used for residences were few and far between. More and more had become local restaurants or shops specializing in farmhouse chic or antiques. At least those that weren't already law firms. So many law firms.

It would be nice to have someone living in that big house on 4th. It had always been a favorite of Ruby's, mostly because it had a large wrap-around front porch with a rounded corner that jutted out like a rotunda. It seemed like a great spot to watch the world go by with a glass of sweet tea. The home was a beauty in red brick with a gabled roof and large wood-framed windows in a rich cream that matched the porch. A house with as much charm as Franklin itself. It had always been a favorite of Pawpaw's, too, which was a high compliment given the number of homes he'd had the pleasure of restoring. The Bennett House on 4th was his swan song. He was tasked with turning it from an office back into a welcoming residence and he couldn't have been happier about it. Ruby got her melancholy about the commercialization of the homes from him and was glad to see one going the other direction for a change. The last project Pawpaw took on before he retired ended up being the death of him after an accident with the wiring. Pawpaw never blamed the electrician for it, but losing much of his motor function on one side of his body took a toll on Pawpaw's spirit as he turned the last parts of restoring the Bennett House over to young James Cavanaugh. The death certificate said Mitch Baxter died of a heart attack. A cold medical way to say that Ruby's pawpaw died of a broken heart.

Arriving at her tour gathering spot on Public Square, a flicker over the rooftops caught Ruby's attention. Storms were building in the distance and moving in from the northwest as they often did, especially in the fall as the warmer days of late September collided with the coolness of October in spectacular displays of lightning and flash floods. She'd make it through her first tour, but the second one was going to be wet if it happened at all. *Good weather for hop frogs,* Pawpaw would have said. *Good weather for a ghost tour,* Ruby thought as she took one last glance at the darkening sky.

Two

Pitch darkness was broken in staccato flashes of white as the house shuddered with each burst of thunder. Rain rushed helter-skelter down the gabled roof of the Bennett House as panes of antique wavy glass trembled in their frames. Pebbles of hail ricocheted off copper flashing along the gutters adding to the cacophony of the storm. Streetlights, nestled among the branches of magnolias, tried to sputter to life as the power surged quickly giving up the ghost and drowning the town in inky blackness.

Inside, the new residents slept fitfully between shrill storm warnings on their phones. Common sense said the sturdy brick walls that had stood since 1875 would make it through the night, but the raging storm outside seemed hell-bent on giving those walls a run for their money. Sounds of wind, rain, and thunder blended into a nightmarish lullaby. Exhaustion turned to sleep as the old silver clock in the foyer chimed once. An almost ridiculously small sound amidst the chaos outside.

The storm took a breath and left the house in a vacuum of silence after the constant assault of noise. From the edges of the silence, another sound emerged. Faint, but building. A slow sharp rhythm followed by several quick raps. With each repetition of the series, the sound grew. Methodical. Hollow. Relentless. Reaching a crescendo, the cadence of the lone drum stopped. Silence once more. But only for a moment. As the lightning flashed once again, the deafening crack of a dozen rifles echoed through the Bennett House. In the bedroom upstairs, a woman screamed.

Mallory Winter sat bolt upright in the carved four-poster bed on the second floor of the Bennett House. Her face, usually beautifully composed, was drained of color. Her thin frame shook as her husband Jake wrapped his arms around her trying to warm the chills of fright. Mallory's scream had given way to gasping sobs. Words were still failing her as Jake gently rubbed her back. Mallory's face was buried in his shoulder and her fingers dug into his back and twisted his t-shirt in a death-grip as if she was terrified to let him go. Not knowing what had frightened her, Jake's eyes tried to scan the darkness as his ears attempted to separate the sounds of the storm outside from any noises that shouldn't be in the house. The only sounds were the pounding of rain on the windows and the rumbling thunder moving into the distance.

"Shhh, Mal. It's ok. I'm here," Jake said rocking her slowly. "It's just the storm."

Mallory didn't answer but shook her head violently.

"A bad dream?"

Once more, she shook her head, but with less ferocity than before. Pulling back from her, Jake brough her arms in front of him and gathered her hands in his. They were shaking uncontrollably even as he rubbed them. "It was just a dream, baby. Come on, lay back down."

Mallory shook her head again, her dark hair tousled and as wild as the blue eyes that looked up at Jake. "Not a dream. I *saw him die.*" The trembling intensified throughout her whole body as she nearly choked on the last words. With a whimper, Mallory fainted into her husband's arms.

Caramel-colored coffee was going cold in the mug between Mallory's trembling hands. Her gaze was intent on the empty space between her and Jake at the breakfast table. Dark circles made her deep brown eyes look sunken. Other than a few moments in a faint, Mallory had been awake since she screamed in the middle of the night. Jake, too. He had his own dark circles, but his bright blue eyes looked marginally less skeletal. Pushing a hand through his hair, not caring that it made the salt and pepper strands stick straight up, Jake raised his cup of lukewarm coffee, but stopped just short of taking a sip.

"I know it seemed real to you, Mal, but dreams—"

"I know what I *saw*, Jake," Mallory snapped. Her dark eyes focused on his face. "I know what I *heard*. Someone shot a man and he died at the foot of our bed."

"There's no one at the foot of the bed, baby," Jake said softly as he tried to put a reassuring hand on her arm.

Mallory twitched at his touch, still jumpy from the night's terror, and sloshed coffee on the table. Leaving the puddle on the antique mahogany was unlike her, but she made no move to clean it up. "He was there. I heard gun shots and opened my eyes. He was standing there bleeding. He looked so frightened. So young." Her eyes glazed once more as her focus shifted back to the empty space between the two of them. Only a couple of feet wide, but it might as well have been miles.

Jake let her sit with her thoughts a few more minutes while he mopped up the spilled coffee and took the cup out of her hands. Pouring the contents down the sink, he rinsed the mugs and put them in the dishwasher. Mallory still sat lost in her thoughts when he turned back to the table. "I know you believe what you saw was real—"

"Because it was."

"—but my job is to help you figure out what it actually was so you can sleep better tonight. That's all." Sitting back down, he took her hands in his. This time, she didn't flinch and looked up at him. "Hey," Jake said forcing a grin through his own exhaustion, "let's get out of the house. Take a walk. Get some breakfast."

Mallory sighed. "I'm not hungry. Maybe just coffee."

Jake glanced at the sink where two perfectly good cups of coffee had just been dumped out. "Coffee it is. Better coffee than the swill I just poured down the drain."

For a moment, Mallory smiled. Fleeting, but a smile nonetheless. "Sorry."

Squeezing her hand, Jake said, "Throw some clothes on and let's go see how this old town fared in the weather last night."

Mallory nodded, pushed her chair back, and took a few steps toward the staircase. Hesitating, she turned back to him. "Come with me?" It wasn't her usual flirtatious invitation upstairs. There was fear behind her words.

"Looks like you guys had a long night, too," Tilly said with less than her usual highly-caffeinated energy.

"You could say that," Jake answered as he paid for their coffees.

"Those were some wicked storms, for sure." Tilly glanced up at Mallory, and raised an eyebrow. "Somethin' on your mind, Mallory? You look a little far away."

"Hm?" Mallory asked. "Sorry, yes, actually. This may be a weird question—"

Tilly perked up and leaned on the counter. "I love weird questions! Whatcha got?"

Mallory hesitated a moment as though she regretted blurting that out. "Well, is there something we should, um, *know* about our house?"

Tilly tapped her fingernails on the register as she thought. "It's old, so there's a lot to know about it. Most of the interesting stuff happened before my time, though. It's been offices as far back as I can remember. Not much interesting there. It was a recording studio at one point. Does that help?"

"I'm thinking before that. Something a very long time ago?"

Tilly shrugged. "You need Ruby Baxter for that one. She'd know. She's the tour guide I told you about. If you want Franklin history, she's your girl. If you want to know what's going on around town in the present day, that's me."

Mallory shifted uncomfortably and took the coffee the barista held out to her. "That's ok. It's probably nothing anyway."

"Wait a minute!" Tilly's eyes widened. "It wasn't the weather that made your night long, was it? Something happened! What? What was it?"

"Most likely just a bad dream Mallory had," Jake began, "but she can't seem to shake it." Customers had begun filing into the line behind them and Jake made a move to make space for them in front of the counter.

"Tell you what," Tilly said as she entered the order of the woman behind them. "You two find a table and enjoy your coffee. I'll text Ruby and see if she can meet us here. I've got a break soon and I want to hear all about it!"

"I don't want to put anyone out," Mallory insisted.

"Nonsense!" Tilly said cheerfully. "I love this stuff and you'll really like Ruby. It'll do her some good, too. Her grandpa died recently and she could use a good project to take her mind off things."

"If you're sure," Jake said with a smile full of gratitude for Tilly's enthusiastic offer to help.

"Positive. I'll find you in a few."

Three

Hey, Rube, need you at the coffee shop
What's up?
The Winters are here
Who?
Bennett House. Just get over here. They were asking about the house. Wife seems nervous about something. Told her you could fill them in on the place.
Thanks for volunteering my services
Anytime. Come on! Break in 5
On my way. You owe me
London Fog on the house
Deal

Dressed in dirty jeans and a wadded ponytail wasn't exactly how Ruby wanted to meet the hot-shot newcomers in town, but they would have to take what they could get on short notice. She didn't have time to go home and change. At least she had slapped on some mascara and lip gloss before she walked down to the cemetery to check on Pawpaw. The mess at the gravesite wasn't as bad as she feared. Then again, how much damage could a storm do to a mound of dirt and some dead flowers? The mound now looked a bit like melting chocolate ice cream with dead flowers as morbid sundae toppings. Ruby was sure Pawpaw would have come up with some goofball name for an ice cream flavor to describe it. All she could think of was Death by Chocolate. Pathetic effort.

Tilly waved her toward the far end of Onyx and Alabaster's bar top where the drinks were placed for pick up when they were busy. "On the end. Give me a sec," Tilly said as she rang up another customer.

Ruby checked the cup for her name and wrapped her hands around the signature black paper cup. The warmth felt good on her fingers chilled from being out in the cool fall air. Since she didn't know who to be looking for, Ruby scanned the tables of the narrow coffee shop from the doorway that separated the coffee house from the design store. Onyx and Alabaster lived its brand in all the ways. The coffee shop itself was black with large black and white marble tiles on the wall behind it with the name in chic thin gold lettering. Interior brick over a century old that ran the length of the side walls was painted a matte black. White marble tables were dotted along the narrow space and the black chairs tucked under them blended into the walls and floor. In the high industrial ceiling, massive black and gold light fixtures bathed the space in warm light. Black and white modern art on the walls broke up what could have been a dungeon of a space, transforming it instead to a chic modern one. Her favorite table, though, was the large gold velvet horseshoe sofa with its glossy white marble and gold gilt table.

Mid-morning on a weekday, the handful of tables were sparsely populated, mostly by regulars with laptops in front of them. As she surveyed the customers, a gaggle of Brentwood moms sporting designer athleisurewear that would never see a drop of sweat nudged past her to take their coffee with them to scout the design shop for something they would tell their husbands later that they 'just had to have.'

"Come on," Tilly said as she swung around the counter and pointed to the large table in front of her.

Tilly slid into the gold horseshoe sofa next to a couple that definitely didn't fit the bill of the Winters that Ruby had conjured up. Rather than the snappy dress of a lawyer and the latest fashion of a designer, the couple in front of her was dressed casually in jeans. The woman wore a tank and a thin hoodie jacket with her dark hair wadded in a messy bun on top of her head. The man had on a sweatshirt and was running his fingers through his silvering hair trying to tame it down, but only making it stick up more with each pass. The only indication of power or money was the word Yale in large white letters on Jake's sweatshirt.

Tilly gave them both a huge grin and commenced with introductions. "Ruby, I'd like you to meet Jake and Mallory Winter."

The couple both smiled and said the obligatory how-do-you-dos, but Mallory seemed to be getting more uncomfortable by the second. Ruby wasn't sure what was making her so nervous, so she decided to just dive right in. "Ruby Baxter. Nice to meet you both. Tilly says you have some questions about the house?"

Mallory glanced at Jake who took the lead. "When we bought the house, we were more into things like square footage and renovation type things. We really didn't ask about the history of the place. We know the sign in the yard says Walter Bennett House 1875, but that's all we know. Old homes tend to have stories and we thought maybe ours does, too."

"Well, it was built in 1875 by Mr. Walter Bennett like the sign says. He was a pretty prominent businessman. In fact, his family was well-known around here for a long time. They had a hardware store on the corner of 4th and Main for decades. The house itself stayed in the family until the 1960s. It's been a few things since then, recording studio, engineering firm, but the late 60s was the last time it was a residence until you came to town."

Mallory shifted her weight, tucked one of her feet underneath her on the seat, and hesitated before she spoke. "You do ghost tours, too, right?"

Ruby nodded. "I do, pretty much every night of the week this time of year. Fall and ghost stories are a popular combination with the tourists."

"Do you get many locals in your groups?" Jake asked, jumping in as Mallory swallowed her sip of coffee.

Ruby chuckled. "No, not really. You may have noticed all the churches around here. My Pawpaw always said that we live in the big shiny brass buckle of the Bible Belt. The only spirit the locals are going to talk about is the Holy one at Sunday service. They know the stories are there, but they like to keep them in the confines of the tours for tourists."

"Pretty conservative place, huh?" Jake said, more than asked.

Tilly laughed. "Yeah, you could say that. Nice folks, a little narrow-minded about some things, but really nice. I think hauntings make things more interesting," she added twirling the pink ends of her hair.

Mallory rubbed at her temple. "That's one word for it. Not sure it's the one I'd use, though. Tell me, Ruby, has our house ever been a stop on your ghost tour?"

Ruby studied Mallory's face for a moment. She looked tired and tense. There was something more than curiosity behind the question. "Your house? No. The one across the street has occasionally. The red brick with the wraparound porch. Apparently, there's a lady in white that looks out the window. Haven't seen her myself, though."

"You believe in those things?" Mallory asked quietly. It wasn't judgement. It was as though she was looking for reassurance.

"I do. I mean, I hope there's a way to see the dead after they've gone. I'd hate to think the last time I saw my Pawpaw was the last time I'll see him."

"And nothing has ever happened in our house? No hauntings?"

Ruby shook her head. "If there had been a restless spirit in that home, a renovation would have been the perfect time to find out. That kind of thing tends to stir up energy in the house and irritate the spirits. If anything was going to happen, it would have then and I'd know about it. My Pawpaw spent plenty of time in that house working on it. He never mentioned anything to me."

Jake ran his fingers through his hair again managing to lay it down a little bit. "Your grandfather worked for James?"

"No, actually James took the project over from him before he was able to finish it himself. There was an accident with the wiring and Pawpaw got a bad shock. Nerve damage was pretty severe and he lost the use of one side of his body. James took it over more out of respect for my grandfather than anything else. He had more than enough business, but he always liked Pawpaw."

Mallory reached a hand out to pat Ruby's. "I'm so sorry for your loss."

Ruby curled her fingers around Mallory's. "Thanks. Mallory, why don't you tell me why you're really asking me these questions? What happened?"

Mallory tensed and Ruby thought she was going to pull her hand away, but she didn't. Instead, she relaxed and squeezed Ruby's fingers, grateful for the opening she was nervous to create herself. "I-I saw something last night." Her eyes left Ruby's and flitted to her husband. "Jake thinks it was a nightmare from the storm, but –"

"You know what you saw," Ruby finished.

Mallory nodded and Jake rubbed her back gently. Rather than being dismissive of his wife, it was clear he cared about her and was only trying to ease her fears by rationalizing what happened. There was no doubt in Ruby's mind that Mallory believed her own eyes.

Tilly leaned in closer as her curiosity peaked. "Can you tell us what you saw?"

The rims of Mallory's dark eyes began to redden as tears gathered. She pulled her hand away from Ruby's and began twisting her wedding ring nervously as she slowly told her story. "The storm had been so bad and the alarms kept going off. We hadn't slept much in between. I finally was able to drift off, but it didn't last long. I heard gun shots. It sounded like rifles. Several of them. It startled me awake and when I opened my eyes –" She stopped as a chill went through her.

"It's ok, Mal, you can tell them," Jake said softly. He pulled Mallory closer as her gaze lost focus, staring at empty space somewhere in the middle of the four of them.

"It was a man. Standing at the foot of the bed. They, someone, shot him. H-his head jerked back. Blood went everywhere. Then he just dropped to the floor when I screamed. They killed him. H-he was dead and then he was just...gone." Tears streamed down her face unchecked as she stayed in her unfocused trance, reliving the horror of the night before.

Ruby spoke softly, "Can you tell me how he was dressed? His clothes might help me with a time period."

"Like a soldier. Short coat. Long pants. They were both so ragged. Hanging on him so loosely. He was so thin. Frail and frightened."

"What color were his clothes?"

"I don't know. Everything was gray. His clothes, his face. The house was dark. No power. I only saw him for an instant in the flashes of lightning."

"Civil War?" Tilly asked Ruby.

"I'm not sure. Could be. The Battle of Franklin was a horrific thing, but the house wasn't built then, so a soldier from that time doesn't make sense."

"Did the battle happen in town? Maybe it's the land, not the house?" Jake asked.

"There was likely some fighting in town, but most of it was south of here. Carter House and Lotz House down Columbia Avenue were ground zero. A bunch of buildings here around this part of town were field hospitals. Over forty buildings were. Those are often said to be haunted by soldiers who died there waiting for care. Lots of dead and wounded. Around ten thousand causalities -- both sides combined."

"My god," Jake whispered.

"Any tragedy of that size in so few hours can cause a massive energy release. Souls get caught and some don't realize they're dead. Lots of reasons for hauntings. It just doesn't line up with where your house is, though. And nothing has ever happened there before."

Tilly glanced at her watch. Her break was long over but being between the morning and lunch crowd, she didn't rush off. "Could the storm have stirred it up? Lots of lightning."

"Possibly, but it seems like it would have stirred up something that makes more sense than the execution of a Civil War soldier," Ruby said. Her fingers traced a line in the marble table as she thought. "I just don't know."

"If Franklin is so conservative in their views about ghosts, how do you know so much about all this?" Jake asked.

Ruby smiled. "That would be my grandmother's doing. She grew up in New Orleans. Down there the dead and the living walk side-by-side. My love of old houses came from my grandfather, but it was my grandmother who kept me entertained with ghost stories. And she seemed to be pretty in tune with them. If you didn't know her, you'd have thought she was crazy. I'd catch her talking to herself, and she'd just tell me there was a little lost spirit who needed some company, that's all. She passed several years ago." Ruby sighed. "Too bad we don't have her and Pawpaw to help. They'd know exactly what was going on."

Mallory smiled at her. "I think maybe it's your turn to carry on the family business. They seem to have taught you well."

Tilly elbowed Ruby in the ribs. "That's exactly what I keep telling her!"

"Would you mind coming by the house before your tours tonight?" Mallory asked. "Maybe being there will give you some feeling like your grandmother had?"

"Sure, I'd be glad to, although I can't promise any feelings. I've been a little curious to see it all finished, anyway."

Cell numbers exchanged and a time set, the group each went their separate ways. Ruby wasn't sure what to think about the Bennett House being haunted, especially by Civil War soldiers, but it was definitely more interesting than coming up with her own ways to stall applying for the job with James Cavanaugh.

Four

Ruby stood on the sidewalk outside the Bennett House for a moment taking in her grandfather's handiwork. Not much had changed on the outside of the house except for making the front door more inviting and putting elegant fans on the porch ceiling. In the rotunda, Mallory had hung a large upholstered daybed swing made of antiqued black wood. Bolster pillows and a quilt draped over the back made it an inviting place to curl up with a book. Three rocking chairs lined the porch along the side of the house and a cozy pair of Adirondack gliders with a small mosaic-topped table sat beside the front door and faced the street. Ruby imagined Mallory placing them there with the intention of watching the town go by with a cup of coffee in the morning or a glass of wine as the sun set. After last night, Ruby doubted Mallory would be relaxing at the Bennett House any time soon.

Ruby's finger had barely left the doorbell when Mallory opened the door, startling her. A small squeak accompanied her heart leaping into her throat.

"I'm so sorry," Mallory said. "I didn't mean to frighten you. I saw you walking up. Come on in."

It was months since Ruby had last been inside the house and there were still a few major projects undone at the time. The kitchen cabinets were installed but the countertops and finishings were still left to do, some of the lighting had yet to be installed (left undone after Pawpaw's electrocution), along with some of the detail trim work. Now, complete and furnished with Mallory's designer touch, the Bennett House was a show place. In the entry hall, the sweeping staircase that curved at the top had a polished deep mahogany rail and treads accented by white spindles and stair fronts. The interior doors had deep casings detailed with trim molding and glass transoms over them that tilted out to allow air to circulate. Double-sided fireplaces in all of the downstairs rooms had hand-carved mantles and old iron coal grates. The hallway back to the kitchen and dining room, with their own double-sided fireplace dividing the spaces, showed some of the original small bricks that had been modernized with a gleaming coat of white paint. Antique furnishings in the rooms were accented with an occasional sleek accessory seamlessly blending the old and the new. "It's beautiful," Ruby said trying to take it all in. "Pawpaw would've loved to have seen this. It meant a lot to him that it was a home again."

"I'm glad he would have liked it," Mallory said with a hint of a smile. "It was a fun project finding places for our things and adding some local items."

"So often these old places look like time capsules or museums with heavy old furniture and art. This doesn't feel that way at all. You need to go work your magic on some of the other houses around here."

Mallory managed a chuckle through her exhaustion and strain. "That's the general idea. Come on, I'll give you the tour. Maybe along the way, you'll get a sense of what's going on here."

Jake rounded the corner of the entryway and apologized to Ruby for not meeting her at the door. "Client call. Am I in time for the tour?"

Mallory nodded and led the way explaining various pieces of furniture and their origins along the way, but leaving plenty of silence for Ruby to get her own feel for the place. Ruby wasn't sure what it was she was supposed to be picking up, but went along with it since it seemed to make Mallory feel better having someone else believe her. There were many times Ruby wished she possessed her grandparents' traits, Pawpaw's creative talent and Mawmaw's intuition with the spirit world, but she was just ordinary Ruby. Her only talent was knowing more about history than anyone had any use for. As far as Jake and Mallory Winter were concerned, she may have already shot her wad on useful information.

As they reached the upstairs bedrooms, Mallory hesitated on the threshold of their room. Jake put his hand on the small of her back and gave her a gentle nudge. "It's ok, Mal."

Mallory nodded and stepped inside ceasing her narration entirely. Ruby stood in the center of the room and turned slowly around. A high carved four-poster bed sat across the corner of the room, whose two walls were almost entirely framed windows. Deep crown molding wrapped the room in a rich cream contrasting elegantly with the slate gray of the walls. A small chair and footstool sat under one of the windows with a book laid open and facedown. The cover was old leather, worn from time and countless page turns. In the center of the room, a simple chandelier twinkled in the light streaming through the expanse of windows. All of the elegant simplicity seemed specifically designed to showcase the mirror that hung across from the bed.

Hanging horizontally over a low chest of drawers, the rectangular mirror was framed in layers of molding with detailed medallions at the corners. It was large and heavy, but reflecting the stylish room and glittering crystals of the chandelier seemed to lighten the massive piece. The size lent balance to the huge bed and seemed as though it had been made exactly for the room.

Ruby studied it for a moment more. "Was that always just a mirror?"

Mallory shrugged. "I'm not sure. It came from an antique store in town and was sold the way it is. Why do you ask? Do you think it was part of another piece of furniture? A dresser, maybe?"

"No, actually, it looks like it might have been part of a mantlepiece. Do you mind if I look at it a little closer? I geek out about old things like this."

"Knock yourself out," Jake said with a grin.

Ruby walked over to the mirror and shivered as the temperature dropped. She couldn't see an air vent, but there must have been one under the chest causing the chill. She refused to believe the house was drafty. Pawpaw wouldn't have stood for that. Running her hands along the bottom of the mirror frame, she felt for any indication that the piece had been cut from a large mantle. Tucking her fingers behind the front molding, she hit paydirt. Saw marks, not smooth honed wood. "There it is," she said. "The front couple layers of the molding were added to hide the separation, but you can tell from the back where it was cut away. It was once a mantle alright."

"Really?" Mallory asked.

"Yep. See for yourself. Feel right here," Ruby said as she stepped back to let Mallory wedge her fingers behind the frame.

As Ruby moved in front of the glass, she glanced at her reflection and froze. Her mouth opened in a silent scream as her eyes locked on the image where her reflection should have been. Color drained from her face and she began to sway on weak knees.

"Ruby!" Jake leaped over to her and grabbed her arm, catching her before she fainted. Mallory spun away from the mirror wide-eyed. Ruby gasped for air and sputtered trying to find words all the while unable to tear her gaze away from the mirror. Jake set her gingerly down on the floor as Ruby continued to fight for breath. "Get a cold cloth. She's burning up," Jake said sharply sending Mallory scurrying into the bathroom to get a wet washcloth.

By the time Mallory returned moments later and placed the cool cloth on Ruby's forehead, Ruby's breathing had steadied some but was still labored. "Can you tell us what happened?" Mallory asked, kneeling on the hardwood next to her.

Ruby's eyes were still glued to the mirror. "Not my face." Her voice was strained and hoarse.

"Maybe you saw Mallory's as you changed places," Jake, ever the realist, offered.

"No," Ruby said shaking her head slowly. "A man's face."

"The soldier?" Mallory breathed.

Slowly, almost painfully, Ruby pulled her gaze from the mirror and locked eyes with Mallory. "Yes. Dead. So much blood. So much." Ruby's face went ashen and she fainted in the middle of the Winters' bedroom floor.

Ruby's head throbbed and she really didn't want to talk anymore, but she answered Mallory's barrage of questions anyway. Coffee seemed to be Mallory's answer to everything that ailed anyone, but Ruby would have preferred a stiff drink after what she saw. Still, she thanked Mallory as she took the steaming cup and sipped it. Jake sat opposite her at the kitchen table and tried to interject some reality into the conversation about the mirror.

"But, are you *certain*, Ruby?" he asked for what seemed like the hundredth time.

"Jake, if I could unsee it, believe me, I would. I'm certain."

Mallory nodded. "That's how I feel, too. It's like the image is seared onto my brain. I can't shake it, and it doesn't seem to fade. I can see it now as clearly as I saw it last night."

"Right. And if anything, it's as if the image gets clearer and more detailed. Like, the shock is passing and I can focus on the features better, as horrible as they are," Ruby explained.

Jake's brand of skepticism was going to take more than a couple of ghost stories to shake, but he was at least not making the two women feel any more insane than they already did. "So, both of you saw a young soldier who appeared to have been killed. When Mallory saw him, he seemed to be standing at the foot of the bed, but the mirror is off to one side. So, she couldn't have seen the same image you did, Ruby. I mean, she didn't see him in the mirror."

"Right," Ruby said. "I only saw him from the shoulders up. She saw almost all of him. "

"And in both visions, he had been shot?" Mallory and Ruby nodded. "Where?"

"His face," they answered in unison. "Over his left eyebrow," Ruby added. Mallory nodded in agreement.

Jake drummed his fingers on the table as he thought. "So, we've established that you both think you saw the same soldier."

Mallory glared at her husband. "We *know* we saw him."

Ruby sighed as strain weighed on her. "Jake, I know this is hard for you to believe. Really, I do. As much as I was wanting my grandmother's spiritual sensitivities to be the real deal, I was struggling to truly believe Mallory," Ruby admitted. "But, when you see it for yourself, things change." The entire experience had taken a lot out of her and she wasn't in the mood to debate all things esoteric with the pragmatic attorney.

Despite her mood, Jake continued to try to find the logic of it all. "But it still makes no sense that it was a soldier, right?"

"As far as I know, it doesn't. The Union troops occupied Franklin, but it wasn't a place where they kept prisoners of war or anyone who would have been shot like that. There may have been a few soldiers to break through the Union lines and make it to town, but that would have been a huge exception to the rule. With as many rifles as Mallory heard, it makes a lot more sense that it would have been a battlefield death. And that, again, doesn't really line up with the age of the house or even the land it's on."

The three sat in silence for a while considering the various logical and spiritual avenues that could lead to the answer of the fallen soldier. Soon, the clock in the entryway chimed five o'clock and forced Ruby's thoughts out of the Civil War and back to the present. Two tours to do before she could crawl into bed. Ghost tours, no less.

Tossing back the end of her coffee, she pushed her chair back. "I'm sorry I haven't been more help."

"It's ok, Ruby. At least I don't feel as alone as I did this morning." Mallory replied with a wan smile. "Come on, I'll walk you out."

"Thanks. I need to grab my purse from the sofa in the living room on the way."

Jake began clearing the coffee cups as Mallory led Ruby back to the living room in the front of the house. "Are you sure you left it here?" Mallory asked.

"Yes, I set it down when we were talking about the sideboard." Sure enough, there was no purse on the sofa.

"Jake?" Mallory called into the kitchen. "Did you put Ruby's purse somewhere?"

"Purse?" he called back as cups and utensils clanked in the dishwasher. "No, haven't seen it."

"Never mind, then," Mallory answered. "Well, it has to be here somewhere." The two women pulled sofa cushions away and looked on the floor around the furniture.

"Well, this is just silly," Ruby grumbled. "I mean, I know it's small, but it's not invisible."

Mallory put her hands on her hips in frustration. "Tell you what, I'll retrace our steps while you go do your tours. Maybe you meant to set it down here but put it down somewhere else. It's been a long day and you had quite a fright. Could be you're not remembering correctly. I'll text you when I find it and you can come by and pick it up."

"I guess, but I'm sure I put it here," Ruby said with a frustrated shrug. "Thanks, Mallory. I'll see you a little later."

"No problem," Mallory said. "And," she added putting a hand on Ruby's arm, "thank you for believing me."

Ruby gave a short laugh. "Kinda hard not to, now."

Walking into the entry hall, Mallory and Ruby stopped in their tracks. Hanging on the brass door handle was the missing purse. Ruby's mouth dropped open and Mallory blanched.

"Um, I know I didn't hang it *there*," Ruby whispered. "Jake wouldn't have done that as a joke, would he?"

Mallory slowly turned to look at Ruby. "No, he wouldn't be that insensitive. That's bizarre. Not sure I like being in this house just the two of us. I don't suppose you want to stay here tonight?"

"No offense, but not on your life."

The Five Bloodiest Hours

In the waning moonlight, clouds of ragged breath blended with the steam from sweating backs of soldiers as they dug the cold hard ground of Carter Hill. Others wielded whatever tools they could find to dismantle slave cabins beside the empty cotton fields. Horses whinnied and pawed at the dirt as they dragged the beams toward the growing line of trenches. Skeletal soldiers in tattered blue uniforms worked tirelessly building the breastworks in the frigid darkness before dawn, trading their remaining strength and energy for the warmth the work brought.

Mounted officers followed the length of the trenches bring built to span the horseshoe bend in the Harpeth River behind them. Bridges had washed out weeks before as the river passed flood stage. With the trenches complete and armed, Union troops would have a veritable fortress in the direct line of the progress of the Confederates. Gen. Schofield would be pleased to know he had managed to outplay his West Point classmate on the battlefield like he had often done on the chessboard. At least, it seemed so. Gen. Hood's temperamental impulsiveness made him an unpredictable foe.

Shovels in frozen hands cut into the ground with ceaseless repetition. With each turn of the dirt onto the berm in front of them, men steeled their nerves. Prayers were said. Thoughts wandered home. Home. Somewhere that seemed so far away for the troops from Ohio, Missouri, and other places the boys, turned into men by war, never thought they would have to leave. Defenders of the home front had become strangers in strange places longing for familiar faces and surroundings knowing they may never see them again.

Still, they dug. Knee-deep ditches deepened and wooden cabin beams topped the berms giving riflemen a place to stand and fire, then drop down and reload. Each inch further into the ground meant another inch of protection and, so, they dug. Fingers purpled in the freezing cold. And still they dug. Icy mud caked on frozen feet made calloused by months of walking shoeless across the Deep South in pursuit of their enemy. And still they dug.

'Enemy' was such a strange word for many in the ranks. There were so many other words that could be used to describe the men and boys in gray who would soon be taking aim at them. Brother. Friend. Neighbor. Son. But they couldn't think those words. Words with familiarity were traded for words that made pulling the trigger easier. Nameless. Faceless. Rebel. Enemy.

Five

Night settled over the historic downtown with none of the weather theatrics of the night before. Clear skies twinkled with stars alongside a sliver of moon that offered beauty if not illumination. Streetlights glowed in warm circles along the tree-lined sidewalks. Leaves rustled as a chill blew through the branches. One by one, lights in the few remaining downtown residences winked out as the town settled in for a more restful night. Except for the Bennett House.

The soft glow of lamps shone from the arched windows around the house. Each room bathed in soft pools of light to keep the unknown at bay. Light that would allow Mallory Winter to face the night. The silver clock in the entry hall chimed quietly as each hour passed. Eventually Mallory no longer heard it and slept fitfully next to her husband who had long since drifted off.

Quiet reigned in the house for hours before being broken by the faintest sound. Then another. Jake stirred. Once more, the delicate sound. This time, Jake woke thinking it was Mallory whimpering in her sleep. Putting his arm across her to comfort her, he closed his eyes. As sleep played at the edges of his mind, the sounds came again, but not from Mallory. Jake's breath stilled as he listened to the night. His heartbeat pounded in his ears drowning out everything until the sounds came once more, and louder. Laughter. Children.

It was the middle of the night. What were children doing playing outside at this hour? Taking a deep breath to quiet the pounding of his heart in his ears, Jake listened again. It wasn't coming from outside. It was coming from the next room.

For a moment, he debated about whether or not to wake Mallory. If he got up to investigate, he would surely wake her and he wasn't sure she could take another fright. It had to be a dream, he told himself. There had been so much talk of ghosts and hauntings that he was dreaming about them now. That was the only thing that made sense. Closing his eyes, he rolled over and took a deep breath.

For a moment, he found sleep again, but only a fleeting moment. Sleep began to dissipate as a strange feeling worked its way to the front of his consciousness. A sense of being watched. Squeezing his eyes closed tighter, he scolded himself and the ridiculousness of his growing uneasiness. Still, the feeling persisted. Stronger and insistent. Deciding to put the foolishness to rest once and for all, Jake opened his eyes in defiance of his fear.

Cold air rushed into Jake's lungs as he opened his mouth to scream, freezing his voice in his throat. Standing beside the bed were the spectral figures of two small children, toddler twins, tears streaming from sunken eyes. Pale, fragile, and sickly, the little boy and girl looked at Jake with pleading and fear. As they shimmered back into the ether, Jake's scream released in a burst of pure horror.

―――

The small silver clock ticked in the entryway as silence settled between the three people in the kitchen. Every creak of the tree branches in the wind outside seemed to echo in the stillness. Traffic rumbled past the house as business in town continued on its merry way, oblivious to the terror behind the stalwart walls of the Bennett House.

"Children?" Ruby asked. "Are you certain?" The irony of her asking those words of Jake wasn't lost on her. He'd asked her the same thing repeatedly yesterday as his skeptic's mind grappled with her vision of the soldier in the mirror.

"Yes, I'm certain," he answered. His hands trembled despite his best efforts to still them by lacing his fingers together on the kitchen table. "A boy and a girl."

Ruby sat back in her chair and sighed. "Well, at least you know we aren't crazy. Believe in all this stuff now?"

"I don't really have much of a choice, do I?" The circles under Jake's eyes aged him considerably more than the streaks of gray in his hair ever did. The house was wearing on him as much as it was wearing on his wife.

Mallory said little as Jake explained to Ruby what he saw in the night. Rather than being relieved that her husband now believed her story about the soldier, she seemed more nervous than ever about being in the house. "But what do the children have to do with the soldier's battlefield death? Children wouldn't have been out there, too, would they?"

"No," Ruby replied shaking her head. "And it doesn't seem to line up with Jake's description of them, anyway. They weren't shot."

Jake nodded. "They seemed sick. Sunken eyes. Listless. Afraid. I think they died from their illness."

"Which, again, doesn't go with the soldier's death," Ruby finished.

Mallory twisted her wedding ring, her usual nervous habit. "The mystery is interesting and all, but how do we get rid of these things? We can't live in a haunted house forever."

"I mean, you *could*," said Ruby. "They don't seem to want to hurt you. You've had full apparitions two nights in a row. The amount of energy it takes for that to happen is staggering. If they wanted to hurt you, they certainly have the energetic strength to do it. I think they want something else."

"What?" Mallory asked.

"I'm not sure. Maybe they want to be remembered. Maybe they need help crossing over. Maybe they have unfinished business."

Jake ran his fingers through his hair. His hands still shook with unsettled nerves. "How do we find out?"

"And how do we help them?" Mallory added.

Ruby sat for a moment not wanting to accept the only answer she could think of. It was certainly not something a sane person would do. Not something she had ever done in her life. Then, there was the other side of the coin – what if it didn't work and only made things worse? Without any other ideas, she offered, "We ask them."

Jake and Mallory stared at her, unblinking. "A-Ask them?" Mallory stammered finally. "Even if we wanted to, which I certainly don't, how would we even do that?"

"Um, I'm not totally sure. My grandmother just talked to them. I never asked her how. Since these don't seem to fit anything with the history of the house or the land, maybe the spirits are attached to something in the house. If we can figure out what, maybe we can use the object as a focal point to try to reach them that way."

"If we find out what they are attached to, can't we just get rid of it?" Jake asked.

"You could do that, but it just passes the haunting on to someone else. If you destroy it, it may release the spirit and cause more problems. Think of it this way, if you destroyed my house, I'd be pretty pissed off at you."

Jake shifted in his seat, his exhaustion from his sleepless night catching up with him. "No pissing them off, then. So, what do we do?"

"I say we start figuring out what brought them here. Narrow down what the host objects are."

"How?" Mallory asked.

"Make a list of where anything antique came from. Anything you know about any of the pieces. Basically, inventory your house. Once we have a list, we can look for anything in common that might tie the two hauntings together. They may be in the same object, or different ones. While you work on that, I'm going to go see an old friend of my grandmother's. Maybe there's something she can tell me about how Mawmaw talked to her spirit friends."

With a plan in place, Mallory and Jake at least had somewhere to direct their nervous energy for the time being. Even if the plan meant opening the door to more contact with spirits than they really wanted. Ruby set off in search of the one person she could think of in all of Franklin who might be able to help.

Six

Down Adams Street, away from the large Victorians, the craftsman style homes seemed to shrink the further they got from Main. Off the beaten path of tourists and investors, the houses began to more closely resemble the residents who had called the town home before the boom of historical revival a decade or so ago. Happily forgotten, the residents lived in the same homes they grew up in and would likely pass down.

Pawpaw's house was one of these. Like the saying goes about the plumber with the leaky pipes, the house wasn't one that benefitted from his restoration talents. Peeling green paint and cracked concrete steps waited for the master's touch that would never come. A garden once kept by Mawmaw had only the straggly remains of whatever perennials continued to push through the seasons year after year. Ruby had the best of intentions when it came to the garden, but never seemed to have the time to follow through. Or the heart to. Something just felt wrong in messing with Mawmaw's flower beds. Once in a while, Ruby would stick some red begonias in the bed closest to the front steps. The hummingbirds and butterflies seemed to like them and they had always been a favorite of Mawmaw's for that reason. They also didn't require much attention from Ruby who inevitably forgot to water them.

Inside, the house was one of those time capsules Ruby mentioned to Mallory but would never have her change. At least for a while. Growing up, the rooms had been cozy and fashionable, but as time and trends marched on, the little house on Adams was left behind. To be fair, it wasn't because Mawmaw was out of touch with fashion. She was, but that wasn't the reason for the stalled interior design. That was entirely Pawpaw's doing. Ruby had been in middle school when Mawmaw first got sick. By high school, she was gone. Years of smiling through her suffering finally came to an end. After losing Ruby's mother when Ruby was only two and then losing his wife, Pawpaw couldn't bear to change the house. It seemed too much like losing his wife and daughter all over again. The décor seemed to be his way of keeping the precious memories made in those rooms alive. Now that Pawpaw was gone, Ruby finally understood that feeling.

The house across the street was an entirely different story. Dorothy Wallace, Miss Dot to just about everyone in town, changed her paint color on the slightest whim and put whatever flowers her heart desired in the front garden, whether they matched the house or clashed terribly. At the moment, some bright yellow pansies were adding to a late-sixties-inspired hot pink of the siding. A splash of orange from the pumpkins on the porch completed the retro palette.

The woman behind the bright house was equally colorful. For years she ran a small restaurant on Main Street until rents skyrocketed with the influx of yuppies. Hanging up her apron and coconut cream pie recipe, she retired but kept her place as the person all of old Franklin came to for advice. Mostly because she was one of the few underground fortune tellers and psychic advisers in town. 'Underground' might have been a bit of exaggeration. Everyone knew she did it, but she never advertised her services. Mostly because it was illegal in Franklin. Fortune-telling had been outlawed in the municipal code in the seventies and no one ever bothered to change it, being the buckle of the Bible Belt and all. Ruby often wondered why, with all the progress, the city officials left that antiquated law. Was their traditional faith so fragile that they were threatened by women with rocks, candles, and cards?

Miss Dot knew her old age could let her get away with things and used it to her advantage, not to mention the advantage of anyone who came to her needing advice. Today, that would be Ruby. As she climbed the steps to the porch, wind chimes tinkled merrily in the breeze, crystal prism pendulums sending rainbows splashing across the wood siding. Tired faded floral cushions sank into worn wicker chairs on the porch. One cushion had tiny holes in it and the chair itself had twigs of the wicker weave poking out courtesy of Stanley, the obese black cat that only half-cared that Ruby had woken him up with her approach. One green eye slit open as he yawned then closed again.

"Don't knock yourself out with the warm welcome there, Stan," Ruby said with a chuckle as she rang the bell next to the warped screen door.

"Hold yer horses!" Miss Dot hollered from somewhere in the house.

"It's me, Miss Dot," Ruby called.

"Door's open!"

Ruby pulled the screen door wide with a loud squeal and pushed open the currently purple front door. Miss Dot came out of the kitchen drying her hands on a dishcloth. "Is this a bad time?" Ruby asked.

"Any time God sees fit to grant me is a good time. Come on in." Miss Dot waved the dishrag at the sofa as she took her spot in the wingback chair in the corner between the window and the fireplace. On the table next to her, a stack of well-worn tarot cards sat at the ready. A perfect vantage point for keeping warm and an eye on the neighborhood. Ruby settled into the sofa and pulled her legs up under her. Simple but tasteful furniture filled the room serving as a blank palate for seasonal changes in décor. Fall color was woven into the sofa pillows and throws that made the room cozy and inviting. "Alright, what's on your mind? And don't say 'nothing'. You look like you haven't slept in a month of Sundays."

Leave it to Miss Dot to shoot straight from the hip. "I was doing okay until a couple of days ago. Met the new couple that moved into the house on Fourth that Pawpaw had been working on," Ruby said.

"And they're what you're losing sleep over?" Miss Dot asked.

"Sort of. You remember how Mawmaw used to talk to the spirits around her?"

"Lord, yes, that woman could find company in a cave, I swear. What got you thinkin' about that?"

"The Bennett House is haunted," Ruby said simply. Miss Dot raised an eyebrow out of interest not derision, so Ruby continued. "I tell ghost stories for a living, but I'm not fond of having them happen to me."

"So, you've experienced something there yourself?" she asked leaning forward slightly.

Ruby nodded and explained everything she, Mallory, and Jake experienced over the last couple of days at the Bennett House. Once in a while, Miss Dot's eyes would widen, but mostly she remained unphased. After Ruby finished the tale, she sat for a moment and let it all sink in.

"So, you've got ghosts that don't belong that have shown up with the new people and you want to know how they got there and how to get rid of them. Is that the long and the short of it?"

"Right."

Miss Dot sat for a moment in silence before she spoke. "I think you're lettin' the location of these spirits cloud what you already know about them."

Ruby wrinkled her brow. "How do you mean? I don't know anything about them at all."

Miss Dot chuckled. "No one knows this town's history like you do. Stop and think for a minute. If I can figure out who these three spirits are, you damn sure can."

"But—"

"Don't argue with me. Think. Who do you know that was killed in the Battle of Franklin with a shot over his left eye as the mortal wound?"

Ruby sat and shuffled through her mental Rolodex of historical figures of Franklin trying to find one that fit the description. Then it hit her like a ton of bricks. "Shit! It's Tod Carter!" Ruby mentally berated herself for being so stupid. Of course, it was Tod Carter. Theodrick "Tod" Carter was the middle son of Fountain Branch Carter who built the Carter House on Columbia Avenue. It had been occupied by Union troops as a field office during the battle. That house and the Lotz House across the street had been ground zero in the horrifying Confederate loss. Tod Carter had been wounded on the battlefield even though he was carrying furlough papers that could have spared him the fight if he chose, and was brought back to his childhood home where he died two days later.

A smile crept across Miss Dot's face. "I knew you'd get there. Now, let's focus on the children. You know who they are, too."

Now that she was thinking straight, this one came easier to her. "The Lotz kids. Julius and Julia." The toddlers were the children of Albert and Margaretha Lotz, who were German immigrants that bought land from Fountain Branch Carter and built their home just over one hundred paces from the Carter House. The legends around the death of the twins had been debated by historians, but Ruby steered away from the most commonly told lore that the twins drank from a creek that was poisoned by the Union forces. It just didn't make sense that the troops would poison the water supply they themselves would be using as they occupied the town. More likely the twins drowned playing by the water or contracted typhoid, even though records and diaries from the time villainize the occupying troops in their deaths.

"Alright, so, we know who the spirits are at least," Miss Dot said with a satisfied smile. "Now all you have to do is figure out what they want. What's your plan for that?"

"All I can think to do is ask them," Ruby said with a shrug. It was admittedly not much of a plan.

"And if they won't talk?"

"Hell, I don't know," Ruby said leaning back on the sofa. Her exhaustion was catching up with her making her irritable and frustrated. "I don't really know what I'm doing here. I need Mawmaw."

Miss Dot shook her head and tisked. "Nonsense. You got plenty of her in you. Trust it and give yourself some credit. So far, it sounds like you know what you're doing. Figuring out the host item is a great start. From the sounds of things, you might have more than one. But," she said squinting at Ruby, "you're not gonna like what I have to say next."

"Great. Just say it."

"You're gonna have to spend some time in that house, child. You can't talk to spirits if you don't meet them where they are."

"Fabulous." Ruby sighed and closed her eyes.

"And, you need to be ready for there to be some resistance. Some don't like to be confronted. Approach with caution."

"Nothing about this sounds like something I want to do."

Miss Dot laughed. "I expect not. When you open yourself up to the dead, you may get more than you bargain for. Just remember, the dead aren't much different from the living. If they were good people in life, they're probably fine in death. Some people are assholes on both sides of the veil, so keep an eye out for those folks."

"Don't suppose you want to come with me?" Ruby asked.

Miss Dot's old eyes twinkled. "Tempting. You don't need me, Ruby. You can do this."

The Five Bloodiest Hours

The gray pallor of dawn eased into morning as the sun warmed the slick clay of the road north from Spring Hill to Franklin. Union cannon wagons that slipped past the sleeping Confederates had carved deep ruts causing the soldiers to stagger even more than their haggard exhaustion. Rest was not to be found until someone won the war. Though none would say it, many didn't care who anymore. Horses stumbled and rocked their riders nearly off their backs. Except for Gen. John Bell Hood who was strapped onto the back of his mount every morning by his men after the loss of his right leg at the hip from an injury at Chickamauga and the severe injury of his left arm in battle at Gettysburg. His very presence on the horse reminded his men that no matter their complaints and ailments, they were of little consequence to the general.

The ragtag forces slowed their advance, knowing there was a possibility of the enemy lying in wait just over the hill. Scouts were sent, and soldiers took advantage of the wait on the reports to rest weary limbs. Whispered conversations between officers were relayed through the ranks by those close enough to overhear. Caution was being employed even though the Union was expected to be making a run for Nashville. Hood was putting nothing past Schofield and his ability to stage a dangerous gambit to outplay the rebel leader.

As the sun reached its zenith, Gen. Hood and his commanding officers commandeered the Harrison House a mere two miles to the north while the tattered ranks rested behind the safety of the hills between them and their foe. The stately brick colonial with its towering Greek revival front portico quickly transformed into a field office once more. Proximity to the main road between Spring Hill and Franklin made the home a frequent commodity for the forces that skirmished in the area. On this day, the house would bear silent witness to the opening of the gates of Hell.

The scouts reported back to the Harrison House faster than the weary men hoped. Topping Winstead Hill, they quickly discovered there was nowhere for them to hide. Every tree between the hilltop and the Federal entrenchments had been felled to build the breastwork headboards and to prevent Confederate snipers hiding behind them. All that was left was open field between opposing sides. The gambit had been put in play.

Cresting Winstead Hill, shock filled the mounted officers and foot soldiers who gazed toward the town below. Eyes that expected to see the blue backs of Union troops on their way to Nashville were met with a staggering vision of entrenchments that stretched from one edge of the horizon to the other. And not just a single line. Between the first and third line of trenches, the iron artillery waited coolly for their enemies to challenge their power. Training field glasses on the Union's western flank, more artillery was seen waiting in the decaying Fort Granger along the railroad tracks. There, unseen by his old friend on the hill, Schofield oversaw the rebuilding of the rail bridge that would move his supply wagons onward as he lay in wait for Hood to advance.

Words failed the men standing at the feet of the mounted commanders. Words would have done no good had they made themselves present. Hood would pay them no more heed than those that spilled forth from the mouths of his leaders. Seething with venom at being outplayed yet again, the general would hear nothing of retreat. To a man, the officers pleaded with Hood to reconsider his timing. To wait on more troops and artillery that had yet to make it to their location from the south. Just one more day, they begged. Make the enemy wait and wonder while they regrouped, rested, and reloaded. It was sadly wasted breath, especially given that it would be some of the last taken by many on that rise. Precious breath gave life to impassioned words that hung useless among the men.

Back down the hill in the front parlor of the Harrison House, more words were wasted in pleas and lamentations. Heedless, Hood's words were final. Out-prepared, out-manned, out-gunned, they would make the fight. Words that would kill.

Seven

Rather than spend more time in a haunted house, Ruby met the Winters at Onyx and Alabaster to go over Mallory's itemized list of antiques. She knew Tilly would be there and had to be chomping at the bit for an update. Sure enough, as soon as Ruby walked in, Tilly put in her usual order and signaled she'd catch up with Ruby in five.

In the gold velvet horseshoe booth where they met for the first time days earlier, Jake and Mallory had spread out some papers across the marble table. Ruby came prepared with her copy of *Franklin: Tennessee's Handsomest Town, a Bicentennial History,* an out-of-print book she had paid way too much money for a couple of years back. When it came to details of the town, as long as they were before 1999, the book was a veritable bible. It may not contain anything about hauntings, but there was plenty of history and tragedy between the pages. Hopefully, whatever and whoever they encountered in the Bennett House could be explained with it.

"Wow, that's quite a list," Ruby said as she scanned the three legal pad pages of notes on the table.

"I tried to separate it into things that were brought with us and things we bought here. Most of the large pieces have been with us a while," Mallory explained. "I'm not thinking those would have anything to do with the hauntings, but I wrote them down anyway."

Ruby nodded. "I think what we're looking for will be local, but you never know. I'm not ruling anything out."

"One cinnamon orange London Fog," Tilly said as she handed Ruby her drink.

"Thanks, Til."

Tilly settled in next to Ruby in the booth. "Well, this looks like quite the project going on," she said scanning the papers and the thick history book. "Somebody gonna fill me in?"

The trio caught her up on the hauntings and Ruby filled all of them in on her conversation with Miss Dot. Once everyone was on the same page, they began scouring the list of antiques for anything that might seem like a host item for the Carter and Lotz families. Like Mallory said, most of the larger pieces had come with them from other places, mostly up north. Nowhere that Tod Carter or the Lotz children would have been. The list of pieces that had been bought locally was almost as long, but contained more small items. It seemed that Mallory had decided to redecorate completely with the purchase of the historic home.

"Everything from vases to paintings to mirrors," Jake said as he ran a finger down the list.

"Mirrors," Ruby said quietly. Her mind went back to the image of Tod Carter in the bedroom mirror where her own face should have been. Knowing who it was made the image less terrifying and more sad, but still wasn't a comfortable thing to focus on. There was something about the mirror that stuck out to her, though.

Jake broke into her thoughts. "Something significant about mirrors, Ruby? Other than seeing a soldier in one?"

"Maybe," Ruby answered. "Maybe it's just seeing him in one. I'm not sure."

"What's the old tradition about mirrors and the dead?" Tilly asked.

"I'm not sure where it started," Ruby began. "I've heard it's a southern thing, a Jewish tradition, and all sorts of other origins, but basically, the thought is that when someone dies in a home, all the mirrors should be covered to prevent the soul from being caught inside it."

Jake leaned back and chewed on the inside of his lip for a moment. "Now that you mention it, I've heard that one, too. Not likely people were thinking about covering mirrors in the middle of a massive battle."

Ruby nodded thoughtfully. "I'm sure you're right. That could mean that the mirror on your bedroom wall was in the Carter House when Tod Carter died."

"That's a little unsettling," Mallory said.

"Not as unsettling as having a spirit stuck in it," Tilly replied.

"Not helping, Til," Ruby said dryly.

"Sorry."

Jake shook his head. "She has a point, though. The mirror itself is no more or less unsettling than any of the other antiques we have in the house. It's what you *saw* in the mirror that makes it unsettling and the fact that Mallory saw him *outside* of the mirror."

"Which means he may not be trapped in the mirror as much as it's connecting him to the Carter House," Ruby added as she pulled the yellow page over that had the bedroom mirror recorded on it and jotted the note about the Carter House next to it.

"What about the Lotz kids? What were their names?" Mallory asked.

"Julius and Julia."

"Right, but Jake didn't see them in a mirror. They were next to the bed."

Jake nodded. "That's where I saw them, but I heard them before that. Giggling that seemed to be coming from the guest room."

"Is there a mirror in there?" Ruby asked.

Mallory shook her head. "No—" she checked the list again. "Wait, there is. I hadn't thought about it being a mirror but there's a mirrored piece in there. It's shelves with mirrors behind them to showcase the backs of whatever porcelain pieces are put on it."

"I can't imagine anyone putting porcelain in a bedroom for toddler twins," Tilly said with a shake of her head. "Asking for trouble there."

"It wouldn't necessarily have to be in their room. It could be any room in the house where the deceased were. And not necessarily where they died, either. In fact, the kids may have died at the creek, but would have been laid out for a wake in the house. Just like Mallory didn't think about the piece of furniture being mirrored, the Lotzes may have forgotten, too. Or, since they were German immigrants, it may not have been a tradition they practiced." Finding the piece on the list, Ruby once more noted where the mirrored shelves may have originally lived.

"So, we have an idea of what their host items are, but we aren't any closer to figuring out why they are so active in the house," Jake said.

"Which leads us to the only idea any of us, including Miss Dot, have had for solving that part of the mystery," Ruby added. "We have to ask them."

"Like a séance?" Tilly asked.

Ruby grimaced. "I hadn't thought about it that way, but, yeah, I guess so."

"Don't we need someone more, I don't know, *qualified* for this sort of thing?" Mallory asked twisting her wedding ring again. "No offense, Ruby, but I don't really want a bunch of ghosts running amuck in my new house. It's already overrun."

"No offense taken. Miss Dot seemed to think I was capable of it for some reason. I think she's wrong, but I'm not sure we have much choice in the matter unless you want to recruit a psychic from Nashville or somewhere."

Jake shook his head. "I'd rather keep this within the confines of Franklin and their too-conservative-to-talk-about-hauntings selves. Not sure I trust anyone outside of our circle not to go sensationalizing things. We just got here and that's not exactly the way we want to get our names out to the public."

"Then, we do this on our own, I guess," Ruby said with a resigned sigh. "Just know I make no guarantees about anything. I've never done this before in my life."

"So, when is this séance, and can I come?" Tilly asked.

Ruby shrugged and looked across the table at the Winters. "Your call."

Mallory and Jake exchanged looks. "The sooner the better," Jake said. "Sure, Tilly, you're welcome to come, too."

The sooner the better might have worked for Jake and Mallory, but Ruby would have been happy putting it off as long as possible. Nothing about this sat well with her. With no experience at all in this kind of thing, there were only two ways it could possibly go an neither of them was good. Either they would sit there feeling like idiots talking to spirits with no effect whatsoever, or all hell would break loose. "Okay, but I think I need to do a little research on this first," Ruby said. "I don't want to go into it half-cocked and cause some sort of spiritual Armageddon. I'm going to get one of the other guides to take my tours tonight. Til, can you meet me at Dot's after you close? We're gonna need her help."

"Can do. Is it weird that I'm excited about this?" Tilly asked.

"Yes," the trio answered in chorus.

Eight

Wind blew gently through the monuments of Rest Haven Cemetery. In the branches of the century magnolias, birds chirped and rustled the huge green leaves. Squirrels chewed twigs off of oak trees as they mined for acorns among the limbs. In the far edges, cedars stood shading a section completely devoid of headstones but surely not devoid of dead. Ruby pulled her sweater tighter around her to ward off the chill. It didn't help. Sweaters don't do much against a chill that's deep inside.

Ruby paused at a pair of newer stones. Low, garishly dark gray amid the lighter stones aged by time. The dates were old. Replacement stones for those lost in the flood a decade earlier. While it was nice to see that someone still cared enough about the people buried there, the new stones seemed awkward and out of place. Too modern for the old cemetery. Too modern for the people they represented. Rather than embracing the past and its traditions of the standing rounded-top headstones, history had been discarded. It rubbed Ruby the wrong way. Her mother's headstone, as well as Mawmaw's, was the old style. It had been important to Pawpaw that they kept the tradition of the family plot. Somewhere in a shop, someone was making one for him, too.

Pushing the thought of the cold stone that would memorialize such a warm man out of her mind, Ruby sat on the border next to the mound of dirt. While she inevitably felt drawn to his graveside, she felt disconnected from him even more as she sat there talking to the dirt. The dirt wasn't him. What was under the dirt wasn't him, either. But if those things weren't him, what was? Lines of life and death seemed more blurred to her than ever before.

She was too little to remember her mother's death. All she remembered was the wistful smiles that would settle on Mawmaw and Pawpaw's faces when they spoke of the daughter they loved and lost too soon. Ruby never knew her father. He died before he could even marry her mother. Both taken by car accidents on separate occasions. Maybe that was why Ruby rarely went anywhere she couldn't walk to. Maybe that's why she stayed in the small town.

Mawmaw's death had taken so long that it seemed more like a relief for her when it finally did come. She seemed reluctant to leave Ruby and Mitch, but looked forward to seeing her precious daughter again. In many ways, death was peace for Mawmaw, and to a certain extent for Pawpaw who had watched his beloved suffer for so long. Pawpaw's death was different. He didn't want to go yet. Didn't want to leave Ruby. Didn't want to leave his work and the town that held precious friendships and memories. Yet, there he was. Under the dirt.

Ruby wondered what Pawpaw would think of her having a séance to talk to a dead soldier and a pair of twins. He tolerated Mawmaw's spirit conversations, but never really believed her. He just figured if it made her happy, that was all that mattered. Mawmaw believed and he never made her feel silly for it. This, somehow, seemed different. This wasn't chatting with a passing ghost. This was calling them forth.

Or was it? More likely just some theatrics and talking to thin air. Ruby felt inadequate and out of place since Pawpaw's death and this looming expectation of her amplified the feeling. She only knew who she was in relation to caring for him and the business. She was no psychic medium, that was for sure, even if Mawmaw really had been. She'd never before had a conversation with the dead. If she had been able to do that, she would have gotten to know her mother or visited with Mawmaw again. She would have talked to her Pawpaw one more time. No, she was just Ruby Baxter. A tour guide in a small town who had no idea what she was doing about pretty much everything.

With days getting shorter as the end of daylight savings time neared, the sun that lit Miss Dot's living room earlier was sinking behind the Tennessee hills. Green leaves began to give way to golds and reds on some of the trees that turned first. Bradford Pear trees in front yards boasted reddening tops. Crepe myrtles deepened their green leaves to purples. Before long, the hillsides would begin to turn into beautiful washes of color as the sun bathed them in a warm golden spotlight. For now, the waning summer greens were losing their vibrance and dulling into an army drab before the spectacular show to come.

Stanley once more greeted Ruby with mild derision as she and Tilly disturbed his evening nap in the last moments of sunlight. One green eye surveyed the intruders before deciding they were not worthy of opening the other one. A quick scratch behind his ears from Ruby was rewarded with a half-hearted purr before Stanley's eye closed in dismissal of the girls.

Once they were settled inside, Miss Dot brought a tray with tea and slices of her famous coconut cream pie. Scraping off a scoop of meringue, Ruby let the sweet goodness take her mind off the matter at hand for a moment. A brief moment.

"You know I haven't done this before, either," Miss Dot said as she settled into her usual chair. Her pie plate balanced on her knee while her fingers absently drummed on the top of the tarot deck on her side table. "I'm not sure how I can help you."

Ruby sighed and took another stab at her pie. "You read cards for people all the time. How do you keep yourself out of trouble with the spirits who might be a little nasty?"

Miss Dot laughed and shook her head. "Child, the spirits aren't coming to me through the cards to sit down and have a chat. Not like what you're about to do. Cards and séances are very different things."

Tilly sucked on the end of her fork for a moment as she thought. "They must have something in common. You have to get their attention before they will tell you things in the cards, right? How do you do that?"

Miss Dot nodded her gray head. "Well, it's all about setting your mind on the spirits you want to hear from and letting them know you're listening."

Ruby frowned. "So, I just need to focus on Tod and the kids and tell them I want to talk to them? That's it?"

"Pretty much. At least for the cards. You're wanting to do something a lot more complex, though. An actual conversation may take a bit more energy and focus. More atmosphere. More for you than the ghosts. The more intention you put into getting the mood and space feeling right, the more you are focused to receive what they have to give."

"This is starting to sound as ridiculous as it feels," Ruby groaned.

"Do you want my help or not?" Miss Dot asked shaking her fork at Ruby.

Attitude corrected from the scolding, Ruby replied, "I want your help. Sorry."

Tilly wiggled excitedly in her spot on the sofa. "So, we're talking candles, incense, and stuff?"

Miss Dot nodded. "If that's what feels right."

"None of this feels right," Ruby said. It might have seemed sassy to Miss Dot, who, in all fairness, was trying to help, but she couldn't help it. "Aren't the spirits going to pick up on the fact that I'm absolutely faking my way through this whole thing? Isn't that going to be a turn-off for them?"

"Probably."

"Then, what do I do?"

"Don't fake it," Miss Dot answered. She was nothing if not a straight-shooter. "You have to believe in what you're doing. Do you want to help Mallory and Jake or not?"

"I mean, I do. I feel like after all this, I have to. I'm just not sure I can."

Miss Dot leaned back in her chair and drummed on the tarot cards again. "See, there's your problem. You're helping out of obligation. That's not the right reason to help anyone."

Ruby set her pie aside and pulled her knees up to her chest. "I really do want to help them, but I don't know that I can. I feel like a charlatan taking advantage of people from out of town. I happened to know some history about their house. That's it. How in the hell did a conversation about that turn in to all this mess?"

"The Winters trust you, Ruby," Miss Dot said flatly. "It's time you did, too."

Tilly squeezed Ruby's hand. "Maybe creating the right atmosphere will make it feel more authentic instead of like you're putting on a show. It's all in how you look at it."

While Tilly's optimism was a little annoying, Ruby wondered if maybe she had a point. Maybe with all four of them in a candlelit room participating, it would seem more authentic than it did sitting at Onyx and Alabaster or Miss Dot's living room talking about it. "Alright, I'll try to get into the spirit of this even though I feel idiotic. What do we need?"

"That's better," Miss Dot said, blue eyes twinkling.

The Five Bloodiest Hours

Desolation spread its arms wide between the breastworks and Winstead Hill. Almost two miles of empty land. Barren fields. Shelterless expanse. Cannons faced southward, pointed at an enemy yet unseen. The sound of drums had been carried by the wind from somewhere behind the rise. With each beat of the distant rhythm, the stomachs of the men at Carter House churned and tightened. Each knew the same was true for the foe that advanced. Only the leaders seemed unafraid of what was coming. Pillars of military prowess confident of victory that hinged on the actions of the men beneath them. The men in the ranks had seen such confidence before and knew that it was certainly fallible.

In the trenches were farmers, shoe makers, bankers, shop owners, and all sorts of others. Military experience was limited mostly to whatever they gained since they enlisted. The glory of the uniform and the noble cause it represented to each side had long since lost its luster. There was no glory in watching wounds fester or men die in their own diseased filth. There was no glory in starvation and frostbite. No glory in the tears they silently shed in the night. Survival was in their own inexperienced hands no matter the calculated expertise of those who directed the troops from above the ranks.

With each beat of the drum, each stab of the shovel, each step north, the thread of hope was stretched thinner.

Nine

Since both apparitions had been seen in the master bedroom, it had been agreed among the inexperienced séance team that it would be the location for the ritual. Rationally it made sense, but no one really knew if it made any spiritual sense. Rational sense was all they had to go on.

"So," began Jake, "are there any special things we need for this thing?"

"Candles," Mallory answered confidently.

Ruby looked at her with mild surprise. "Good place to start."

"Right," Mallory agreed. "There are some in the kitchen. Jake, can you get those? Ruby and I can gather some from around the house."

"On it," Jake said as he headed downstairs.

Ruby and Mallory split up and began to gather the various tea lights and larger pillar candles Mallory had in each of the rooms of the house. After a few minutes, Ruby made her way back to the bedroom with her arms full of clinking votive glasses and larger candle holders. Jake had found a collection of candles in the kitchen ranging from votives to birthday cake candles, all of which he proudly placed on the bedside table with a flourish.

Ruby glanced down at the tiny colorful cake candles. "Seriously?"

"All you said was candles. I brought what I found," Jake said with a shrug.

"Well, if one of our ghosts is angry about a forgotten birthday, you'll be the hero. If not, well, it's a little silly," Ruby replied with a grin.

As Ruby and Jake began to sort the candles Ruby had found, Mallory walked in carrying a couple of jarred candles in one hand and a large silver candelabra in the other. "Do you think the spirits will prefer the apple cinnamon scented one or the holiday pine one? I couldn't find one with sage."

Ruby and Jake stared at her for a minute. "Scented candles?" Jake asked.

"Well, they always use incense at these things and we don't have any of that. I thought this might work instead," Mallory replied in all seriousness.

"Who always uses incense at these things?" Jake asked. "How do you know what people use at séances?"

"*Ghost Hunters*," Mallory replied with a dismissive wave.

"*Ghost Hunters*," Jake echoed.

"The tv show," Ruby replied as though it was a perfectly reasonable explanation. "And not just that one. Lots of them do séances. They don't all use the technology."

"Mallory's eyebrows flew up. "Oh!" she exclaimed. "Do we need a spirit box to talk to them?"

Jake looked perplexed. "A what?"

"No, I don't think so," Ruby said ignoring Jake's question as she helped Mallory set out the candles.

"Hang on a minute you two," Jake said loud enough to be heard over their conversation. "Since when do you watch those paranormal shows?"

Mallory cut her eyes over at Jake and gave him a sheepish grin. "Guilty pleasure. Sometimes I watch them to take a break when I'm working on a particularly tough design."

"Odd choice, Mal. Not like you're going to get any inspiration from a deserted insane asylum," Jake said wrinkling his forehead trying to understand this new side of his wife.

"That's just the point," she replied. "It's the furthest thing from design and a good mental break," Mallory explained. "I just can't watch them at night," she finished with a shiver.

"And you?" Jake asked Ruby.

Ruby shot him a look and rolled her eyes. "Hello, ghost tour guide, remember? Kind of comes with the job."

"Right," said Jake. He rubbed the back of his neck and shook his head. "I'll leave you two experts to set it all up then," he said as he sat on the foot of the bed. As the two women worked on preparations, he shrugged once in a while and muttered, "*Ghost Hunters*. She watches *Ghost Hunters*. Huh."

Tilly arrived with a bundle tied up in a scarf from Miss Dot just as Ruby and Mallory were finishing up. Before long the séance scene was set. Candles had been placed on the floor in a large circle in the middle of the room with one in the center as a focal point. Miss Dot's tarot cards, along with a guide book since Ruby had no idea how to read them, were placed at her spot along with a clear quartz pendulum. Not that Ruby knew how to use that either. More candles were set on the chest of drawers and side tables. The flickering light added a mystique to the room that seemed more eerie than stylish since the hauntings began. On the chest of drawers, the holiday pine candle burned adding an earthiness to the smell of warm wax. The space was not short on atmosphere, even if Ruby was short on confidence.

"What do we do now?" Mallory asked as she blew out the match from lighting the last candle.

"We sit inside the circle of candles," Ruby answered trying to sound more confident than she felt.

"Do we hold hands or something, like in the movies?" Jake asked. It was a sincere question. Having managed to come to grips with Mallory's television show choices, any flippancy he may have had initially was gone. As for the idea of a haunted house, his disbelief had evaporated when he'd seen Julius and Julia Lotz at his bedside.

Ruby shrugged. "I suppose we could try that."

Tilly sat on the floor cross-legged and held her hands out to each side. "I'm all for holding hands, if for no other reason than to know someone else is here with me. Someone living, I mean."

"Holding hands, it is," Mallory said as she stepped gingerly over the lit candles and sat across from Tilly near the large center candle.

Ruby and Jake took their places in the circle across from one another. Once they were in place, the reality of what they were about to attempt began to dawn on them and a heavy silence fell over the room. Ruby could barely hear the tinkling chime of the silver clock in the entryway over the rushing sound of her heartbeat in her ears. She held out trembling hands to Tilly and Mallory as she took a deep breath.

Repeating aloud some of the steps Miss Dot suggested, Ruby began the séance. "Close your eyes and clear your mind of clutter and doubt." She paused for a moment as she tried to follow her own instructions. Clearing her mind of doubt was going to be impossible, so she moved on. "Focus your thoughts and energy on the spirits in this house. Spirits that have something to say. Spirits who need a voice. Focus on giving them that voice tonight." This time she paused longer to allow everyone time to rein in their wandering minds. Feeling Tilly and Mallory's hands begin to relax in hers gave her some confidence to continue.

As she spoke, Ruby turned her attention from the ones gathered in the circle to the spirits. "We know there are spirits here with something to tell us. You've made yourself known and have our attention. We want to help you, but we can't do that if we don't know what you want or need."

Even through closed eyes, Ruby could see the light from the center candle get brighter and the flame warmer. Not only did the spirits have her attention, she had theirs. Even with the warmth of the candle, her back went icy cold as if all the heat had left the room except for within the candle circle. A chill went through Tilly causing her fingers to twitch in Ruby's hand. Air moved across the skin on Ruby's cheeks, gently at first, then with more strength stinging her skin like a winter wind. Mallory's hand tightened around her fingers. She felt it, too. For a moment, Ruby almost lost her concentration as she realized it was actually working.

As she regained her focus, a heaviness settled over the room and Ruby started to feel a wave of nausea wash over her. Her hands went clammy and her cheeks flushed. There was no way she was going to get sick now. Pushing the queasiness down, she said, "I know you're here.

We can feel you. Thank you for letting us know you can hear me. You must have something to say to work up so much energy. Please, we want to hear from you. What is it you want to tell us?"

As she spoke the question, the room went completely still. A vacuum of silence surrounded the four in the circle. Ruby's heart sank with her failure. Before she had the chance to wallow in her self-doubt, a rifle shot rang out downstairs with a deafening crack. Then another and another. A bloodcurdling shriek rattled the house as the gunfire became more intense. Smoke stung the nostrils of the four panicked people in the circle. As their eyes flew open, they were dumbstruck at the scene around them.

War had broken out all over the house. Blinding muzzle flashes surrounded them as their ears rang from the shots. Screams of men were drowned out by the death throes of horses and the thunder of cannon fire. As the battle raged on, figures of the soldiers began to materialize in the smoke. Some bore rifles and bayonets. Others wielded axes and farm tools. Anything and everything that could have been scrounged by a soldier in the Civil War. Jumping up and racing to the staircase, Ruby saw a soldier downstairs take aim at another one and pull the trigger. The shot missed its mark but took a chunk out of a gold-gilt mirror frame before embedding in the wall behind it.

"The bullets can hurt you! Get down!" Ruby screamed at the others. How the spectral bullets were actually causing damage, she didn't know, but knew that she didn't want to find out if the damage was permanent.

Ruby raced downstairs with Jake on her heels begging her to stop as other sounds blended with the cacophony and chaos of the battle.

"Ruby!" Jake shouted. "What the hell are you doing?"

"How can I help them if I don't see what's happening to them?" she shouted back as she raced through the rooms ducking rifle-fire.

"Get down! You'll be killed!"

"I have to find out what they want! I have to find the way to stop it!"

The sounds around them intensified. Women screaming, children crying, bells clanging, men arguing. Some of the scenes were war while others were more personal conflicts between civilians. As the soldiers continued their fight, other spirits began to step through the haze, each in their own hellish loop. The sickly Lotz twins huddled in a corner and cried helplessly as a soldier was bayonetted in the heart in front of them. Blood spurted from his chest between fingers that gripped the wound as he staggered out of the room. Another man opened a door and was shot by an unseen gunman. Chaos and violence took over every room in the Bennett House.

Mallory's scream from above stopped Ruby and Jake in their tracks. Turning and looking up to where she was standing on the upstairs landing, they saw a young woman hanging from the stair railing, her face contorted as she spun slowly, her bare feet dangling. Tilly backed away from the stairs and cowered in a bedroom doorway as two men stepped out of each side of the upstairs walls. Each man had a pistol in his hand and vengeance in his eyes. Shouting around them drowned out the words they spat at each other as they took aim.

All around the house, men fell from gunshots, stabbings, and bleeding out from war wounds as women sobbed over dying children and clutched pregnant bellies as they succumbed to hemorrhaging. As the chaos peaked, the smell of smoke changed from gun smoke to wood smoke. Spectral flames licked at the walls and ceilings as men with their clothes aflame screamed and thrashed. As she stared in terror at the melee around her, a voice whispered in her ear. She could almost feel the breath on her neck with the words 'Not dead.' The entire tragic past of Franklin was on display.

Jake wheeled around and grabbed a wild-eyed Ruby by the shoulders. "How do we make it stop? How do we send them back where they came from?"

Ruby blinked hard. "I—I don't know! This wasn't supposed to happen. None of this was supposed to happen! They were just supposed to talk!"

The soldiers moved their battle back into the entry hall where Jake and Ruby argued. A rifle shot hit the wall behind Ruby and sent plaster showering down on her. Screaming, she buried her face in Jake's shoulder as they dropped to the floor out of the line of fire. Pushing her back and grabbing her face with both hands, he looked hard into her eyes. "You were able to bring them out. You have to be able to put them back. Think! How can you do that?"

Fear gripped Ruby as her whole body shook violently. If she didn't stop this madness, someone alive was going to be killed. "They all came out when I gave them permission to speak to us. Maybe I can tell them they don't have permission anymore."

Jake nodded. "It's a long shot, but better than waiting on one of them to kill us in the cross-fire. Do it."

Ruby took a deep breath and tried to still the trembling in her legs enough to climb the stairs. Halfway up, she stopped and gripped the railing. "Enough!" she shouted to the house at large. "Stop this right now! All of you! You had your time to speak your piece, and now that time is done!" The din around her began to quiet as she spoke. Images began to fade. Even the smell of smoke began to dissipate with the haze. "You no longer have permission to communicate with us like this. We still want to help you, but this is not the way to do it." Images faded into a lingering mist that filled the house like a dense fog. "I will not give up on you, but you must be patient. Leave Mallory and Jake alone. We know you're here. We won't forget. And we will help you. Just give us time to figure out how."

Exhausted, Ruby collapsed onto the staircase as the fog cleared and the sounds silenced enough to hear the silver clock on the entryway table chime midnight.

Ten

The gray light of dawn streamed through the bay windows of the Bennett House parlor when Ruby began to stir. Her head pounded and she didn't want to open her eyes even to the faint light. Quiet and stillness surrounded her giving Ruby hope that the spirits had returned from whence they came. Her mind sifted through the images from the séance failure. So much death and violence. So much that Franklin covered in their façade of small-town perfection. How much pain, historically and presently, did the structured beauty hide? How many suffered in silence like the spirits in the mirrors had for so long? What if no one ever gave them permission to speak? Would the pain of the past repeat itself?

So much pent-up suffering had been unleashed at once. She expected Tod Carter and the Lotz twins. Those spirits would have been enough to handle mentally and emotionally, but there were so many that needed help. They had come from everywhere at once. Did every mirror that Mallory bought have someone trapped inside? Or had she somehow tapped into all of the haunted souls in town? How was she going to find out without repeating the spiritual onslaught from the night before? And would they survive it again if she did?

Opening her eyes, blinking against the pink hues of morning, Ruby found herself on the living room sofa. Tilly slept sprawled on the plush rug with her legs halfway under the coffee table. Jake and Mallory were each curled up in an armchair. It seemed all three of them had been keeping watch over Ruby until exhaustion finally got the best of them. On the wall behind Mallory was the gold gilt mirror that had been shot in the opening of the melee. The chunk wasn't missing anymore. No bullet hole in the wall behind it. Scanning the room, she realized that all the damage was gone. No more crumbled plaster. No more splintered furniture. Would the same have happened if any of them had been struck in the crossfire? Could the spirits locked in a never-ending war actually kill them?

Groaning with the headache pain, she closed her eyes again. Mallory stirred in her chair and yawned. Ruby heard her sit up with a sigh. "I'm so sorry," Ruby whispered. "Did I wake you?"

Mallory shrugged. "I don't think so. More the crick in my neck than anything else, I think. Some coffee and ibuprofen and I'll be fine."

"I could use some, too, if you don't mind. My head is killing me."

Mallory nodded and waved her into the kitchen. Putting on a pot of coffee, she pulled out two glasses of water and a bottle of Advil. "Help yourself," she said setting them on the kitchen table in front of Ruby. "You had quite a night. I'm not surprised your head hurts."

"I'm not the only one," Ruby said popping a couple of the pills into her mouth and washing them down. "We all had quite a night."

Mallory sat down next to Ruby and patted her hand. There were tiny creases at the edges of Mallory's eyes that Ruby hadn't noticed before. Dark circles seemed to have deepened even more since Mallory's first encounter with Tod Carter's ghost. The whole experience was aging the once vibrant and stylish Mallory Winter. "As far as rough nights go, I think you win this one," she said gently. "Once you collapsed, it seemed like you were reliving the whole thing over and over in your unconsciousness. You scared us, if I'm honest."

"Scared me, too," Ruby confessed. "I don't remember anything after the staircase."

Mallory nodded her head slowly. "Probably best."

In the other room, Tilly and Jake had begun to stir with the smell of the coffee brewing. Mallory pushed herself out of the chair and busied herself getting creamer and sugar out along with four coffee mugs. Always true to form with her coffee cure-all. Coffee was poured between yawns in relative quiet. Each one at the kitchen table seemed lost in thought or too tired to think. After a while, conversation slowly picked up along with the caffeine.

"I know this is all as new to you as it is to us, Ruby, but what do we do next?" Jake, ever the pragmatist, asked.

Ruby rubbed her temples. "Why ask me? I clearly don't know what I'm doing."

"Not true," Tilly said. "You know how to reach them. They came out because you asked them to. They left because you told them to. What you lack is control of the situation."

"Like I said, I don't know what I'm doing."

Mallory patted her hand again and let it rest on top of Ruby's. "She's right, hon. Give yourself some credit. For something none of us expected to work, it was remarkable. Maybe more than we could handle, but you actually did it."

"And we know a lot more than we knew before," Jake added. "If there is such a thing as looking at the paranormal logically, we have a head start on figuring this out now that we've seen them all at once. All we knew about was the soldier and the kids. Now we know that every mirror in the house must hold someone that needs or wants something."

Ruby nodded and winced as the pain in her head refused to abate. Every thought about the night before made it throb harder. "We also know that a lot of them do not get along. Clearly some of those soldiers don't know or care that the Civil War is over. Duels and feuds over a hundred years old are still raging. Violence, fear, and pain seem to be the reigning themes. That makes the whole thing a lot more concerning, but you're right. At least we have more information now." Nothing about the information she gathered in the chaos of the night made her feel any better about the job at hand, but it was better than operating in the dark when it came to how to end the hauntings.

Tilly smiled over the edge of her steaming coffee mug. "See? That means, as horrible as it was at the time, you did a good thing."

Ruby sighed. "Okay, I'll concede to being able to bring them out and put them back even though I have no idea how I did it, but I don't have a clue about what we do next and I'm too exhausted to think about it."

Mallory nodded. "You need some rest. Maybe not sleep since that seemed to be a bit nightmarish for you, but rest. Personally, I could use a hot shower." She paused for a minute and wrinkled her forehead. "Is someone going to be watching me from the bathroom mirror?"

"Ew," said Tilly. "That would be awkward."

Knowing the mirror wasn't contractor standard issue and instead a repurposed antique, Ruby said, "I'd cover that thing if I were you. I asked them to leave you alone, but a lot of them *are* soldiers after all. Maybe don't tempt them."

Taking her cue from Mallory, Ruby took a long, hot shower comfortable in the fact that the bathroom mirror in Pawpaw's old craftsman cottage was only as vintage as the early 80's and not likely to be playing host to a randy spirit. She had to admit, it helped her feel more like herself again. But not quite. Something about last night lingered. Not so much the images. Those did more than linger. Those had been seared on her mind. Something more about being able to wing a séance on her first try. Catastrophically, but still. Maybe Miss Dot was right. Maybe there was more of Mawmaw in her than she thought.

Much had changed about her life in the past few weeks and none of it seemed real as she sat in the cozy outdated living room where she had spent so much time with Pawpaw talking about his latest project and odd historical facts Ruby found in her latest library book. Normal conversation seemed like a nostalgic luxury she could no longer afford. Even if she could afford it, there was no one left to share it with. Surrounded by spirits, she was desperately alone. Even Tilly and the Winters, as invested as they were in her at the moment, lacked the permanence of family.

Pulling her long damp hair to the side, she worked it into a thick braid as she leaned back in Pawpaw's recliner. There was comfort in the feel of the worn fabric on the arms and the familiar creak as she pulled the lever to release the footrest. It still smelled like him. Old Spice aftershave and sawdust. Exhausted and emotionally drained, Ruby closed her eyes and let the tears pour unchecked down her cheeks for the first time since Pawpaw's heart attack. If she could reach so many souls at once, why couldn't she reach him?

Enveloped in the comfort of her grandfather's memory, sleep eased over her worn out mind and body. Horrors of the night seemed held at bay by the warmth and peace of her childhood home. Tears dried on her cheeks in salty streaks and her breathing finally found a natural rhythm. As is so often the case when the body and mind have had more than they can handle, sleep was heavy and dreamless. By the time she woke, the sun had just begun to graze the tops of the hills. Her body had recovered some of its strength, but there was still the problem of the mirrors looming over her along with the expectations of Jake and Mallory that she could do something about them.

She had to find a way to connect with the spirits in the mirrors without drawing them out into the open. That was too dangerous for everyone involved. Her thoughts wandered back to the first experience with the mirror in the bedroom where she glimpsed Tod Carter. Something about that image became clearer as she thought about it without the initial fear and disbelief. There was a moment before the bullet ripped through his head that he had looked at her. He had *seen* her. Really seen her. Had he known that she could reach him before she knew it herself? Had he seen her for who and what she really was even when she couldn't?

There was only one way to find out.

The Five Bloodiest Hours

Two years of sporadic occupation. Two years of divided loyalties. Two years of walking on eggshells with soldiers and neighbors alike. Two years of life in a tinderbox set too close to a flame. Now, there were sparks.

Uniforms once deep blue and crisp were faded and weary. Citizens once proud and outspoken kept conversations to the mundane and innocuous. All watched. Waited. Wondered how and when it would all end.

Holding a collective breath, a strange semblance of normalcy eventually took root. Soldiers who were encamped on the perimeter came into town with passes from commanding officers. Food was served, goods sold, neutral niceties exchanged. The raucousness of the initial months was curtailed by severe orders and punishments from the officers to protect the decorum of the citizenry. Friendliness was not required, but decency was. The penalty for violating the rules of civility were steep. The penalty for spying, steeper. And so, the town remained on tenterhooks.

Sound traveled far and clear in the crisp dawn air of early winter. The murmur of voices. The crack of an axe on wood. The rustling thud of a fallen tree. Thousands of men may have crept past Hood's sleeping forces in Spring Hill, but they would not go unnoticed by the citizens of Franklin.

Before the sun broke free of the horizon, the lightest sleepers stood in open doorways understanding immediately the sounds floating toward Main Street. Curiosity drove cautious steps into the pre-dawn darkness closer to the source only to have them retreat again to the safety of their homes. Safety that was fragile at best. Plans for the day were forgotten. Meals unprepared. Chores left undone. In their place, parlors hosted hushed speculation.

A few of the bold asked passing Union soldiers what they should prepare for. The answer varied. Some would say there was little to be concerned about as Schofield was merely making a show of strength to hold Hood at bay while the bridges were rebuilt and troops moved north to Nashville. Others warned of Hood's rashness and rage while suggesting that basements be made ready for shelter.

The men who remained in town, too old, too infirm, or too neutral to fight, began to prepare shelter for their families. Women tended to children with their terror buried beneath a lapful of sewing or other tasks made meaningless the moment the breastworks were thrown up. Preparations were made under the guise of normal chores to keep the trembling in their hands concealed from small eyes that would not understand the uncertainty and fear.

In truth, no one knew what to do to be ready if the skirmish became a battle. Baskets of food were packed as if for an afternoon picnic on the banks of the Harpeth in the springtime. Water was fetched from wells and cisterns. Some thought of chamber pots. Most lugged mattresses off beds and laid them on the dirt floors in the spaces under their homes and businesses. None of these things would be needed for a skirmish on the outskirts of town. None would be of any great use should the battle breach the entrenchments and pour into the sixteen main blocks of the terrified town. Basements offered some protection from muskets and rifles, but little against cannon fire. Should the Confederates push the Union back toward the town, the incoming shelling could be catastrophic. It made no difference where loyalties lay at that point. Artillery didn't care whose side the people of Franklin were on.

Eleven

Ruby stood in the middle of the Winters' bedroom to the side of the mirror that held the spirit of Tod Carter. The last time she looked into the glass, she witnessed a brutal skull-shattering death. Blood everywhere. Terror. Knowing that the ghost was trapped in the loop of his death made her hesitant to step in front of it. If she couldn't reach him, she would be reliving it with him once again and Ruby wasn't sure she could stomach it.

Her thoughts had been so focused on what was inside the mirror that she almost hadn't seen what was on it. At first glance, it seemed like the silvering on the back of the glass had tarnished in places. Separating what was reflected in the glass from the glass itself, Ruby saw the darkened places for what they really were. The palm of a hand and five fingertips. It was as though someone inside had pressed their hand against the mirror and left the imprint.

Jake let her gather her thoughts for a moment before he broke into them. "How are you going to do this, Ruby?"

Staring at the print, she couldn't help but wonder if Tod Carter was showing her the way. If he really had seen her the first time, maybe the connection was strong enough for him to be guiding her. It was time she put her disbelief in her own abilities to the side and believed in him at least. "I think he's telling me what to do."

"Who is?" Mallory asked.

"Tod Carter. Do you see it?" Ruby stepped closer to the mirror but was careful not to stand where she would see her reflection. "There. In the corner."

Jake and Mallory looked where Ruby was pointing and squinted. "Damage from last night?" Jake asked.

Ruby shook her head. "I don't think so. Look closer. Do you see what it is?"

"My god," Mallory gasped. "It's a handprint."

Ruby nodded. "And it wasn't there before. I think Tod Carter is trying to help me help him."

Jake ran his hand through his hair slowly as he reached the conclusion Ruby had. "So, the way to connect to the spirits individually is a physical connection to the mirrors?"

"It would appear so. When I asked the question about what they wanted to say without focusing on specific people, I connected to all of them. The energy behind my effort was too scattered. Touching the mirror must be the way to narrow the spread."

Mallory twisted her wedding band. "What are you going to do?"

"He reached out to me; I'm going to reach out to him."

Stepping closer to the mirror, Ruby closed her eyes, but her memory betrayed her by replaying the scene she couldn't forget. Realizing she was going to have to face the horrors, she opened her eyes. Her own reflection was transparent and layered over the face of a young soldier until hers faded completely. His face was dirty and drawn thin from years of struggling for survival against the harshest odds. Slowly, he raised a hand and pressed it against the shadowy print on the glass and nodded at her. Behind the exhaustion in his eyes, there was compassion. It was as though he could feel Ruby's fear.

Fingers trembled as Ruby willed them to reach out toward the mirror and Tod Carter's hand. Every bit of common sense said what she was trying to do was impossible. Every shred of street sense told her that no one sane went looking for ghosts much less trying to actually connect with one.

Her hand hovered a few inches from the glass. The temperature dropped around her as an electricity built in her fingers and stung her palm. From the center of her hand, she felt a tug toward the mirror that became stronger and stronger until her skin finally pressed against the cold glass.

With a flash of light, she was enveloped in acrid smoke. Gun smoke. Chaos like the night before raged all around her, but instead of spectral shadows, the images were solid and vibrant. The men and horses around her were real. But she wasn't. Ruby was the specter. She was the ghost among them.

Bullets screamed past her and ripped through soldiers sending blood spurting across anyone nearby. There was so much blood that solders couldn't possibly have known what was theirs and what wasn't. From the hillside above her, cannon fire shook the ground as men rushed to load the next rounds. The bullets came from the breastworks below like a hailstorm, ripping through anything solid they encountered. Raining hell on the desperate men charging toward them. Men like Tod Carter who stood beside her with papers in his trembling hands. The look on his face was not fear. The trembling was rage. The papers in his hand were furlough papers. Papers that should have meant that he was with his family, not standing on the hillside above his home watching the ravaging of the land and imagining the worst of his loved ones inside the house.

Shoving the furlough papers inside his coat, the young soldier set his sights on the enemy entrenched in his front yard. Raising his gun to his shoulder, he fell in with the men who charged the line of soldiers that were spilling over the breastworks to meet the enemy barreling down Winstead Hill.

In the next moment, Ruby was lying in a muddy field surrounded by the dead and dying under the cold night sky. Shrieks pierced her ears as men realized they would die where they fell. Horses in their death throes sent chills through her. A gurgling sound next to her pulled her attention away from the mass of carnage. Turning, she saw the familiar form of young Tod Carter, so soaked in blood he was almost unrecognizable. In the mirror she had seen only the shot to his head. It may have been the mortal wound, but it was far from the only one. Riddled with gunshots, Ruby couldn't believe he was still breathing. How could anyone survive such an onslaught?

Another moment, another scene. This time, the young soldier was on a makeshift operating table with a surgeon standing over him. There was no need for anesthesia as the surgeon worked to stem the bleeding of the many wounds. Tod was unconscious from loss of blood. As the surgeon bent over his patient, family in the entry way paced and cried. Fountain Branch Carter pulled at his hair and said nothing. The father of the fallen soldier was deathly pale. The only one who seemed to have control over their emotions was Moscow Carter, Tod's older brother. Moscow had taken advantage of his furlough papers and rode out the siege of his family home in the basement. It seemed that tending his brother was an act of penance for not being beside him in battle. Even Moscow's stalwart face drained of color as the surgeon straightened his back and held a bloody bullet up and inspected it for missing fragments. Dipping it in a small bowl of water to rinse the blood off, he then handed it to Moscow with a grim nod before beginning to pack the wound the bullet left behind.

The next scene brought with it a heaviness rather than the adrenaline-fueled energy of the previous ones. Ruby stood beside the fireplace that glowed with low coals, neglected as the gathered family focused their attention on the pale form laying in the center of the room. Over the fireplace, Ruby saw the mirror reflecting the faces of brothers, sisters, and a bereft widower who must have been relieved that his beloved Polly had not borne witness to the destruction of her home and the brutal killing of her son. Tod's breath was labored and rattling. The end was near and there was no fight left in him. He had fought to protect his home and family and lost. Now, he was losing the fight with his own body. Tod Carter died in the home and the town he could not save across the hall from the room he was born in surrounded by family he could no longer protect. Family he could not bear to leave alone to pick up the pieces.

As the visions of the past faded and his story drew to a close with his last breath, Ruby found herself looking into the shadowy eyes of Tod Carter's ghost through the mirror. He seemed expectant; waiting on her to speak. "There are no words."

He nodded solemnly.

"You stayed behind to look after them, didn't you?"

Once more the soldier nodded.

"And now, you're alone."

Tears gathered in his eyes. "Yes" came the hollow voice. Barely a whisper.

"How can I help you? How can I end this hell you're trapped in?"

"Take me home." A tear slid down his cheek making a track in the battle grime.

Once more, he nodded at Ruby then looked at his hand. She realized he was about to pull it away and panic and sadness consumed her. For a connection she feared moments before, she couldn't bear to let it go now. A sob choked her as she promised him, "I will."

Twelve

Ruby sat cross-legged in the half-dead grass of Rest Haven Cemetery in front of a chipped tombstone. A small iron cross rusted next to it marking the grave of a Confederate soldier like several others dotted around the family plots. This particular stone was short with a slight curve on top. Nothing spectacular or noteworthy about it. Except the name. Theodrick, 7th son of FB and MA Carter, Born March 24th, 1840, Died December 2, 1864. A distance away were other Carter graves. Two wives of Moscow Carter and their children, one named for Theodrick that died the day it was born. Sadly poetic. Perhaps other family graves were there but missing headstones. As it was, though, Tod Carter's stone was as alone as his spirit.

Ruby stared at the stone as she adjusted her view of cemeteries. For two weeks, she had come every day to Rest Haven to talk to Pawpaw as though his spirit might be at his grave listening to her. Now, knowing she was sitting beside a grave for someone whose spirit was in a mirror, she began to wonder if Pawpaw heard anything she'd said to him. The idea of being heard was the one thing that was keeping her from being crushed by her grief. The one thing that made her feel like she wasn't completely alone in the world. Now, there was a hollowness that begged to be filled; an emptiness that, if Ruby wasn't careful, could consume her.

And yet, it was that same emptiness that brought perspective. Could it be that the emptiness was the reason the spirits chose her as their voice? Tod Carter's pain at being alone after spending his life and death looking after his family and their home was almost tangible as he spoke to her. She understood that feeling too well now. It was a pain she wouldn't wish on anyone. Ruby may have disagreed with his reasons for enlisting, but his isolation and sorrow were something she could relate to. It wasn't a soldier she was helping as much as another soul. She had known pain and sorrow for two short weeks. He had felt it for over 150 years. He wasn't the only one. There were so many.

Now that she knew how to reach the spirits in the mirrors individually, the next step remained unsolved. How was she going to get the mirrors back where they needed to be? And a step after that- how was doing that going to bring the spirits the peace they wanted? Could they send themselves on to the other side once they were back in the space they were connected to, or was that something she was going to have to do?

"What have I gotten myself into?" she asked Tod Carter's stone. No answer. She knew there wouldn't be.

Long days of summer were fast becoming the long nights of winter as fall settled in more and more. The sun seemed increasingly in a hurry to dip behind the buildings and hillsides every day. Shadows stretched across Main Street and shaded the sidewalks as shoppers pulled their jackets tighter as they walked. Hours before, it had been warm enough in the sunshine to not need them at all. Some days were balmy enough for short sleeves, while others were frigid. And one of those days could immediately follow the other. Fall in Tennessee was a fickle thing.

After walking the couple of blocks to Onyx and Alabaster in the gathering chill of late afternoon, Ruby was greeted by a warm wall of air as she pulled open the black door.

Sitting at the large table, Tilly grinned and slid a black cup over to Ruby. "Your usual."

"Thanks, Til."

Niceties exchanged, the four got down to the business at hand. Ruby explained her thoughts about using her authority, albeit weak, as a historian for getting the mirrors to the places they belonged in once they figured out where that was. "Of course, there are some issues that come with all this that I'm not sure how to tackle," she added as she finished.

"Like?" Mallory asked.

"Well, we don't know how to get the spirits to go to the other side. What if we get the mirrors back to the right houses but end up spreading hauntings around town like a virus."

Tilly nearly choked on her coffee. "Oh, god, I hadn't thought of that."

"Certainly don't want that to happen," Jake said. "What other issues?"

"Well," Ruby began, "how do we convince people to take the mirrors? I mean, do we just say, 'Hey, we have this haunted mirror that needs to be in your house, but don't worry, we're pretty sure once it's back in there it won't be haunted anymore.'?"

"Yeah," Jake said running his hands through his hair. "Not sure that's going to go over very well."

Tilly shrugged. "With some folks, it might. Depends on who it is. Most people wouldn't believe it was haunted anyway. At least, they wouldn't admit it. I guess we could always just not tell them."

Jake shook his head. "We're getting into some moral issues now. We can't just lie to people to get them to take the mirrors, even if it's a lie of omission. It's unethical. But, I think we've wandered into the weeds here. Let's take one mirror at a time. We know where the bedroom one goes and we know Tod Carter wants to go home."

"Right," Ruby said, "but the Carter House isn't going to appreciate the haunting of the mirror like, say, the Lotz House would. They're all about historical accuracy. We can't just tell them the mirror is haunted by Tod Carter. They'd laugh at us and certainly wouldn't take the mirror."

Mallory, who had been seemingly lost in her own thoughts for a while, spoke up. "No one lives in the Carter House anymore. It's a museum. So, are we really morally obligated to tell them about the spirit trapped inside? It's not like we are sending a ghost into someone's home and making them live with a haunting."

The other three sat and pondered her words for a moment. Patrons of Onyx and Alabaster came and went, ordering lattes and pastries, exchanging greetings, and going about their merry way oblivious to the struggle over paranormal ethics happening in the front booth.

Tilly broke the silence first. "She has a point."

"Well, people *do* work and visit there every day," Jake said, his attorney's mind clearly not sure about the moral implications. "I don't like the idea of not being upfront with the people we're saddling with our ghosts." Clearly, Jake was digging in with his moral high ground, even to the point of going against Mallory, which Ruby never thought she'd see.

Ruby chewed on her lip as she thought for a minute longer. "I don't know if I can get Tod Carter out of his mirror or not, but I don't think he's dangerous if I can't. It would be me he would be angry at, not the employees and visitors. I just need to explain to him why those people are in his house. His whole goal in staying behind was to protect his family and the home. Surely he'll be able to understand that the museum people are trying to do the same thing."

Jake shook his head slowly. "For the record, I'm not okay with lying to the museum about the mirror."

"Noted," Mallory said curtly.

"I'm not thrilled about lying to them either, Jake," Ruby said. Her voice was showing the strain of her own internal struggle with the issue. "I grew up with these people. They trust me and here I go lying to them to protect a spirit that until a couple of weeks ago, I was sure didn't really exist except in my grandmother's head. I've had to come to grips with a lot of things I never thought I'd have to lately and lying to people on top of it all isn't something I'm excited about adding to the list. But here we are."

Tilly twisted a strand of hair around her finger and shrugged. "Or, maybe it's time the people of Franklin faced the ghosts of their past." Three pairs of eyes stared at her, stunned by the poignance of the statement that came from the least poignant of them all.

"She's right," Ruby said quietly. "It might be time for that, but I'm not sure a museum run by The Battle of Franklin Trust is where we start with that very noble cause. Their mission is facts. I don't see them counting Tod Carter haunting a mirror among those facts."

Mallory nodded. "Which brings us right back to what I was saying."

Jake shot a glance at her then sighed, clearly outnumbered in his moral battle. "I guess we don't really have a choice then, do we? Either we lie about the mirror, or we sentence Tod Carter to an eternity of suffering. Morality seems to have a huge gray area when it comes to the paranormal," Jake said with a frown. Ruby wondered if that was the face he made when he lost a case in court. He took Mallory's hand by way of apology and added, "Alright, let's go with attempting to explain it to him so he won't terrorize the employees and visitors. That is *if* we can't figure out how to get him out of the mirror and to where he really belongs."

Ruby sighed and laid her head on her arms crossed on the table. "I have no idea how to do that."

Mallory reached out and patted her arm. "You will, Ruby. You will."

The Five Bloodiest Hours

The sounds of shovels, shouts, and maneuvering artillery carried across the fields to the dilapidated remains of Fort Granger. Built on Roper's Knob, it overlooked the entrenchments from the top of a bluff, but was still below Winstead Hill. Some of the artillery had been positioned in the fort and aimed southward. Knowing it would help the men on the western flank was one thing, but its true purpose was to provide cover for the work going on with the bridges. Having been washed out or burned, there was no passage over the Harpeth River that would support the wagon trains that were needed for the march to Nashville. Digging in and fighting Hood's army wasn't a sure victory. Win or lose, whatever was left of the Union troops had orders to get to Nashville. To do that, they would need bridges.

Only the rail bridge had enough structure left to work with, and so it would have to do. With Hood breathing down his neck, Schofield couldn't take the time to rebuild anything from the ground, or water, up. He had already sent word to his superiors that he wouldn't be able to hold Hood the three days they ordered. Holding him for the night was the most Schofield could hope for and that meant a pressing need to clear a way out of Franklin for the wagons.

Spurred on by their general's supervision, beleaguered men dragged lumber to the train trestle. Arms burned with the strain and stomachs rumbled with nerves and hunger. Still, they worked on, never ceasing. There was no time for complaint. No time to rest. Some poured their focus into the work at hand to keep from looking up the hill from whence the enemy would surely come. Others kept one eye on their work and one on the hill. Still others worked like blind men, their focus trained entirely on the south. Many wondered if their general should be commanding at the front lines of the breastworks instead of the bridge while others realized the front lines meant little if there was no way out of town. None spoke a word about it. There was neither time nor energy to spare for speculation.

All that mattered was the bridge. Buildings were dismantled. Non-essential parts of the fort were pulled down. Any lumber and materials that could be scavenged, were. Bit by bit, board by board, beam by beam, the rail trestle became a hodgepodge of a wooden bridge that would provide an escape route for the supplies that were the life-line of the men bound for Nashville.

Periodically, as the work progressed, one of the wagons would be pulled out onto the expanse to test the structural soundness. While this meant a stoppage in the work, it was better to lose one wagon to the river from a failure in the bridge strength than the entire train. Men watched with bated breath as the wheels slowly turned. Wood creaked and popped, but held as the wagon inched forward. The mule in the harness resisted, but was eventually persuaded to take a few more steps. As the bridge bore the weight of the wagon, men began to breathe once more. Only briefly, however, for the wagon had to be backed down again for the work to continue. If the bridge safely bore the weight forward and backward, they assumed it could survive more than one wagon moving across. With as many as needed to go over, it would be a gamble regardless of the quality of the makeshift engineering. It didn't matter how great the risk. It was the only card they had to play.

Thirteen

Ruby tried to blame her irritation at giving ghost tours on the cold, but that wasn't it at all. If she was honest with herself, and she rarely was, she'd have to admit that it was the fact that the stories were pretty much just that. Stories. Exaggerations based on the imaginations of individuals that spun into larger tales as they were repeated through time like a game of telephone. Other than the people who owned the homes, there was little that could be proven about any of them.

It was the history of the houses that drew Ruby to being a tour guide in the first place. She took the job after college to help Pawpaw with the bills even though he told her she didn't need to. As a kid, she didn't see herself as a freeloader. What kid really does? As an adult, however, there was no way she was not going to help with something. True, she helped with the business, taking calls from clients and work crews while Pawpaw was on the job site (he was never really one for a cell phone), but that wasn't contributing financially. Ruby decided to put her history degree and knowledge of the town to use as a tour guide. She wanted to do a regular history tour, but they only needed ghost tour guides at the time, so that's where she ended up.

Having been so fully immersed in hauntings, it seemed almost disrespectful to be telling the tales she did every night. Exaggerations at best; utter fiction at worst. Ruby couldn't imagine how indignant the spirits would be if they heard the nonsense being told about them. Or not told. How many spirits were left out of the stories? Did they hear her going around town talking nonsense about others and wonder why she wasn't telling people their story? Judging from the chaos at the Bennett House the night she opened Pandora's box, there were a lot better stories she could be telling if she had a mind to. Something inside her went a little sick at the thought of that. Now that she had actually seen them, actually talked to Tod Carter, they were no longer characters in a story. They were real people with real souls that needed real help. And they were all looking to her to do it.

Having no earthly idea where to start with sending spirits to the other side, wherever that was, she found herself seeking out Franklin's sage once more. Sitting on Miss Dot's floor against the sofa, Ruby laid her bead back on the cushion and closed her eyes. "I can probably lie my way into getting the mirror back into the Carter House, but I don't know how to get him out of there. He asked me to take him home. I don't think he meant just back to the house."

Miss Dot nodded as she picked up a few tarot cards form the stack on the side table and let them fall back down one at a time. "I'd say you're right about that. The building doesn't hold anything for him anymore. Some residual energy, sure. He grew up there and died there. That makes sense. But, home is gonna be where his family is and they've all gone over as far as we know."

"So, how do I get him there, too?"

"Well, you didn't know how to talk to them all and you managed to figure that out. You didn't know how to talk to them individually, and you figured that out."

Ruby shook her head as she stared up at the ceiling. "Nope, Tod showed me that one. If his handprint hadn't been on the mirror, I wouldn't have thought to touch it like that. The ghost gets credit for that one. I just get credit for the séance from hell."

Miss Dot laughed. "You need to give yourself some credit, child. He may have given you a sign, but you were the one who followed your instinct and reached back out to him. Now, think. If he showed you how to reach him, he might have given you something to work with for getting him back."

Ruby closed her eyes. The images of Tod's final moments played through her mind. Details seared in her memory. Could something in them be the key to how to release him from the prison of the mirror? Battle, injury, and surgery seemed unlikely places to focus. The last scene was of his family gathered and mourning as he died. Family he stayed to protect. That thought led back to her reasoning earlier with Jake. "Tod Carter stayed to protect the house and family," she said bringing her thoughts aloud. "He doesn't need to do that anymore. The family has gone on and the house is protected as a landmark now."

"Does he know that?"

Ruby looked up at Miss Dot. Could it be that simple? "No, he doesn't. If he knew that, he'd have no reason to stay."

A smile crept through the wrinkles on Miss Dot's face and settled around her eyes and mouth. "So, now, you know what to do. I knew you'd figure it out."

"Each of the spirits is here for a different reason. From what we saw that night, most of them are fighting for something or have suffered in some way. If I figure out what their reasons are, maybe I can show them that their reasons can be let go of."

Miss Dot's smile faded as she nodded. Her pride at Ruby's finding the solution was replaced by caution. "That will mean talking to each one. Understand that many may have had an agenda in life that they still hold on to. While our young soldier and the Lotz babies, for example, might be honest about their intentions, some of those others, especially the ones who died with spite in their hearts, might not be so truthful. Approach with compassion, but also with your wits about you."

"Good advice."

"And get some rest. You're no good to anyone, living or dead, if you're too exhausted to take the strain of what the spirits have to show you." Her gentle smile returning, Miss Dot rose from her chair and took a few steps toward the kitchen. "Why don't you stay here tonight?

Memories can be just as hard to sleep with as rowdy ghosts," she said with a nod toward Pawpaw's house across the street.

Ruby got up and hugged her. "What would I do without you?"

"Not have pie before bed, for one thing." With a wink, Miss Dot went happily humming into the kitchen.

Fourteen

Having called ahead and explained the finding of the mirror that belonged at the Carter House, one of the senior members of The Battle of Franklin Trust met Ruby and the Winters at the Carter House visitor center. In the back of Pawpaw's truck, the mirror was wrapped and padded carefully even for the few short blocks they had to drive to get it from the Bennett House to Carter Hill. As Ruby got closer, her stomach knotted up and her palms went clammy. By the time they parked, she was feeling a little faint. Determined not to let her own insecurities keep her from doing right by Tod Carter's ghost, she swallowed her fear and put the truck in park.

"Ready, kiddo?" Jake asked.

Mallory squeezed Ruby's hand. "You can do this."

Jake nodded. "Of course, you can. Once we get them convinced to take the mirror, we'll ask to be shown around so you can have some time with our young soldier. Hopefully, he'll see reason."

Ruby took a deep breath and slowly released it. For a moment, her head felt light, but she soon regained her composure enough to appear in control of her nerves to the outside observer. "I'm ready."

The trio climbed the shaded steps up to the visitor center. Inside, they were met by an older gentleman in a gray suit. "You must be Ruby

Baxter," he said holding out a hand to her. "I knew your grandfather well. Good man. I was sorry to hear of his passing. I'm Bob Lawrence."

Ruby shook his hand. "Thank you, Mr. Lawrence. This is Jake and Mallory Winter."

"Glad to meet you both. Please, call me Bob."

Jake and Mallory took turns greeting Bob as Jake thanked him for seeing them.

"Nonsense. It's my pleasure. Anytime we have an artifact returned to the house, it's a good day. We've tried to gather as much as we could. Moscow sold off a lot of it, but we've been piecing things together for a while now. This mirror of yours definitely has my interest."

"From what I can tell, like I said on the phone, it appears to have been cut from the mantle to be a separate piece. Some molding has been added around the frame, but I'm certain it's from the best parlor fireplace. Would it be possible to take it up to the house to be sure?" Ruby asked.

Bob grinned and nodded. "I don't see why not. Tours don't start for another hour or so. Should give us plenty of time to see what's what before the visitors come through."

Securing the help of some men with longer and stronger arms than Ruby and Mallory, Bob and Jake helped unload the mirror and carry it up the hill past the berms, cannons, and outbuildings that were riddled with bullet holes from the battle. The farm office had taken particularly heavy fire. Hardly a board in the siding could boast not having had a bullet go through it. The pit of Ruby's stomach thrummed and churned as she realized how many soldiers on either side might have had these very sights as their last.

With some precarious maneuvering up the covered back porch steps, past a cannonball hole that had a piece of metal screen over it to preserve it from invasion by birds and insects, and through the entry hall, the mirror finally was set down in the best parlor. Several pieces of furniture that had been present in the house the night of the battle still sat in their places. A cabinet with glass doors and two ornate sofas sat against the walls. In the center of the room was a small square table with a field desk on it that was on loan from the family of Gen. Jacob D. Cox, the officer who had commandeered the house for use by the Federal troops.

Ruby could feel a surge of energy coming from the mirror, as though Tod realized where he was. Knowing she couldn't give away anything she was feeling, Ruby instead turned her attention to the woodwork surrounding the fireplace. Sure enough, much of the trim work matched the original trim of the mirror. It was the right width, too. Now, all she had to do was convince Mr. Bob Lawrence of that.

The men unwrapped the bubble wrap and quilts that had protected the glass on the drive over to reveal the lost mirror of the Carter's best parlor. "Imagine it without those extra layers of molding," Ruby explained. "Those were added later to conceal the fact that it had once been part of a mantle. If you turn it over, you can see the places where it was cut away from the larger piece. I'd imagine there's at least an indention or some scarring on the mantle against the wall that matches."

Jake helped Bob lift it and examine the underside. "I see, I see," Bob said thoughtfully as he ran his fingers along the sawn edge. "And the molding does indeed match. Wood is the right age. Glass looks right." He stood up and took a step back to examine it in comparison to the existing fireplace surround and mantle. "You're right. It's been painted over enough that it would be hard to notice where part of it is missing, but there is indeed a matching scar on the mantlepiece. I can't believe after all this time the mirror has found its way back home."

At the word 'home', the mirror practically hummed with energy. Ruby couldn't believe no one else could feel it. Hair on her arms stood on end and a tingling raced along her skin. It was like standing too close to a bolt of lightning. Tod Carter knew he had made it home.

Jake glanced over at Ruby who nodded. "Mallory and I are glad to donate it to the museum if you'll have it, Bob."

Bob chuckled and shook Jake's hand. "I'd be a fool to turn you down. There's some paperwork, of course."

Mallory smiled sweetly. "Of course."

Shaking his head and chuckling again, Bob said, "I just can't believe how these things have a way of finding their way back here. That field desk there," he said gesturing to the middle table, "that came from a man who was on the tour. Mentioned that he'd inherited it and asked if we'd like to have it on loan. I'm telling you, we're lucky to have good folks like you helping us out."

A twinge of guilt over her omission of the truth about the mirror soured the moment for Ruby. Jake winced a little, too. Mallory, however, was nonplussed.

Jake shook hands with Bob and asked if he might show him and Mallory a little of the house before they got on with paperwork. "I know Ruby was hoping to get some photos of the mirror back in the house where it belongs, as well."

"Of course!" Bob said. "Take your time, Ruby. Catch up when you're ready. If we aren't in the main house, we'll be in the visitor's center."

"Thank you. I'll be there shortly, I hope."

Bob led Jake and Mallory out. Both turned as they got to the door and mouthed 'good luck' to her. She was going to need every bit of that luck, she was afraid.

Once she had the parlor to herself, Ruby took a few photos in case Bob asked to see them before kneeling next to the mirror that had been left propped against the fireplace after examining the back. Reaching trembling fingers out, she touched the place where Tod Carter's handprint had been.

Her own reflection began to fade as his shimmered into view. His face seemed expectant and confused. Hesitantly hopeful. "Am I—am I home?" he asked.

Ruby nodded and a tear ran down his cheek. His eyes looked past hers as he searched the room around her. Confusion replaced the joy as his eyes met hers again. "You know they aren't here, Tod. You told me yourself."

His face fell as he nodded. "I know."

"They've gone on, Tod. The house is safe, too. It's a museum."

Surprise came over the young soldier's face. "Why?"

"Because what happened here was a tragedy for both sides. The museum preserves the house to help people remember that. There are people who will always protect it now. Your job is done, Tod." Tears in her own eyes blurred her view of his face as tears rolled down his face.

The connection between her soul and his was so strong it almost hurt. "You can rest now. You can go home."

A sob rocked Tod's body as relief washed over him. "Home?"

Ruby nodded. "Home," she whispered. "To your family. They're waiting for you."

Nodding, Tod Carter placed his other hand against the glass and let his forehead rest between his hands, a gesture of both gratitude and peace. Ruby did the same, meeting him hand to hand, forehead to forehead. "Thank you, Ruby," he whispered. "Thank you."

"You're welcome." As she spoke, she could feel warmth where there had been the familiar cold that always accompanied the visions of Tod Carter. Pulling her face back from the glass, she saw him nod and smile as his image faded and her reflection solidified. Then, he was gone.

Fifteen

It wasn't a feeling Ruby had expected. She thought she would feel a sense of relief at sending Tod Carter to the other side where he belonged, but she hadn't counted on the sense of loss that went with it. They didn't talk about that on those reality shows with the mediums. They seemed detached from those they helped. She felt anything but. Something about the experience with his ghost felt like it was a part of her own soul's journey. Maybe it was.

Tilly thought it was silly to feel so melancholy about something she should be proud of, but Ruby couldn't help it. Even if she wanted to wallow in yet another loss, she didn't have time for it. There were more souls that needed her help, and she couldn't just leave them in the mirrors while she felt sorry for herself. Jake and Mallory seemed encouraged by the fact that she had been able to get Tod Carter to willingly give up his guardianship of his family and house and had faith that she would be able to do the same with the others. Ruby wasn't so sure. Miss Dot's words of caution about some spirits perhaps being unwilling to give up their earthly agendas had her worried.

Rather than tackle a mirror with an unknown entity in it, she chose to work with the Lotz twins next. Hopefully, they would be pliable and willing to return to their parents. She was going to need some cooperative spirits to hone her skills of releasing them before she tackled ones that might put up a fight.

The guest room where the Lotz mirror was reminded Ruby of a high-end boutique hotel or a magazine page out of a Restoration Hardware catalog. Tailored bedding and sleek lamps blended with an antique headboard, dresser, and the mahogany piece with mirrored shelves. A slim vertical mirror was framed by the layers of small shelves on either side. On the shelves were tasteful and chic knickknacks and a few old books that added warmth and hominess. Even though the mirrors on the shelves were all separate, Ruby hoped the piece behaved as one when it came to the twins and focused on the center glass.

Ruby glanced at Jake and Mallory who nodded. "Go ahead, Ruby," Mallory said. "You can do it."

Taking a deep breath to steady the fluttering in her chest, she raised her hand as she stepped in front of the long mirror. Before she even touched the glass, the twins began to come into focus as her reflection faded. As her hand made contact, the toddlers both nodded at her.

In an instant, she was beside a running stream that was as real as she had been on the other side of the mirror. Water gurgled as it splashed over rocks and swirled against the bank. Julius and Julia Lotz played by the water floating leaves in the eddies as their sister Matilda, only slightly older, poured water from tiny tea pot into a tiny tea cup in front of a porcelain doll. The water dribbled out and the little girl screwed up her face in a pout as she realized the tea pot was empty. Going to the stream, she dipped the tea pot in and filled it back up, pausing for a moment to watch the leaf Julia was floating before scampering back up the bank to her tea party.

Julius picked up a stick and leaned out from the bank to try to free his leaf that was stuck on a rock. Julia watched for a moment, then left her leaf to float away as she scrounged for her own stick. A moment later, both children were busied trying to free the bright yellow leaf from the stone as Matilda Lotz chatted happily with her doll and drank creek water from her miniature tea cup with delicately painted blue flowers.

The pastoral scene changed quickly into one of wild panic. Julius tripped and caught Julia's stick trying not to fall into the creek, but only succeeded in pulling them both into the flowing water. The place where they landed was deeper than where the leaf had caught on the rock and both toddlers plunged under the icy water. With the shock of the cold, both gasped taking in water as they thrashed trying to stay on the surface. The current pushed the flailing children closer to the bank as Matilda realized what was happening. She raced toward the creek toppling her tea set that cracked on a tree root. Scrambling down, Matilda grabbed Julius by the hair and one arm and pulled the screaming child out of the water before going after her little sister. Soon, three soaking wet children lay panting and coughing in the mud on the edge of the creek.

Another scene shimmered into focus with Matilda gathering the pieces of the tea set up in her skirt and tucking her doll under her arm. The toddler twins coughed occasionally as they sat in a patch of sunshine drying out and poking brightly colored leaves onto the end of a stick. With her toys gathered, Matilda left the twins to their play and trotted back up to the house.

Once more the scene shifted to one of fear and panic as the twins began to cough and gasp for air. Julius doubled over, vomited, and choked as Julia tried to stand, but collapsed wheezing and turning a horrifying gray color before vomiting herself. Color drained from their faces as their little lips turned blue. They were suffocating right in front of Ruby while she helplessly watched as a ghost in their reality. Tears rolled down her face as she realized the children were dying alone on the edge of the creek, sick and afraid. Ruby wanted to gather the twins in her arms, but she couldn't touch them. Their death had to play out without her intervention. There was nothing she could to do to stop something that happened over 150 years ago no matter how much her heart broke for the children. After a few excruciating minutes, the children collapsed in each other's arms as they took their last breaths together.

The heart-breaking vision faded as Ruby's ghostly reflection once more overlayed the twins in the mirror. Sobs shook Ruby's shoulders as she struggled to force back the grief of their death so she could help the children find their peace. "I'm so sorry," she whispered through her tears.

Julius and Julia nodded.

"I want to help you, but I need to know how."

A tear rolled down Julia's cheek as she seemed unable to find the words she needed.

Ruby spoke again, hoping to hold their images there while they found their voices. "Many people thought you were poisoned by the water, but you weren't, were you?"

Julius shook his head.

"Matilda drank the water, too, and she was fine," Ruby said.

Julia nodded, still crying.

"Was your death caused by falling in the water?"

Both children nodded, seeming to perk up some at having her get closer to the reason behind their deaths.

"But you didn't drown in the water. You died later on the bank." Ruby paused as the twins looked at her expectantly. She was close, she knew it, but hadn't quite hit on the real cause of death. Her mind spun through every theory that had been put out there about the deaths of the Lotz twins from poisoning to drowning to illness and none of them quite fit what she witnessed. As she struggled with her own thoughts, a third ghostly image played in the mirror. The children struggling in the water at the moment they both gasped in lungs-full of water. "That's it!" Ruby exclaimed as it hit her. Something she had read ages ago in some college science class. "Dry drowning! You did drown, just not in the water! Lack of oxygen explains the pallor and the water in your systems explains vomiting that made everyone assume you were poisoned."

The twins' faces brightened as Ruby figured out the truth behind their deaths. That knowledge seemed to bring them some peace, but it wasn't enough to free them from the mirror. There was something else they needed.

"How can I help get you out of this mirror? Do you know what you need?"

Julia's face saddened as a tear rolled down her pale cheek. "Papa. Mama."

Julius nodded. "Home."

"You want your parents," Ruby said as her own tears started falling again.

The children, barely older than babies, began to cry along with Ruby. Their grief at dying alone was almost palpable it was so intense. They wanted to go home so they could finally be with the parents they had missed for over a century and a half.

Ruby nodded at the precious little faces in front of her as she said, "I'll take you home. You'll see them again." It was a promise she was determined to keep.

The Five Bloodiest Hours

Battle brings with it the terrors of the thin line between life and death. In the heat of the fight, humanity is lost as survival becomes paramount. It is in the dark moments before and afterwards that the rays of light shine through and humanity can be found, though it hangs by a thread.

On Fair Street, just two blocks from the center of town, haggard and emaciated men willed one foot to follow the other down the rutted dirt road. Only momentary relief met them when their commanding officer stopped in front of a home with a large front yard. Men leaned heavily on the front fence or sat on their packs as the officer approached the house.

In the clear air, the men heard a request for the use of the yard to pitch tents and rest. For a moment, their spirits rose as far as exhaustion would allow. As the woman shook her head, they fell just as quickly. Eyes that could barely hold themselves open watched to see if the officer would commandeer the yard despite the woman's objection. Instead, they watched the officer turn back to them with tears in his eyes. But not tears of anguish. Rather tears of gratitude.

One by one, the men in blue filed past the older woman who held her front door open for them. Each muttered thanks as much as their extinguished strength would allow. One by one, the men in blue found a place on the floor in the parlor and entryway to lay their bedrolls. One by one, the men in blue found rest in the home of a southerner. One by one, the men in blue and the woman shared moments of humanity in the face of battle.

Nearby, more soldiers at the end of their strength sought refuge in a home on Fair Street. There, the weary men were met by an older father and his daughters. With more reluctance than the woman, the man allowed the soldiers to rest. Having spent his boyhood at the knee of his father listening to tales of battle, he knew the terrors the men had faced and would see until the war reached its end. He knew how many would suffer the losses of friends and comrades. He knew how many would die.

As the men rested in near silence, each contemplating the same things the father knew in his heart, the daughters served warm drinks and what food they could spare. Each soldier expressed humble gratitude knowing the gesture was sincere as it had not been forced. The weight of the impending battle was not lost in the midst of the humble hospitality. Knowledge that the moment of rest could be shattered in an instant was never forgotten as coffee was poured and whiskey added to fortify the men who could barely sit up to drink it.

One of the men seated against a wall next to the piano ran a finger along the carved wood. Tears gathered as thoughts of music and conversation in parlors before the war drifted through a mind too exhausted to fight the pain of knowing he may never see those times again. Kneeling beside him, one of the daughters held out a cup and glanced at the hand, weathered and cracked from cold and toil, lovingly resting on the piano leg. Standing, she looked back at her father, who nodded. Placing her tray on the top of the instrument, she sat before it and opened the lid to reveal the shining ivory keys. Her sister joined her and for a few precious moments, music filled the room as tears fell down dirty bearded faces to the man.

None were immune to the beauty and pain of the moment. None were immune to the thought that this could be the last music they would hear. None were immune to the depth of the humanity they had been granted. None were immune to the fact that, with the first cannon shot, the moment would be shattered.

Sixteen

Ruby sat on the floor in the middle of the Winter's guest room staring at the mirrored piece of furniture in front of her. Like the vision of Tod Carter, witnessing the death of the Lotz twins sapped her mentally and emotionally. How many more of these scenes would she have to witness? How long could she withstand the strain of watching people die before it broke her?

Mallory sat on the floor next to her and patted her knee. Jake sat on the end of the guest bed. Neither intended to push Ruby to speak, but she felt compelled to anyway. "I know how they died," Ruby said softly.

"Were they sick?" Jake asked. "They looked so ill when they came to me."

"Yes and no," Ruby answered vaguely. "They fell in the water, but their sister pulled them out. She thought they were fine, but they had inhaled too much water. It took a little while, but they began to get sick and struggle to breathe. They drowned on the bank. Alone."

Mallory choked back a sob as her heart broke for the children. Tears began to well up in Ruby's eyes again. Jake's face fell as he tried to keep his composure. "Dry drowning?" he asked.

Ruby nodded. "I believe so. Their sister drank the water, too. It wasn't poisoned. Dry drowning is the only thing that explains it all. And the vomiting and their color from oxygen deprivation explains why their parents and others believed they were poisoned."

Mallory shook her head. "I don't understand. Why were such small children alone by the water?"

Ruby shrugged. "I don't know."

"Parents nowadays would be charged with neglect," Jake said bitterly.

"Times were different then," Ruby said. "In all of the diary entries and documents from the time, no one seemed to blame the parents as much as they blamed the Union. Maybe blaming the Union troops was their way of protecting the parents from the shame of not being with their children when they drowned. Maybe it was just one more way to justify their hatred of other human beings. Who knows?"

Mallory sighed. "It's such a shame. Such a sad loss. I can't imagine the pain those parents felt no matter what the cause was."

Jake nodded. "They certainly suffered for any part of it that was their fault. So, what do the twins want? How do we help them get out of that piece of furniture?"

Ruby stood up and stretched her back. "They want the same thing Tod did. They want to go home so they can see their family again."

Mallory stood as well and walked over to the mirror. Unlike Ruby, Mallory's reflection was clear and defined. The strange reflections seemed to be confined to Ruby. "So, like the Carter's mirror, we need to find a way to convince a museum to take this piece?"

A slight smile played on Ruby's lips. "Yes, but this one shouldn't be as tricky."

"How do you mean?" Jake asked.

"The Lotz House may be a museum, but unlike the Carter House and Carnton Plantation that are run by The Battle of Franklin Trust, the Lotz House embraces its hauntings. In fact, they even do ghost tours at night around Halloween. I think they will be more than happy to take the haunted mirror back." She paused for a moment. "The trick may be getting them to let me release the kids, actually."

Mallory frowned. "Surely they wouldn't make the children stay imprisoned in there!"

Jake shrugged and slapped his hands on his thighs as he stood up from his spot at the foot of the bed. "The way I see it, the gift of the mirror includes releasing the kids. If they can't agree to that, no deal."

"And what if they refuse and don't take the mirror?" Ruby asked.

Jake's lawyer side grinned. "Trust me, they'll take the mirror. They can always tell the story about how the mirror used to be haunted by Julius and Julia Lotz."

"Fair enough," Ruby laughed. "I'll make some calls and let you know what I can work out."

The beautiful white Lotz House was only 150 paces from the Carter House, sitting next to a small office building that reflected the glorious hideousness of 1970s architecture and orange brick. Unlike Carter House, none of the land remained around it. Instead, there was a gravel drive and parking pad tucked in amongst the surrounding buildings and intersection. No visitor center building greeted guests and no walk through the grounds before reaching the home. Despite its humble surroundings, the house itself was a showcase of woodworking mastery. Albert Lotz built the home with his own hands as a catalog of his work that potential clients could use to choose the elements they wanted to add to their own homes. Outside, the white wooden siding framed intricately carved window casings; the bottom floor windows being different from the second floor to showcase different styles available to clients. Columns graced a covered porch whose ceiling was painted in the traditional southern pale blue, commonly known as 'haint blue.' Legend said the color would keep ghosts, or 'haints', out of the house. Whether or not that was true, it was certainly good at preventing bugs and birds from making their homes up there. Hanging from the balcony railing on the second story of the porch was a red flag signifying the use of the home as a field hospital following the battle of Franklin. To drive home the point of its connection to the battle, a cannon sat in the front yard.

While it lacked the official museum accouterments of a visitor center and original furniture that the Carter House had, the curators had packed every nook and cranny with as much period furniture as they could to add to the feeling of what the home might have been like when the Lotz family lived there. Only a couple of original pieces remained with the house. In the first-floor hallway were glass cases housing artifacts like Minie ball bullets, field backpacks, and other items from the Civil War recovered on the grounds and in the area. One of the most prominent features of the Lotz House that Carter House couldn't boast was an archeological dig in the basement. It was there that the Lotz family lived for months while Albert rushed to repair the severe destruction after the battle as soldiers were being treated by army surgeons around him. His careful craftsmanship of the original home contrasted sharply with the rushed placement of floorboards and other repairs made from whatever tools and materials Albert could scrounge, including nails from the shoes of the seventeen horses that died in battle in his front yard.

Ruby had no trouble convincing the Lotz museum director to take the mirrored piece as a donation from Jake and Mallory, and even seemed eager about the ghosts of the children that were currently occupying it. Not only had the house seen its share of ghost tours, it had been used by more than one paranormal investigation group, including a local one that had their experiences nationally televised. It was that fact that made Ruby concerned about the museum allowing her to free the twins once the piece made it safely back inside.

As with the Carter mirror, Jake, Mallory, and Ruby had carefully wrapped the mirrored piece for the short journey in the back of Pawpaw's old truck. Gravel popped and crunched under the wheels as they pulled up the drive to the front of the Lotz House. On the porch, the director and another docent rose from their chairs where they had been awaiting the group and the long-lost Lotz mirror.

"Welcome, Ruby!" a tall thin older man said holding out a hand to her.

"You must be Andrew," Ruby said shaking his hand.

"I am," he answered with a smile then turned to Mallory and Jake. "Andrew McHale. You must be the Winters. I can't tell you how excited we are to get this piece of the home back."

Mallory and Jake both shook Andrew's hand. "We're glad to help," Jake replied. "We love the piece but it's always better to have things where they truly belong."

"And where others can appreciate their beauty," Mallory added.

"Indeed." Andrew agreed. "Let's get it up to the Red Room and you can tell me more about our little stowaways."

With the help of the other docent, the group of five got the piece up the narrow staircase and around the turn to the Red Room with more ease than the three of them did getting it out of the Bennett House guest room. True to its name, the room where the piece was brought to rest was wallpapered in a rich red and filled with dark wooden furniture. The piece was placed in a corner next to the fireplace on the south wall of the home. Originally, there would have been a window where they stood the mirrored shelves, but the wall and its windows had been blown out by cannon fire and Albert couldn't get glass to replace the ones that were lost. So, he rebuilt the wall without any windows at all.

Once the quilts and bubble wrap were removed, Andrew stood back to admire the new addition to the room. "It really is an interesting piece. I believe we have some porcelain we can place on the shelves, too, to make it truly authentic to the time period."

"It's perfect," Mallory said taking in the room. "It's as though the spot in the room was just waiting for it."

"High praise from a designer," Andrew said with a grin. "Maybe it was." Turning his attention to Ruby, he finally brought up the subject Ruby had been nervous about since her first call to him. "So, tell me about the children in there. We've always thought they were haunting their bedroom, but perhaps we have someone else making mischief in there."

Ruby shrugged. "You must, because the twins are in there," she said waving a hand at the mirror. "I'm positive of that."

"I don't mean to sound ungrateful or disrespectful, but how do you know?" Andrew asked.

Jake answered for her as Ruby hesitated in her own self-doubt. "I've seen them myself. Not in the mirror, but at the side of the bed. When we tried to talk to the spirits to see what they wanted, we all saw them. Then, Ruby was able to focus her efforts a bit more and connect with them through the mirror."

Andrew's eyes widened and his scruffy eyebrows raised. "Really?"

Ruby nodded and smiled sheepishly. "Yes," she answered softly. "It's not something I'm used to and it sounds so strange to hear what I've done said out loud."

"Fascinating stuff, though, Ruby! What a gift to have!" Andrew exclaimed. "How do you connect with them?"

"By standing in front of the mirror and putting my hand flat on the glass."

"Amazing. How did you discover doing that would help you connect with them?" Andrew asked clearly enamored by the paranormal side of things as much as the historical.

Ruby cut her eyes over at Jake and Mallory, who looked as apprehensive as she did about answering that question honestly. As much as she liked having an ally in her spiritual weirdness, she wasn't keen on letting anyone outside their circle know how Tod Carter guided her to connecting with the spirits in the mirror. "It was an accident, actually. I put my hand on the glass and there they were."

Andrew exhaled and shook his head. "That must have been startling."

"At first it was, but the kids just wanted to tell their story and get back home so they could join their parents again." Ruby relayed the story the twins had shown her to Andrew knowing he would actually believe her. As she got to the end and the death of Julius and Julia on the creek bank from dry drowning, he was enthralled.

"I've been saying something similar for years," Andrew said nodding thoughtfully. "It had to have been drowning, but dry drowning makes so much sense. While I can't very well say that to anyone in the historical community since I can't prove it with documentation, it's good to know for myself. Always feels good to solve a historical mystery, even if one must keep it a secret."

Ruby was genuinely glad that Andrew was pleased, but still felt uncomfortable bringing up the subject of releasing the twins from the mirror. Partly because she wasn't sure if he would resist in order to keep the haunting going, and partly because she was afraid she would end up with an audience while she did it.

Mallory seemed to sense her uneasiness and squeezed her hand. It was a simple gesture, but it was becoming one Ruby truly appreciated. So many years had passed since her mother or grandmother had done the same thing when she felt unsure of herself. "It's time, Ruby," Mallory whispered.

Ruby knew it was, too. Her skin had been tingling since the mirror entered the house and the sensation was only getting stronger. It was as though the children were begging her to release them. Nodding and squeezing Mallory's hand back, she released it and cleared her throat. "Um, I guess we should get to the other part of all this. I'm sure the kids are eager to get out of that mirror."

"Can you feel them?" Andrew asked. Ruby nodded. "Fascinating stuff," he said again. "Do you think I could see them when you connect to them?"

Jake shook his head. "Not like Ruby can. All Mallory and I have been able to see when she connects to the mirror are shadows moving. It's enough to know they are there, but not clear enough to really see what's happening."

Andrew's face fell slightly, clearly disappointed about not being able to see the children for himself. "Ah, well. I understand. It would have been an incredible thing to experience, though."

Mallory shuddered. "If you say so. Myself, I'm happy to keep it to shadows."

"Is there something in particular you need? Lights off, candles, anything?" Andrew asked. "Seems like everyone we've had in here to investigate needs different things to be successful."

Ruby shook her head. "No, just me and the mirror. It's more about convincing them they'll be ok than anything else. No real hocus pocus to it."

"Fascinating."

Given that he made no move to leave her to it by herself, Ruby tried to square with the fact that she was going to have to do the connection to the children with an audience. Swallowing her fear and trying to calm her pounding heart, Ruby focused on the mirror and what the children needed. Releasing them was more important than her own insecurities. She also reasoned that experiencing it for himself may help convince Andrew that ghost stories weren't all about the show and selling tickets as much as real stories about real people.

Giving her a wide berth, Mallory led Jake and Andrew to the other side of the room. Ruby was grateful for Mallory's consideration and made a mental note to thank her for that on the way home. Ruby took a slow deep breath to calm the shaking in her hands as she stepped toward the mirrored piece of furniture and placed her hand on the center glass.

As her own reflection faded and the twins shimmered into focus, her nervousness vanished as her heart broke for the children. Where Tod Carter looked hopeful with his tears, Julius and Julia looked terrified. Being so young, they faced the fear of leaving the known world of the mirror and stepping into the unknown. Even if their parents might be there, it was still frightening.

"It's alright," Ruby said gently. "I'm here. Everything is going to be ok," she reassured them even though she really had no idea if it was or not. Suddenly, a thought hit her that almost made her release the mirror. What if where she was sending them to was worse, not better than where they were? What if she was sending them from a place of loneliness but still being part of the world in some way to oblivion and nothingness? If that's what she had done to Tod Carter, she couldn't fix it now.

As Ruby hesitated and her expression changed, Julia's lips began to tremble as tears gathered in her eyes. Julius tried to be stronger than his sister, but was teetering on the edge of crying himself. "Home?" he asked as a sob choked him.

"Yes," Ruby answered. "You're home now."

"Papa?" Julia asked.

Ruby shook her head. "He's not here, but this is the house he built."

Julius nodded. "Can we go now?"

Ruby tried to smile. "That's up to you. Do you want to go?"

Both of the children nodded.

"Your father's house is a museum now." Confusion on the faces of the children led her to explain what a museum was. "It's a place where people come to learn about the past. They come to learn about your family and the house your father built. Your family and this home are important things to the town of Franklin. People will know your story for a long, long time. We won't let you be forgotten."

Through their tears, the children smiled. Julia put one of her little hands on the mirror. "Ruby."

As tears began to roll down her face, Ruby put her other hand flat against the little girl's. "Julia."

Julius followed suit, putting his little hand next to his sister's and touching Ruby's through the glass. "Thank you, Ruby."

"You're welcome, Julius. I'll miss you. Both of you." She couldn't say anything else. Sobs choked any other words she might have wanted to say.

Julia smiled as her tear-filled eyes brightened. "I hear them. Calling us."

Julius nodded. "Calling us home."

Ruby's sobs rocked her body as the children began to shimmer and fade, leaving only her own solid reflection in the mirror.

Seventeen

Emotionally and physically spent, Ruby sat down heavily in one of the rocking chairs on the Lotz House front porch. She wiped the remaining tears from her eyes with her sleeve and dropped her head into her hands. Much like Tod Carter's return to the ether, sending the Lotz twins home left her with an emptiness and grief she didn't particularly like. Ruby had enough grief in her own life at the moment. She wasn't sure she had it in her to keep taking on the loss of the souls in the mirrors.

Her thoughts were interrupted by the quiet presence of Andrew McHale. He gently closed the front door behind him and stood on the porch with his hands in his pockets looking at some nebulous space between him and the horizon. After a long moment in thought, he sighed and said, "I've spent my whole life searching for facts about people of the past. I thought I knew them. Thought I understood them as real people. I was wrong. It wasn't until you and your mirror came along that I finally felt them for who they truly are. It's a gift I will forever be grateful for."

Ruby stared at Andrew. "I'm not sure I follow."

He chuckled and settled into the rocking chair next to her. "I've dedicated so much of my career to the Battle of Franklin and the Lotz family. When you spend so much time studying a place, events, and the people they impacted, it feels as though you are connected to them. Similar to how you feel connected to friends in your life, even though the people of history are long dead. The story of the Lotz twins is a sad one, but even so, it has been a fascinating mystery for me. I think I lost something of the sadness in my quest to solve it. Today, watching your heart break for the children, it reminded me that their loss was felt so deeply by the ones who loved them and the reason for the loss is secondary to that pain. Being able to feel that is a gift, and one I will not soon forget."

"I knew the connection was something important to the spirits trapped in the mirrors, but I never thought about it impacting the living," Ruby said quietly.

"Perhaps it's time to change your perspective. What you're doing is important to people on both sides of the glass, Ruby. This town has spent a long time preserving a history they don't truly understand. They protect the aesthetics but know little of the people responsible for creating them. It's time Franklin came face to face with its past so they can appreciate it for the right reasons."

"Not the Disney version they've created," Ruby said with a frown, thinking back to her own thoughts about that same thing.

"Exactly. It's a lovely façade, to be sure. Pristine and welcoming. But it was a tumultuous history that created it. It's time they saw it for themselves. It's a gift you can give to both the living and the dead."

"That sounds like a lot of responsibility," Ruby said.

Andrew smiled warmly at her. "Did you think about it like that when you first connected to the spirits? Or did you simply do what needed to be done to help them?"

Ruby sat in thought for a moment. She had felt inadequate for the task at hand when this started, but knew the spirits deserved peace. "I guess it was a little of both, but knowing they deserved to feel the peace of finding where they belonged was more important than anything else. I didn't think I could do it and felt the weight of the task, but not a sense of greater responsibility to the town or mankind. I was too focused on the dead to worry too much about the living, other than the Winters who wanted their house back." She paused as another thought formed. "I've been feeling like my purpose died with my grandfather. He was always what I felt responsible for protecting. He was the one who loved this town so much and wanted to preserve it."

Andrew smiled again. It unnerved Ruby a little how much the historian seemed to see inside her. "Perhaps," he said, "your grandfather has sent you the mirrors to help the granddaughter he loved find purpose in the town he loved." Slapping his hands on his thighs, he rose from the chairs with a sigh. "I'll go check on Jake and Mallory and see if they have any questions about the exhibits. Take all the time you need out here. I'll keep them occupied until you come in and say you're ready."

"Thank you, Andrew," she said. "For everything."

With a nod, Andrew went back inside leaving Ruby to ponder his words and rest from the exertion of helping Julius and Julia go home.

As she sat rocking and staring at the construction going on across the street where the old Piggly Wiggly once was, she began to digest the words the historian left her with. Maybe Andrew McHale was right. Maybe Pawpaw meant for her to be part of all this so she could connect with him through the town itself. It had been her home, but she, like so many residents, took a lot of the history for granted even though she knew it well. It was more textbook than personal to Ruby. But not to Mitch Baxter. The town had a soul to Pawpaw, one that had been lost on Ruby. She could see that now. He wasn't just helping his clients when he restored the buildings around Franklin. He was honoring the residents of the past that had contributed to the town in their own ways. Restoring their houses brought something of the past owners back to the town. Back home. And for the ones reluctant to leave for one reason or another, Ruby could do the same now. She could bring them home.

Part of truly being home is the acceptance and welcome of those you are coming home to. Perhaps shifting her perspective to encompass the service being done for the living as well as the dead would create that sense of home for all of them. The dead could find their way back to their loved ones and the living could have a very real experience of connection to those that went before them in the town's buildings. Rather than hiding the ghosts in the mirrors, maybe she needed to let the building owners see the shadows like Andrew had. If it had a profound impact on him, maybe it would do the same for others who didn't know the history as well as he did. Maybe it would inspire them to dig deeper and appreciate more. If Pawpaw had been responsible for leading her to the mirrors to help her connect to him through the town, she hoped he would be glad she could connect more people to the town as a result.

Feeling more rested and focused, she rose from her rocking chair and stretched her back. From the porch, she could see the Carter House and her thoughts returned to the memory of Tod Carter. "Thank you," she whispered to him hopeful Tod could hear her from wherever he was. "Thank you for showing me what to do. And, Tod, if you see Pawpaw, tell him I love him and miss him." She opened the front door and rejoined the Winters as Andrew began telling them about the family hiding in the Carter House basement during the fighting in their own front yard.

The Five Bloodiest Hours

Children sat at their mother's feet half-heartedly playing with China dolls and toy soldiers, each more interested in the conversation of the adults than their toys. The adults cast furtive glances at the children as they talked quietly in vague terms they hoped were keeping the terrible truth of the situation from the little ones. Details may have been lost on the young, but the hushed tones of the conversation were enough to spark fear in their tiny hearts. It hadn't been long before that they had heard such murmurings and seen their mother dab at her eyes with her lace handkerchief. That time, the hushed conversations came after the tragic loss of their twin siblings. Little ears strained to decipher what tragedy brought on the cryptic conversations in the parlor this time.

Despite the pleading of the little ones, the older children of the house refused to tell them what was happening. It was plain on the faces of the older ones that something fearful was happening. Ashen complexions and forced smiles gave away the terror that they either felt or suspected. Perhaps they knew only little more than the young ones, but the older children at least understood the gravity of the situation more fully.

The older man from across the road talked rapidly to their papa and glanced anxiously toward his own house. Gestures were made toward the south wall of the parlor they gathered in as he shook his head. Their father disagreed with the other man, but his objections were becoming fewer and weaker as the conversation continued. Their mother said little other than that she trusted her husband to make the best decision for his family. Soon, the conversation stopped abruptly as noises outside drew the attention of the older man and their papa. Both men stood at the window for a long moment in silence. Turning to face the older man, their papa's face had drained of color. With nothing more than a nod, the decision was made.

Voices that had been quiet murmurs moments before spoke with strength and determination even through the fear that accented them. Orders to gather whatever supplies they could carry were given to the older children who immediately went to carry them out. Their mother rose from the rocking chair in the corner and took her smaller children by the hands. Leading them up the staircase their papa had carved with his own hands, she instructed them to choose a toy to take with them while she chose clothes from their large carved armoires. The children didn't understand why their mother needed the clothes since they were already dressed for the day, but didn't question her. There was so much they did not understand and too many questions to ask of their parents who seemed overwrought already. Instead, they turned their focus on putting their toys in a pillowcase to take with them to wherever they were going. China dolls, toy soldiers, a stuffed rabbit, and a small security blanket were lovingly packed together for the journey.

Gathered once more in the parlor, the children noticed the absence of the older man from the house across the street. Instead, there was a soldier in blue standing near the front doorway with his hands behind his back. His features were drawn with exhaustion and his clothes flecked with mud, but he did his best to stand as officially as he could. The youngest of the children could not take his wide eyes off the soldier, torn between fear and admiration for the uniform that was similar to those of his toy soldiers. Noticing the child, the officer smiled down at him causing the embarrassed boy to hide behind his mother's skirt. Curiosity couldn't be quelled for long as the child continued to peek at the soldier while securely attached to his mother.

Once all were assembled, their papa nodded at the young officer who led the family to the front door. Their mother held the smallest of them on one hip and the hand of the little girl as she lifted her proud head high to conceal her terror. Sunshine and pleasantly warm air greeted them as the soldier held the door open. Another officer met them at the bottom of the porch steps and led them the hundred paces across the road through the soldiers who barely noticed the train of civilians picking their way through the mud, men, and weapons that were being moved into place. Ahead, the brick chimneys of the Carter House rose above it all like a beacon of safety from the coming storm.

The little girl watched through the parlor window as her grandfather's long determined strides carried him through the lines of soldiers back across the street. Coming through the front door, he knocked mud from his ravaged front yard off his boots before going into the best parlor where the officers had set up their command. The little girl peeked around the doorframe to try to hear what was said. Words were exchanged in low tones that she couldn't make out, but they were not heated which was a small relief to the worried child. Other children huddled together and pretended to play with toys or listen to their mother read, but her attention was on her grandfather. Her independence and curiosity had made her a favorite of his and she took full advantage of her position among the grandchildren.

Walking across the entryway and into the family parlor that also served as his bedroom, her grandfather smiled down at his little spy and pulled playfully on one of her curls. Following on his heels, they crossed the room to the other adults who had been in whispered conversation since her grandfather had set out for the white house across the street. More words were whispered to the adults before he turned his attention back to the children. Instructions were given as though the plan were going to be great fun. A chance to get dirty in the middle of the day without being scolded for it. They would be helping their grandfather and uncle dig a hole in the dining room floor while they waited for their neighbors to arrive.

The little girl could hardly believe her luck. The arrival of the soldiers that morning had been frightening, but now things seemed to be turning for the better. She had dug for bugs and worms in the garden before, but digging a hole in the house was something unheard of. Her grandfather silenced the excited chatter amongst the children with a finger over his lips. It seemed he wanted to keep the endeavor a secret and that only served to make it more thrilling to her.

With furtive glances to the soldiers still constructing trenches where their cotton fields had once been, the children followed their uncle and grandfather out of the back door and down the steps to the basement rooms. The first and largest of them was the dining room. It was colder down there and the little girl shivered in the chill and excitement. No fire had been built in the large fireplace even though the three house slaves were gathered there. The field hands had fled as the soldiers began dismantling their cabins in the wee hours of the morning. The dining table and chairs had been moved to one side of the room leaving the rough-cut brick floor bare in the center of the room. The sugar safe had been removed from the room entirely and hidden in the storage room. Shovels, spades, and pick axes leaned against the wall in its place. A rug taken from one of the upstairs bedrooms was rolled up and slumped in a corner.

    Her uncle took one of the pick axes and scraped a large rectangle into the stones. Then, he pried one of the bricks out of its place in the dirt floor. Then another and another as the smell of fresh earth filled their noses. Her grandfather and the oldest grandson each took another pick and began to do the same. She and the younger children stacked the bricks out of their way against a wall. Once all of the bricks in the middle of the shape had been worked free, the digging began. Her grandfather handed her a small shovel while the other girls were taken to the next room to begin sorting supplies to be buried in the hole. She dug alongside her grandfather watching and imitating every move he made. She pushed her little booted foot down on the spade and lifted chunks of dirt. She put her clods in the pile with her grandfather's, enthralled by how quickly he could work. In all her eight years, she couldn't remember her grandfather ever doing anything like the work they were doing now, much less with such skill and speed. There seemed to be a sense of urgency in the adventure and so she picked up her pace as well.

    Blistered hands finally were able to rest when her grandfather declared the hole deep enough. All tools were set aside as everyone began to move the supplies into the dining room. Jars of all sizes and sacks of flour were placed at the bottom while dried meats and cheeses were set in gaps around them. Root vegetables were placed on top of these followed by bedsheets to keep the food as clean as possible. Finally, dirt was thrown on top of it all and packed down. The excess dirt was shoveled into the storage room as bricks were put back in place to hide the work that had been done. To disguise it all as much as possible, the rug was rolled out and the table and chairs replaced.

    Exhausted, the children looked at their handiwork and took delight in their grandfather's compliments on a job well done. None of them realized that the work could have been done by others who were stronger and faster, and that, by choosing them to do the work, their grandfather had spared them hours of fear as he distracted them from the war gathering around them like storm clouds.

Eighteen

Ruby stood in front of a tailored rectangular mirror with a whitewashed frame hanging over a sideboard in the parlor room that was serving as Jake's home office while they got settled in. Something was missing in it. There was no drop in temperature as she stepped in front of the glass. No swirling of shadows or materializing spirits. Just her own reflection. "Odd," Ruby said. "I'm getting nothing at all from this one. It's like it's not haunted at all." Glancing over at Mallory, she asked, "Where did you find this one, Mallory?"

Mallory thought for a moment. "Oh, yes. Pottery Barn."

Ruby's shoulders fell and she shook her head in exasperation. "Well, that would certainly explain it. This one wouldn't be haunted, would it?"

"No, I suppose not," Mallory replied sheepishly.

Jake suppressed a giggle at his wife's expense. "At least that's one more to cross off our list. Moving on, then."

"Tell me what possessed you to buy *that*?" Ruby asked Mallory as she looked at the mirror over the powder room sink. There was nothing about the mirror that said 'Mallory Winter' at all. Gold gilt surrounded a round mirror that was domed outwards instead of flat mirrored glass. The effect made anything reflected in it look smaller and farther away than it actually was. On either side of the circle were candlesticks mounted to the frame. Lit candles might have reflected light into the room, but unlit candles just seemed like useless little soldiers standing at attention for no reason whatsoever. The mirror itself was flecked with dark spots where the silvering on the back of the glass had tarnished rendering using it useless for anything but aesthetics. Even that was questionable to Ruby as she stared at the garish thing.

"Honestly, I really don't know," Mallory admitted with a finger on her chin as she stood back looking at it. "I thought the curved mirror would open up the room, but it really is too big for the space."

"That's your only problem with it?" Ruby asked with a chuckle.

"Well, maybe not the only problem. I admit it won't be as hard to let this one go as much as some of the others." Mallory cocked her head to one side and squinted at the bubble mirror. "I wonder who's inside this one?"

"Only one way to find out," Ruby said with a sigh. While the process of reaching the spirits in the Winter's mirrors was becoming more commonplace for Ruby, it didn't make it any less taxing on her system. Each time left her drained, physically and emotionally. The only difference these days was the lack of terror that had accompanied the exhaustion. It was an improvement, she supposed.

"Jake," Mallory called down the hall to the back room Jake used as an office. "You ready?"

"Yep!" he called back. "On my way!"

A moment later, Jake and Mallory stood in the powder room doorway as Ruby stepped in front of the rounded speckled glass. As she did, the temperature dropped and goose pimples rose on her arms. Ruby's reflection was distorted more than usual as it rippled and faded with her touch. In front of her, the face of another soldier materialized in her own reflection's stead. Like Tod Carter, the soldier in gray was young and battle-worn. His brow wrinkled as he blinked rapidly in confusion. Ruby could sense his growing panic and whispered gently, "It's alright. I'm here to help you."

"I don't understand." The words were hollow and seemed to come from across an expanse even though the one who spoke them was inches from her on the other side of the glass.

"You've been in here a long time," she explained. "My name is Ruby. I'm here to help you get home."

"I'm Jasper Patterson. How long has it been?" he asked.

"A century and a half."

His young eyes fell as they filled with tears. "I was supposed to go home. They told me I was going home."

Ruby knew what she had to do, but felt her own fear rising in tandem with the soldier's. She needed to see his story to know how to help him get home, but knew it was going to be gruesome. He had obviously died in battle, or because of it, and nothing about watching that with Tod Carter made her want to see a rerun. Ruby had no choice, though, if she was going to get the soldier out of his glass prison.

"Jasper, do you know what happened to you?" she asked gently.

The young soldier gazed past her into empty space as he thought for a moment. "I was wounded. They said I could go home. I waited for the wagon to take me back home, but it didn't come. I waited and waited for it."

Ruby's chest tightened as her heart ached for the young soldier who waited so long in vain, who died waiting. It was something to go on, but didn't connect Jasper to a building that she could return the ghastly mirror to. "Do you know where you were when you...were waiting?"

Jasper shook his head slowly. "I'm sorry, Miss Ruby, but I don't. I come from Alabama. I'm not sure where I was."

"Can you show me?"

The soldier's face tightened. "Miss Ruby, you don't want to see that. It's...it's too terrible."

Ruby softened her expression as she tried to smile through her heartache at the gentle soul who was trying to protect her from his own horrors. "I've seen the battle already, Jasper. It's terrifying, I know. Can't say I'm looking forward to seeing it, but I need to. I can't help you if I don't."

Jasper nodded slowly and put his hand to hers. In an instant, Ruby was transported back onto the battlefield, but in a different place than before. The Carter and Lotz houses were nowhere to be seen through the smoke from the heavy artillery. Trenches snaked through the wasteland of landscape in front of her. Chaos reigned as ranks and regiments disintegrated into a mass of blood and bodies. Once more, Ruby found herself a ghost in the past as men rushed by her to their death or to the sides of fallen comrades cutting down anyone in their way. Men fought with anything they could get their hands on from muskets, pistols, sabers, and even the butts of guns they could no longer find ammunition for.

Ruby whirled around searching the mass of humanity for Jasper and finally found him kneeling over a fallen soldier pouring water from a canteen into the dying man's mouth. Despite the young soldier's efforts, his fallen friend sputtered his last breath. Realizing his friend was gone, Jasper sat back on his knees and removed his cap as he reached down and closed his friend's eyes with trembling fingers. Wiping his tears away with the back of his hand, Jasper pulled his friend's pistol from his belt and tucked it into his own before picking up his musket. With steeled determination, Jasper stood and spun on his heel to face the enemy entrenchments.

Horror choked Ruby as she helplessly watched Jasper bring the musket to his shoulder and stride toward the onslaught of enemy fire. Her hand went to her mouth as a scream caught in her throat. Bullets flew past Jasper whistling through the smoke and haze. Overhead, grape shot from exploding canisters rained down and took victims all around Jasper. Ruby couldn't fathom how he managed to avoid being hit. Sparks singed the coat that fluttered behind him as Jasper raced into the melee. Over the headboard of the trench, a soldier raised a gun to fire on him, but it misfired giving Jasper a fleeting moment of the upper hand. The young soldier seized the opportunity, yanked the muzzle of the malfunctioning gun, and pulled the startled Union soldier forward. Stumbling backwards trying to regain his balance, the soldier stood up over the protective header for an instant too long. Jasper took his shot at near point-blank range. The musket shot ripped through the Union soldier's gut with such ferocity that daylight could be seen through the wound before the soldier dropped lifelessly into the trench. Adrenaline-driven fear and rage combined to make Jasper momentarily blinded to an enemy soldier approaching from the side. Turning too late, Jasper saw the end of the pistol flash before the bullet caught him in the chest tossing him backwards onto the mangled corpse of the soldier he had just killed.

Another shift in time and Ruby was sitting on the edge of a wagon of wounded being pulled out of the heaviest fire and across the empty fields. Rising in the distance were the chimneys of Carnton Plantation. Gone were the farm animals and crops. Instead, spreading across the vast lawn were fallen soldiers. As the wagon approached, doctors raced to meet it before giving directions to the soldiers in the driver's seat. Some of the men didn't survive the journey from the trenches to the hospital. Those bodies were stripped of weapons and ammunition then laid in stacks away from where the wounded were carried. Along the back porch, doctors scurried back and forth triaging the incoming wounded to sort them once again. Those who might live were put in place to await their turns in the make-shift operating theaters in the home's interior. The ground ran red with blood, and limbs piled up outside the open windows as surgeons removed what they could to help save the men. As his injury was serious, Jasper was carried immediately inside and placed on a cot.

Once inside, a woman knelt over him and gingerly moved his clothes away from the bullet wound dangerously close to his heart. Soft words were spoken as a wet cloth bathed the wound. He groaned and writhed in pain as the woman worked. A little girl who couldn't have been more than nine or ten, stood behind the woman who must have been her mother and ripped strips from a tablecloth to make binding. Her mother wrapped the strips tightly around Jasper's chest to try to stem the bleeding while he waited his turn in surgery. Once he was bound, she held his head as she poured whiskey into his mouth. Ruby realized she was watching the mistress of the house, Caroline McGavock, known as The Widow of the South, and her daughter, Hattie, tending the soldiers using her own linens.

Shifting time again, Ruby found herself standing in the corner of what appeared to be the bedroom of a small boy. Little Winder McGavock's bed and toys had been pushed to one side to make room for an operating table that was no more than a door laid across a pair of sawhorses next to the open windows. Underneath the table was a basket of more amputated limbs. Blood seeped through the basketweave creating a crimson puddle on the polished wood floor. Around the room, men sat slumped against the walls bleeding through the makeshift bandages applied by nurses and Caroline McGavock. Jasper was laid on the operating table, chest bare, his breathing shallow and raspy. His face was gray from blood loss and pain. Ruby watched as the surgeon readied his instruments and ordered chloroform for the patient and wondered what possessed the doctor to think that someone literally dying in front of him could be saved.

Another shift and she was kneeling on one side of Jasper on the Carnton lawn amid the hundreds of dead and dying men. His wound was bound once more where the surgeon had removed the bullet, but his color and breathing had deteriorated significantly. On the other side of him, a nurse knelt and spoke softly to Jasper promising him that everything would be alright and that he would soon be going home. In that moment, Ruby saw the irony of the nurse's words. It was death that would make everything alright by taking his pain away. Home, however, would be elusive for a very long time. The nurse rose and walked away, stepping over other bodies in various states of dying, leaving Jasper to wait. Ruby stayed by his side, an invisible caretaker, until his final breaths rattled his chest and he died alone in his waiting. As Jasper's body went still, she saw a glint of candlelight through the dining room window. The mirror.

As the vision faded and Jasper's reflection once more took its place, Ruby blinked back her tears. "I'm so sorry, Jasper."

He smiled wanly as tears gathered on his eyelashes. "At least this time I didn't die alone."

Ruby smiled. "You knew I was there?"

"This time." There was a strange sense of sadness and gratitude behind Jasper's words that made Ruby wonder how many times he had to relive his death terrified and alone.

"I wish I could have been there for you the first time."

Jasper nodded. "I want to go home, Ruby." Tears choked him as he spoke making it impossible in the moment for him to say anymore.

Ruby fought back her own tears before she could answer him. "I know, Jasper, and I'm going to help you do that. I need some time, and some help." Every fiber in her being wanted to pull the mirror off the wall and take it to Carnton immediately, but she knew this one would be a hard sell. Once again, Ruby would need to reach out to The Battle of Franklin Trust who put no stock in ghost stories. She'd managed to convince them to take the Carter mirror, but wasn't sure she could pull off another miraculous mirror find without looking suspiciously like a fraud. "Can you wait a little longer while I figure out how to do what needs to be done?"

"I've waited a century and a half," Jasper answered forcing a smile. "I can wait a little more."

Ruby nodded. "I *will* get you home, Jasper," she promised. "Soon."

Jasper nodded once more as he began to fade away. "Soon," he replied as he vanished.

Nineteen

Rainwater puddled in the ruts and sunken grave sites as persistent drizzle refused to let up. In the gray mist, the place seemed more forlorn than usual. Ruby stood under the bright red umbrella she used to help her tour groups find her in passing crowds. The vibrant color was a stark contrast to both the weather and Ruby's mood. For a long time, she stood silent and still watching the little rivulets of mud forming in the eroded mound of her grandfather's grave. She needed his advice so badly, but he wasn't around to give it. Part of her was angry at Pawpaw for not being there when she needed him, and the rest of her was wracked with guilt for thinking that way. The result of her internal conflict was the loss of any words for him at all.

As the rain tapped relentlessly on the umbrella, Ruby's thoughts wandered to the Carnton mirror and the conversation she wasn't looking forward to having with Bob Lawrence at The Battle of Franklin Trust. She had managed to convince him of the authenticity of the Carter mirror, but would he buy her undocumented assertions about the Carnton mirror, too? The docents she knew at the Carnton Plantation held very firm to their no-nonsense history of the battle and the role of the house. It didn't feel right to lie about the spirit trapped in the mirror, but would their staunchness keep them from taking it if they knew the truth about it? The more time Ruby spent with the dead who needed her help, the more she felt like their stories were as important as any of the ones told on the tours. Hiding Tod Carter's spirit from Bob seemed like the right thing to do at the time, but was it really? Maybe Tilly was right. Maybe the town needed to face the ghosts of their past. It sounded great in theory, but what if the Trust dismissed her and her haunted mirror making it impossible for her to keep her promise to Jasper?

Ruby knew what she needed to do, but it would have made her feel a lot more confident about it if Pawpaw could tell her she was right. As time passed, she felt him slipping away from her. She was giving voice to so many of the forgotten dead, but the one she needed to hear the most was nowhere to be found. Ruby could reach strangers so easily. Why could she not reach the one who knew her better than anyone else?

———

Ruby counted the third ring of the phone and nearly lost her nerve waiting on Bob Lawrence to answer. Just as she pulled her phone away from her ear to hang it up, she heard his voice on the other end.

"Well, Ruby! Good to hear from you!" he said with his usual good humor.

"Hi, Bob, I hate to bother you, but I'm hoping you can help me."

"Happy to. What can I do for you?"

Ruby paused as she worked up her nerve. "I have another mirror you might be interested in."

"Really? Well, aren't you a lucky charm?" he said with a chuckle. "If you're calling me, I'm assuming it's a Carter or Carnton mirror, then?"

"Well, yes, a Carnton one, actually. But there's something you need to know about it first." If Bob was going to buy into the truth about the mirrors, he was going to need to see them for himself. He'd need to come face-to-face with the ghost of the plantation's past. It was a huge risk, but it was the only way to do the right thing morally for the museum and for Jasper's spirit. "Would you mind meeting me at the

Winter's house tonight? You can take a look at it there and decide if you're interested."

"For a lost Carnton mirror? Absolutely!"

Ruby exhaled the breath she didn't realize she'd been holding. "Great. It's the old Bennett House on 4th. Is six o'clock good for you?"

"Perfect. I'll see you then. Looking forward to it. Thank you for reaching out again, Ruby."

"No problem." *You should probably wait til after you've seen it to thank me,* she thought as she hung up.

"Are you out of your mind?" Jake asked. He stared at Ruby with wide eyes and shook his head.

"Maybe, but I can't lie to him again. It's just not right. If we want history to be accepted and these spirits trapped in the mirrors to be seen as the real people they were, we have to be honest about it," Ruby argued.

Mallory shook her head. "I'm not saying you're wrong about that. You're absolutely right, but you said yourself The Battle of Franklin Trust doesn't put stock in ghost stories."

Ruby sighed. "I know, and that's exactly why Bob Lawrence needs to see the mirror for himself. It worked for *you*, Jake."

Jake held his hands up in front of him. "Don't use me as a reason for this lunacy." Running his fingers through his salt and pepper hair making it stick up wildly, he sighed. "I'm just worried about you, Ruby. That's all."

Ruby softened her defiant expression as she met his eyes. It was hard to be sassy to someone who was genuinely concerned and had hair as crazy as his. "I appreciate that, but what exactly are you worried about?"

The attorney side of Jake came out as he explained as though he was trying to convince a jury. "Ruby, you've been in this town your whole life. People know you. They trusted and respected your grandfather, and I have to think that trust and respect has transferred to you, too. Putting this out there in a town that doesn't exactly embrace their spooks and spirits might strip you of any reputability you have as a historian."

Mallory leaned across the table and put her hand on Ruby's. "He has a point. Think about this."

It had been an impulsive thing to invite Bob to see the mirror and its resident for himself, but she still felt like it was the right thing to do. "You're right. This could definitely hurt my reputation as a historian."

Mallory and Jake relaxed. "I'm glad you see my point," Jake said.

"But," Ruby continued as the Winters groaned, "it's really not about me. It's about Jasper and every other soul trapped in the mirrors in this house. I can't just leave them there, and I can't lie about the mirrors anymore. It cheapens their deaths if I don't acknowledge them to the people who take the mirrors. I'm not ashamed of them and neither should anyone else be."

Jake shook his head and measured his words before he spoke. "It's not a question of being ashamed of them or not. It's a question of belief systems and what truths people are willing to accept. You said yourself this town likes to keep their haunts in the confines of the ghost tours. The Trust is particularly vocal about not entertaining those things. Starting with them might be a tougher sell than you realize. We believe in you, Ruby, but I'm not sure the Trust or rest of town will be easily convinced."

"Or, worse," Mallory added, "condemn you for it."

"Like a witch hunt, you mean." Ruby said pulling her hand away from Mallory and crossing her arms.

Mallory nodded. "Something like that," she said quietly.

"Franklin might be ultra conservative in a lot of ways, but I don't think they would go that far. They don't tolerate scandal very well and certainly wouldn't create one themselves. If I'm condemned, it will be by ostracizing me rather than burning me at the stake. I can handle that."

"But this is your home, Ruby," Mallory persisted.

"I *said*, I can handle that."

Ruby was resolute and the Winters gave up the fight, at least verbally. Their expressions gave away every thought in their heads from concern to condemnation of her idea. Mostly worry, though. Ruby didn't like defying half of the people that believed in her, but she knew Pawpaw would want her to stand up for what she believed was right, even if it cost her reputation. The souls she was trying to set free had sacrificed far more than that. Still, that didn't mean it was easy to do. Hiding behind her wall of determination was very real nervousness that her plan could backfire on her. It was, after all, Franklin, Land of the Reserved.

Twenty

The nervousness had only increased by the time the silver clock in the entry chimed six. Jake paced the hallway like an agitated tiger, and Mallory fussed over tea and cookies, rearranging the tray she was putting together over and over again. Ruby leaned on the doorframe of the hall bathroom and stared at the Carnton mirror, careful not to step in front of it. She didn't want to get Jasper's attention until she needed to. As much as she tried to calm her thoughts and focus on what the trapped soldier needed, Ruby couldn't help but worry about the consequences of her actions.

A knock on the door startled her, making her heart pound in her ears. A cup clattered onto the tray in the kitchen. Mallory must have been startled, too. If Jake was flustered, he hid it well behind his professional courtroom demeanor as he answered the front door.

"Good to see you again, Bob," he said holding his hand out. "Thank you for coming by."

Bob greeted him with a hearty handshake and, "Pleasure's mine. I appreciate the invitation."

"Come on into the living room and make yourself at home. Mallory's putting together some refreshments. Ruby, why don't you see if Mal needs some help while I get Mr. Lawrence settled in."

Ruby was grateful for Jake's instructions. She must have looked as nervous as she felt and sending her to the kitchen was his way of giving her time to collect herself before the big show. Or maybe time to rethink the entire scheme.

"Can I help you?" Ruby asked Mallory, her voice cracking with nerves.

"Not with those shaking hands," Mallory said. "Sit down for a minute and take some deep breaths."

"I don't know why I'm so nervous," Ruby pulled out a kitchen chair and slouched in it. "This was *my* idea and I've done far more frightening things than this lately."

Mallory sat down and gathered Ruby's hands in hers. "True, but at least as much rides on this as on those things. Both are huge and you have every reason to be nervous."

Ruby narrowed her eyes at Mallory. "This isn't helping."

Mallory shook her head. "Let me finish. Yes, this is a big scary thing. A risk. But you've conquered other big scary risks. You can do this, too. I know you can. *You* just need to know you can." Mallory patted Ruby's hands as she released them and stood up. "Now, we better get in there before the men come looking for us. You ready?"

Ruby nodded even though she was far from ready. How did someone get ready for what she was about to do?

Mallory straightened her spine and picked up the tray exuding more outward confidence than she surely felt. Ruby tried to follow her lead, but felt ridiculous instead of glamorous and confident. Giving up and resorting to another deep breath rather than posture to steel her nerves, she followed Mallory to the living room.

Jake and Bob were deep in conversation about Jake's work on Music Row and seemed to barely notice the women weren't there at all. Ruby wished they had dawdled a little longer in the kitchen since they hadn't been missed, but it was too late for that now. Mallory set the tray down on the coffee table and began pouring tea as the men wrapped up their conversation and turned it to include Mallory and Ruby.

Once everyone had tea and a cookie, Bob smiled at Ruby. "I have to say, you've piqued my curiosity, young lady," he said good-naturedly. "So, where is this mysterious Carnton mirror?"

"In the bathroom, actually," Ruby said trying to hold her teacup still in her trembling hands.

Bob raised an eyebrow and chuckled. "I'm sure Caroline McGavock would be amused by that."

Mallory looked at Ruby and grinned sheepishly. Apparently, she hadn't considered the thought of what the mistress of Carnton Plantation would have thought about one of her fine mirrors in a hall bathroom. "It does seem to be quite a demotion for it, doesn't it?" Mallory said. "I'm sure you'll find a much better suited location for it. The dining room, perhaps." Mallory winked at Ruby as she planted the seed for where the mirror had hung in the past and should be put back.

"Indeed," laughed Bob. "Especially since there are no bathrooms in the plantation house." Bob paused and brushed a cookie crumb off of his tie. "Ruby, you mentioned that there was something I needed to know about the mirror?"

Ruby glanced quickly at Jake and Mallory, who both nodded at her. It seemed that since she was determined to tell the truth, they had resolved to support her in her madness. "Have you ever heard about the tradition of covering mirrors to keep the dead from being trapped in them?"

Bob shifted in his chair. "I've heard about it, but I've never been one prone to superstitions," he said with a dismissive wave of his hand. "Folks a long time ago used to have all kinds of strange ones. Can't blame them. They didn't know any better. Why do you ask? You're not telling me the Carnton mirror's got a soul stuck in it, are you?" Bob laughed at what he was sure was a joke.

Mallory and Jake smiled wanly, but Ruby's expression remained serious. "That's exactly what I'm saying."

Bob stared at her for a long moment as the smile ran away from his face. "Ruby," he said at last, "I never thought you to be one to buy into such nonsense, even though you do give the ghost tours."

"I have to agree with you, Bob. And most of the stories I tell on the tour are nonsense. But the mirror is the real thing. If I hadn't seen it for myself, I'd be thinking the same thing you are."

Bob shook his head slowly. "I didn't hesitate to believe you about the Carter mirror. I assumed, given your reputation, that you had done your due diligence about the piece's history. Now, I have to question you. I don't like not being able to trust you, but ghost mirrors are just too much."

Ruby sighed. "I can understand that."

"So, you'll understand that I have to ask you how you knew the mirror in the bathroom came from Carnton?"

Jake stepped in trying to add credence to Ruby's assertions. "She saw it. The spirits in the mirrors show her what she needs to see to find where they belong so she can set them free."

"Free?" Bob asked.

Mallory cleared her throat. "The mirrors are a prison. They can't leave without being back where they first got trapped. Ruby is helping them get there and then release them."

All traces of Bob's jovial nature had vanished. In its place was skepticism and near disgust. "This is sacrilege." He seemed to be struggling with politeness. "I am a director of The Battle of Franklin Trust and a deacon in my church. What would people think if I started spouting the nonsense you are?"

"You mean the *truth*?" Ruby countered. "Do you honestly think everything in the universe and spiritual realm can be explained by science and the church?"

"Indeed, I do. It's faith, Ruby. I may not understand it all, but I know what I believe."

"As do I, Bob. And I believe what I've seen and done. Let me ask you a question – do you believe in angels and demons?"

Bob nodded, but looked at Ruby suspiciously as though he was trying to figure out where she was going with that question. "You've been to church, Ruby. You know what the Bible says about those things. Of course, I believe in them."

"So, why can't you believe that there are other beings, or spirits, too?"

Bob leaned back in the armchair. "Because I've been taught not to believe in them and I have no reason to doubt that teaching. It's superstition and nonsense. Nothing more."

Ruby leveled her gaze at Bob and held it for a moment. "What if I could give you a reason to doubt it?"

Bob scoffed at her. "And how do you plan on casting shadows of doubt on a lifetime of belief?"

"I'm assuming you've never seen an angel or a demon, but you believe in them. You haven't seen a ghost either, but you *don't* believe in them. Let me show you what you've never seen and you can decide for yourself." Ruby crossed her arms over her chest. Her nervousness dissipated as she stood her ground for the benefit of Jasper and the others who needed her. "Or are you afraid I'm right and you can't handle having to change your tune? Are you going to let your own pride get in the way? Pride's a sin, you know. A deadly one."

Bob's face contorted as he struggled to maintain his composure as Ruby challenged his faith and convictions. Purple blotches cropped up on his cheeks and neck as he stifled his anger. Finally, he regained control and said, "Show me your 'ghost,' then, if you *can*, but it will take more than shadows in a mirror to convince me to take it back to Carnton."

Jake and Mallory held their breath as Ruby stared hard at Bob Lawrence. She knew what she had to do, but there was always a chance Jasper wouldn't cooperate. And if he did show himself, would Bob be repentant about not believing her, or would it be the start of the most low key witch hunt in history? She'd come this far. She had to go the rest of the way, whatever the cost.

"Follow me," Ruby said as she rose from her chair.

Without looking back to see if Bob did indeed follow, she walked out of the living room and to the hall bathroom. Standing with her back against the doorframe, secretly letting it hold her up as her knees trembled, she waited for the others to catch up. Bob followed Jake and Mallory, but the deep-seated suspicion never left his face. It was clear he was going to resist anything Ruby tried to get him to see. All she could do was hope Jasper could come through enough to let Bob see a truth he couldn't contradict.

"Here it is," Ruby said stepping aside so Bob could see the ornate bubble mirror.

Bob stepped into the doorway and stared at the gold gilt frame and rounded speckled glass. "It's stunning," he whispered.

"It's a bit much," Ruby replied. "Caroline McGavock was showing off a little with this one."

"Hey," Mallory interjected. "I happen to like that mirror."

Ignoring the objection, Ruby continued, "We're not here to look *at* the mirror. We're here to look *in* the mirror."

Bob made a weak effort not to roll his eyes. "And how do we do that?"

"Through me," Ruby answered flatly. "Step aside." Bob gave her an indignant look. "Please," she added. Bob did as she asked, but remained in the doorway as Ruby took her place in front of the mirror in the small bathroom. With another deep breath, she closed her eyes and raised her hand, letting it hover a moment a hair's breadth from the glass. Steeling herself against the experience of connecting with the dead, she let her hand rest on the glass as her reflection paled to reveal Jasper.

"Miss Ruby," he said with a smile. "Do you have news?"

"Perhaps, but I need your help."

"Anything."

Another deep breath. "I have someone here who can take you back to Carnton so I can release you, but he doesn't believe in you like I do."

"Why not?"

Ruby paused. Jasper knew he was dead, but there was something strange in explaining that Bob didn't believe in ghosts. "Mr. Bob Lawrence helps to run the museum at Carnton. He's not one for ghost stories, so to get you home, we're going to need to show him what you showed me."

Jasper's face darkened. "This man doesn't believe you. He wants proof before he'll help."

"Yes, I'm afraid so."

Jasper nodded.

"Can you tell me what to do so he can connect with you like I do?" Ruby held her breath hoping Jasper knew how. She certainly didn't and hadn't thought about that when she blurted out her invitation on the phone.

Jasper closed his eyes for a moment. His forehead wrinkled between his eyebrows as he thought. Finally, he opened his eyes and nodded. "I think I do, but you have to be part of it or it won't work."

"Tell me what to do."

"Keep one of your hands on the glass and put your other palm across his eyes. He will see what he needs to see."

Ruby kept her hand in place as she turned to face Bob. She repeated Jasper's instructions. "You'll get your proof, but if you move away and break the connection, you may not see all you need to see. That part is up to you and whether you can handle what happens. I've already seen this. It's not easy to stomach."

"Don't worry about me," Bob said puffing out his chest. "I doubt there will be anything to see at all, much less something to be concerned about."

Bob Lawrence's bravado irritated Ruby, but she did her best to hide it. He would see soon enough, and then he would have to eat crow. "Let's get started, then." Ruby did as Jasper instructed. Once her other hand was over Bob's eyes, she nodded at the soldier in the mirror. With a nod in return, Jasper began to send the images through Ruby.

Almost immediately, Bob jerked backwards and pulled away from Ruby's hand. His eyes were wild. "It's witchcraft!" he whispered. His breath was fast and shallow as his fear seized him.

"I thought you said you could handle it," Ruby spat.

Bob scowled. "I can handle a lot of things, but I will not be manipulated!" he thundered.

"Admit it," Ruby shot back, her hand still on the mirror with Jasper watching in amazement as she stood her ground. "You're afraid of what you're seeing. Afraid it will make you question your beliefs. Is your faith that weak, Bob? Is it too weak to stand up to what I'm trying to show you? You seemed damn sure of it a few minutes ago."

"You won't shake my faith with parlor tricks, young lady," Bob snarled, regaining some of his swagger.

"Well, then," Ruby said with feigned sweetness, "it won't do any harm to keep watching what Jasper wants you to see."

Bob looked from Jake to Mallory, who were standing with their feet planted and arms folded across their chests, and back to Ruby, whose eyes blazed. "You're wasting your time, Ruby."

"I'm fine with that if you are, Bob."

Defiantly, Bob stepped forward again and allowed Ruby to replace her hand over his eyes. Once more, she nodded at Jasper who channeled the story of his demise through her. It was no easier to watch a second time. Ruby fought back her tears, but eventually just had to let them stream down her face since she couldn't wipe them away. Bob never made any attempt to pull away. Instead, he seemed glued to the spot where he stood, riveted by what he was seeing. Once in a while, Ruby could feel him flinch in response to some of the more gruesome details. Finally, the heart-breaking tale concluded and Ruby released her hand from his eyes.

Bob's rage and defiance was gone. In its place was fear. His face had drained of color and he seemed unable to speak. Ruby knew he had to believe what he'd seen was real. That Jasper was real. Would he admit it, though? Would he let his beliefs be challenged? Would he let his mind be opened a bit?

"The tea," he whispered. "You put something in the tea." Wild eyes searched Mallory who was outraged at the accusation.

"I most certainly did not!" she shouted.

"You know what you saw, Bob," Jake said taking Mallory by the hand to soothe her anger. "I didn't believe it myself until I saw it with my own eyes."

Bob sputtered angrily. "No, no you've tricked me. I don't know why, but you've tricked me. Made me hallucinate. Why?" he demanded. "Why did you do this to me?"

"Bob," Ruby said gently. She was struggling to reign in her anger, but knew it wasn't going to get her or Jasper anywhere. "All I did was let you see what Jasper showed me so you could see the truth about the mirrors. The truth about the history you work to preserve. There may be angels and demons, but there are also lost souls that need our help."

Bob shook his head violently. "No, this is a trick or witchcraft."

"So, you can believe in witchcraft, but not a lost spirit trapped in a mirror?" Jake asked. "That logic doesn't wash. Either there is more to the universe than your closed mind will admit, or there isn't. You can't have it both ways."

Jake's attempt at lawyering some reason into things didn't land. Bob turned on his heel, and stormed out the front door.

Ruby sighed and looked back at Jasper. "I'm so sorry," she said. "I won't give up."

Jasper nodded. "I know. Thank you for trying."

Ruby smiled at the soldier. "Thank me when I've got you back at Carnton."

The young soldier smiled a tired smile as he nodded and began to fade.

Once he was gone, Ruby finally released her hand from the mirror and turned to face the Winters. "That went well." Ruby let her back slide down the wall as she sank to the hallway floor, worn out by defying Bob Lawrence as much as the ethereal connection to Jasper.

The Five Bloodiest Hours

Behind the rise of Winstead Hill, marching orders were being passed along the brigades. Scouts had reported back with the details of the massive Union entrenchment that cut off any advance to the river. Hood had been advised to wait on reinforcements or reroute the troops around the town. The general refused to hear any opposition to his plan to lay siege to Schofield's army. Weak reasons were given that the alternatives would only serve to give the Union time to advance on Nashville and the troops that waited to rendezvous with them there. No, Hood would face his old friend at Carter House.

The commanding officers weren't the only ones who knew of the scouting reports. Confidentiality wasn't easily kept in the open space of a battlefield. In the ranks, men spoke in hushed tones about the brazen insanity that seemed to have consumed Hood to make him think a head-on attack of three layers of battlements was his best strategy. It wasn't a plan for victory. It was a death sentence.

Toward the rear of the troops, a chaplain sat on his field pack and held a small bible open in his hands. The worn and cracked leather cover had seen many battles, but none like what awaited the men on the other side of the hill. Pages bore the dust of the road and rugged campsites. Those pages fluttered in the breeze as the cleric closed his eyes in prayer. For long moments he sat still. Only his mouth moved as he spoke words kept between him and his god.

Opening his eyes, he saw a ragged line of men approaching. In their eyes was the fear of the condemned. On their shoulders they bore the weight of their cause. In their hands they each held something precious. One by one they sought the solace of the chaplain and asked for prayers of protection and forgiveness of sins should they die. The cleric spoke words he hoped would bring them peace in death if not safety in battle. As each rose to return to their ranks, the soldiers held out watches, photos, letters, lockets, and other trinkets asking that the chaplain ensure their return home should the soldier not survive the fight to carry them home himself. To a man, the chaplain refused, not out of hardness of heart, but because he would not make a promise he could not keep as he would be marching alongside them into the onslaught.

As the last of the men went back to his brigade, the chaplain stood and looked up into the clear blue heavens completely at a loss for words.

Twenty-One

From speakers overhead, jazz music played over the sounds of the espresso machine as Ruby, Mallory, and Jake gathered once more to regroup at Onyx and Alabaster for Mallory's usual coffee cure. Ruby picked at the seam on one of the tufts of the gold velvet horseshoe sofa. Mallory traced the gray veins of the marble table. Jake stared absently at the menu board across the coffee shop. Ruby was glad the Winters weren't the type for 'I told you sos' even if she did deserve it. Instead, they seemed as defeated as she did after the debacle with Bob Lawrence and the Carnton mirror.

Tilly slid into the booth with three drinks balanced in her hands and set them down. "Awfully quiet today," she said as she settled in. "What'd I miss?"

Ruby pulled her tea closer to her and let it warm her hands. "A mess," she said not looking up from the cup.

"And not a fun sort of mess, I gather," Tilly said. "Is anyone going to catch me up?"

Ruby looked at Jake, silently asking him to do it for her. With a nod, he relayed the events of the past few days, concluding with the disastrous channeling of Jasper's death at Carnton to Bob Lawrence and Bob's thunderous reaction earlier in the evening.

Tilly sat in silence for a few minutes as she digested everything. "Geez," she said at last. "That's one hell of a mess, alright. So, what're we going to do about it?"

"That's what we're here to try to figure out," Mallory answered. "But we don't seem to be making much progress."

"Much?" Ruby asked. "Try none at all."

Tilly sighed. "So much for making this town see the ghosts of their past."

Jake leaned forward and took a sip of his coffee. "I don't know. I think that's still a possibility. Maybe we just needed to ease into it instead of streaming an entire death scene into the brain of a Baptist deacon and board member of The Battle of Franklin Trust."

"So, you're saying we should be focusing on people with less of a staunch reputation. Maybe some that have lent their stories to the ghost tour?" Ruby asked.

"Something like that," Jake replied. "If we have mirrors that go with some of those places, that might be a place to start. They might even welcome the haunted mirrors."

"Unless ol' Bob has already spread the word that we're either nutcases who practice witchcraft or nutcases who poison tea," Ruby said dryly.

Tilly shrugged. "Either way you're nutcases with haunted mirrors, so I say go for it."

"Thanks for that moment of clarity, Til," Ruby said rolling her eyes.

Tilly smiled as she slid back out of the booth to get back to work. "You're welcome. Now, go on, you crazies. Go home and get some rest. You've got a lot of ghosts to help."

Ruby held the tarnished silver hand mirror out in front of her, careful not to let her own reflection find the glass yet. Operating under the assumption that the larger mirrors could possibly be from some of the more prominent houses where Bob Lawrence would surely start spewing his venom against Ruby and the Winters, they decided to work on the smaller ones in hopes they would be easier to get back where they belonged. The shops around Main Street were the sources of many of the legends that Ruby told on her ghost tour and most of the second and third floors had been residences around the Battle of Franklin. With any luck, the hand mirror belonged in one of those.

"If we can get mirrors into the shops that welcome the ghost stories, maybe we can head off Bob's witch hunt," Jake said as he sat in his usual armchair in the living room. "If you can get more people to buy into your reputation as a 'good witch' rather than the poisonous heathen Bob would make you out to be, you might be able to hang onto some semblance of your reputation as a historian."

Ruby laid the hand mirror in her lap and raised an eyebrow at Jake from her spot on the sofa. "You may have missed your calling. Maybe you should have gone into PR instead of law."

Jake chuckled. "You'd be surprised how often those two collide."

"He's right, though, Ruby." Mallory set her coffee cup on the side table next to her and brushed a thread off her jeans.

Ruby marveled at how someone who dressed so casually in jeans and a sweater could still exude class. Ruby could be wearing something almost identical and feel like a frump. Of course, being dressed up made her feel like a fraud since it was so far from the girl that was most at home on a restoration site or on the floor with an old book. So, frump it was. "Right. Well, I guess we should get on with it then. Gossip spreads quickly in small towns, so we need to work fast if this plan is going to work."

The mirror in her hand seemed like a good place to start if they wanted to find spirits that may have been less socially prominent than the Carters, McGavocks, and Lotzes. It was silver, which meant it would have been precious to whoever owned it, but it wasn't elaborately engraved or detailed in any way. Just a simple silver mirror. Ruby closed her eyes and hoped returning it would be as simple.

Turning it over, Ruby raised the glass in front of her face to see her own reflection begin to fade. Not having enough room for her whole palm to touch the glass, she placed the fingertips of her left hand to the glass while holding the mirror in her right. As another figure began to materialize, Ruby breathed a sigh of relief that it worked. Overlapping hers, was the face of a young woman of about eighteen years old who looked confused to see Ruby. The woman craned her neck to look around and past Ruby to the room behind her. "Where am I?" she finally asked. There was a trace of Scottish brogue in her voice. For a moment, Ruby thought her plan of finding a mirror that didn't belong to a prominent family may have backfired. The last thing she wanted at the moment was another McGavock mirror.

"You're inside your hand mirror, I'm afraid," Ruby answered. "Can you tell me who you are?"

The girl shook her head and ignored the question. "No, I know I'm in the mirror. It's my mirror. But where is this place? This isn't my house." The woman was brusque and impatient in her speech. Not at all like the others had been. They had all been gently ethereal. This one seemed almost irritated with the whole situation.

"This is the Bennett House on 4th Avenue," Ruby explained. "It's been a long time and the mirror has changed hands quite a lot."

"I don't live here," the woman said shaking her head in agitation. "Where is my family? My father?"

Ruby sighed. "I'm trying to get you home, but you're going to have to help me. I need you to focus for a minute. Let's start again. My name is Ruby and I'm here to get you out of this mirror. To do that, I need to know what happened to get you stuck in here so I can get you back home."

The woman in the mirror stopped her anxious fidgeting and looked at Ruby. "My name is Caroline Clouston. Please don't make me go home!"

Ruby stared back at the young woman whose agitation had become more panic-stricken. This was a turn in the situation Ruby hadn't anticipated. Tod Carter, the Lotz children, and Jasper all seemed desperate to get back home. Caroline seemed terrified at the thought. Clouston Hall sat at the corner of 2nd Avenue and Church Street. It had been the home of a prominent figure in Franklin history, but, thankfully, it was also well-known as haunted. Getting the mirror back into the art gallery that now occupied the space would be easy, but not if Caroline wouldn't cooperate.

"Why don't you want to go home?" Ruby asked.

Caroline's eyes darted around searching the space she could see behind Ruby. "I won't get married. I won't!"

"Calm down, Caroline. No one is going to make you get married." Ruby tried her best to sound comforting rather than condescending, but wasn't sure it came out that way. "You don't have to get married now or ever. I mean, you actually *can't*."

Caroline stopped fretting for a moment and stared at Ruby. "No, I suppose not. I'm in a mirror. No one can marry me in here. Not even that old prune of a man no matter how rich he is. But what if he *can*? What if he can get me out of here?"

None of this was making any sense. Ruby knew the story of the Clouston daughter who was being forced into an arranged marriage and chose to hang herself off the balcony railing in the entry hall rather than go through with it. Clouston Hall and the tale of the young bride's suicide was an expected one on her ghost tours. If Caroline chose suicide over marriage, surely, she knew she was dead. Why did her ghost seem so confused by the whole thing?

"I'm the only one who can get you out of that mirror, Caroline. Not your father, not the old man, only me. I need you to calm down and think for a minute. Can you do that for me?"

Caroline nodded and closed her eyes as she tried to collect herself. After a moment, she seemed calmer as she opened her eyes.

"Better?" Ruby asked.

"Yes," Caroline replied nodding.

"Good. Let's try this one more time. You are Caroline Clouston and I am Ruby Baxter. You've been in that mirror for about one hundred and fifty years. Everyone who can make you do something you don't want to isn't alive anymore." As she spoke, another thought occurred to Ruby that might explain the confusion. "Caroline," she began carefully, "neither are you. Do you know that?"

Caroline looked thunderstruck and her mouth moved silently as words failed her. "*Dead?*" she asked as words finally returned to her. "I'm *dead*?"

"I'm so sorry, Caroline. I thought you knew."

Caroline shook her head. "No, I knew I wanted to be, tried to be, even, but then I was in this mirror and thought it hadn't worked. I didn't know how I got here, but I was away from father and that lecherous old fool so I didn't really care how."

Ruby nodded. "I think we need to figure that part out first before we deal with what to do with you and the mirror. No one should spend an eternity behind a pane of glass."

"It's better than a lifetime with that ogre," Caroline said bitterly.

"Well, it's been more than a lifetime and you don't have to worry about him anymore," Ruby said trying to get Caroline into a more cooperative mood. "Can you take me back to the night before your wedding so I can see what happened that ended with you stuck in your hand mirror?"

Caroline hesitated, but then pressed her fingertips to Ruby's on the glass.

As with the others in the mirrors, Ruby became a ghost in Caroline's past. In the middle of the floor of a small upstairs bedroom, Caroline knelt before a large trunk. Behind her was a tall wardrobe with the doors wide open. On one of the doors hung a beautiful white gown. Her wedding dress. Slowly, Caroline opened the rounded lid of the trunk and ran her fingers gently over the fine fabrics inside. Lifting out lace handkerchiefs and a pair of elegant gloves, she tossed them on the wood floor beside her. A shawl came next and met the same fate as the others. After more small pieces were removed, her determined expression finally brightened as she pulled out a long silky negligée. Caroline stood and held it up in front of her and smirked at it. Then, she reached back into the trunk and pulled out a satin dressing robe. Once more, her expression changed to steely determination. Ruby understood the choice. Caroline was making a statement. Her wedding night would happen only on her terms or not at all. Since her father wouldn't accept her terms, she would make sure her message was clear.

As the scene faded and changed, Ruby found Caroline dressed in the negligée and tying the robe closed modestly at her waist. Bare feet padded softly across the room to her window. For a moment, she looked out into the darkness of the night, her dressing table candle reflecting in the wavy panes of glass. After a while, she turned her attention to the cord tying her curtains back loosely. Never flinching, she worked the cord loose and held it up in front of her, inspecting the length. It must have passed muster because she draped it over her arm and walked over to her dressing table. One slender finger slid through the candle holder loop as she raised the candle up to take with her. Pausing again, she picked up her silver hand mirror with her free hand. For a moment, she looked at her reflection, holding the mirror out so she could see her face and the detailed lacework at the neckline of her negligée that peeked out from the robe. Her head cocked to one side as she inspected the image in the glass. Satisfied with what she saw, she walked out of her bedroom door to the balcony at the top of the staircase.

Caroline sat cross-legged on the floor, the fine fabrics pooling around her. She set the candle down on the floor to one side of her and the hand mirror down on the other. Letting the cord run through her fingers, she found one end of it. Slowly, methodically, and dry-eyed, she worked the cord into a slip knot leaving the end loop open. She then slid her arm inside the loop and pulled on the other end causing the loop to tighten on her wrist. With a deep breath, she loosened it again and got to her feet.

Ruby watched as Caroline Clouston tied the free end of the cord to the balcony handrail and pulled it tightly to make sure it would hold. Then, she slid the looped end over her head and pulled her long hair out of it to hang loosely around her shoulders. Another deep breath. Resolutely, she put her hands on the railing to balance herself as she swung her legs over it and found footing between the spindles. For a moment or two, she stood there with her hands clutching the railing and her bare feet braced. Then, oddly, she released the railing with one hand and crouched to pick up the mirror. Standing again, she looked into the glass. "It's your life to live, love, or die, Caroline," she whispered to her reflection. "Better to die than live without love." With those words, she released the hand holding the railing and let the mirror clatter to the balcony floor as her body leaned backwards. Her feet swung beneath her as the curtain cord jerked taut when the loop around her neck tightened. For a moment, tears rolled down Ruby's face as she watched the lifeless body of Caroline Clouston spin slowly above the entry hall floor before the scene faded for good.

"Oh, Caroline," Ruby sighed as she choked back a sob. "You traded one prison for another. If only you hadn't brought the mirror with you."

Caroline's eyes grew misty as understanding washed over her. "I would have been free. Completely free. Instead—" Tears streamed down her face unchecked as the consequence of such a simple action weighed on her.

"You've paid a heavy price for what you've done, Caroline. It's time for you to find your freedom and rest."

"But, where will I go?" Caroline's voice cracked as sorrow and fresh panic collided. "What I did was a sin. I'll burn in Hell for it! The mirror at least holds no judgement for my choice."

Once again, Ruby was faced with something unexpected from a mirror spirit. One that was actually afraid to go because of what they feared on the other side. The others knew they would find family they loved and lost. What would Caroline find? Family she hurt and betrayed? Fire and brimstone? Ruby had no idea what awaited Caroline beyond the mirror, either.

"Maybe the mirror was your Hell. Or your purgatory. I have no idea about what happens to us once we break free of this earthly plane. I do know that you've been paying for your choice for a long time. You've lost time with your family and friends. Time that may have been spent in a loveless marriage, but for how long? How long would the old man have lived before leaving you with a fortune and a chance to find real love? You gave that up when you made your choice. You sacrificed your future. I have to think that and a century and a half in a hand mirror must account for something in the realm of salvation or damnation."

Caroline's tears slowed down as Ruby talked and a flicker of confidence returned. "Maybe you're right. And maybe I need to face whatever the consequences are. I was prepared to that night. I should be again."

Ruby smiled warmly at Caroline. "Are you saying you want me to take you home?"

Slowly inhaling a deep breath and straightening her posture to the determination she had the night of her death, Caroline Clouston nodded.

"Alright," Ruby answered. "Give me a little time to arrange it with the owners of the Hall. I know them pretty well and they'll welcome the mirror back, I'm sure of it."

Once more Caroline nodded. She attempted a smile, but it was a nervous and weak effort. "Thank you, Ruby." Another nod, and Caroline Clouston pulled her fingertips away from the glass, fading away leaving Ruby with her own reflection once more.

Twenty-Two

"Clouston Hall has been several things since it was built," Ruby explained as she sat in their usual spot at Onyx and Alabaster with Jake and Mallory. "Right now, it's an art gallery. The guys who own it are great and know the place is haunted. They've had enough experiences on their own, not to mention the ones all the other owners have reported over the years. Lots of weird things from noises to things moving around, and even actual sightings of apparitions. It's had a colorful past besides Caroline's death. Like most of the buildings in town, it was a hospital after the battle."

Mallory shivered as she sipped her coffee. "All those wounded and dying. It gives me chills just thinking about it."

"Clouston Hall had its share of horrors, for sure," Ruby went on between sips of her usual tea. "A cannonball came through the roof from the battle. You can still see the burned dent in the wood floor in one of the front rooms. There's a huge blood stain on the floor in another one. Like Carter, Carnton, and Lotz, some of the rooms were used for surgery and others for triage. Amputated limbs up to the window sills, men bleeding and dying, bodies stacked in the basement since no one had time to bury them even if the ground hadn't been too cold."

Mallory's hand was over her mouth and her eyes were misty. "I wonder how many people think about these things when they are touring the battlefield grounds."

Ruby shook her head. "Probably not very many. If we hadn't had personal experiences with Tod and Jasper, I'm not sure it would even affect us as much and we know the details. The plaques and markers focus on military strategy and positions of different regiments. Glory on the battlefield looks a lot different through a century of hindsight. More polished and tidy. Factual, not emotional. Monuments, statues, and paintings tend to only show the brave and determined faces of battle."

Jake nodded solemnly. "I suppose broken men with missing limbs aren't what people want to carve out of marble or paint in oils. Too much time too close to the true horrors of it all."

No one spoke for a few moments as they each thought about what museums should really have in them that might make people think twice about rushing to choose sides and rallying to arms. They listened to the sounds of the coffee shop, the espresso machine, milk steamer, chatter of the patrons, as they looked out the windows to the center of Public Square where four cannon were placed around an obelisk with a Civil War soldier atop it. Children climbed on the cannons and sat on the spokes of the huge wheels dangling their little feet while parents took pictures of them grinning. Other people craned their necks to look up at the soldier known to the locals as 'Chip' because of a chip in the brim of his hat from an accident as he was lifted up there in 1899 for the century anniversary of the town. There was something horrible and darkly poetic about the huge guns becoming playground equipment and photo ops. What was so fearsome and deadly on November 30, 1864 wasn't anymore. Maybe, thought Ruby, it wasn't the guns that were truly fearsome, but the ones who wielded them.

Ruby tapped her fingers on her black cup as she steered her thoughts back to Caroline Clouston and the silver hand mirror. Mallory's thoughts had taken a similar direction. "Ruby, does it seem odd to you that we have Caroline's spirit and not any of the soldiers that died there?"

"In that particular mirror, no," Ruby replied leaning back against the gold velvet upholstery. "It belonged to Caroline and was with her when she died. I'm sure there are soldiers in other Clouston mirrors, though. We just haven't run across them. Just about every building in this town had mirrors in them, except maybe some of the stables, and so many would have witnessed the battle. Not to mention any other murders and terrible deaths. There could be haunted mirrors from this town scattered far and wide."

Jake pushed a hand through his hair. "That's a sobering thought. Just when I was feeling like we were making some progress."

Mallory made an attempt to make the prospects seem less dismal. "For the souls we've helped, we've made remarkable progress. We have to focus on what we can actually accomplish. And we need to get busy. Who knows what road blocks Bob Lawrence will throw our way?"

Ruby groaned. "God, I don't even want to think about him right now."

"You don't have any choice, Ruby. That man could do some serious damage," Jake said. When it came to Bob Lawrence, Jake's lawyer side came out in full force. It was as though Bob was the opposing attorney and Jake was determined to crush him in the closing arguments.

Ruby was grateful for his fire, but the thought of dealing with Bob's crap gave her a headache. She never thought she would want to just concentrate on dead people in haunted mirrors and not the idiocy of the living. "I know he could, but he's one problem among many right now. If we can get the guys at Clouston Hall on our side, that'll go a long way. Whether the others in town want to admit that their own places are haunted or not, most wouldn't argue with you about Clouston Hall."

Jake nodded. "I see where you're going with this. If we can make what we do legitimate with the respected gallery owners and a place that the people all agree about, Bob's words start to lose some power."

"Exactly."

Mallory pushed her empty cup away from her. "So, how to we get this legitimacy thing rolling?"

Ruby looked at her watch. "They should be open now. It's not far. How about a walk?"

"Sounds good to me," Jake said working his way out of the horse-shoe booth.

"Me too," Mallory agreed.

Tossing their empty cups in the trashcan and waving at the baristas who were starting to see the three of them as regulars, they set out for the corner of 2nd and Church.

Clouston Hall was a stately house in red brick with curved windows framed in ivory wood flanking a large front door. A walkway went from the sidewalk on 2nd Avenue up to the front of the house. Behind the home on the Church Street corner was a gravel parking area similar to the one at Lotz. Four chimneys, two on each side, rose up from the roof. Like the Carter House, the Federalist style home had a low second floor and no upstairs windows on the front. In fact, the entire house was similar, right down to the thick molding arch over the front door. The difference was found more with the interior finishes. Where Carter was more stately and less ornate, it was clear that Edward Clouston meant for his home to be a display of the wealth to the people he entertained there. And entertain he did. As a friend of the prominent McGavocks and McEwens, he became friends with some powerful politicians, including the governor of Tennessee. Clouston's exquisite town home played host to three Presidents of the United States – Jackson, Polk, and Johnson. However, even his elite social circle couldn't save him from making bad investments. Eventually, Edward Clouston lost his fortune, including Clouston Hall.

Ruby opened the front door and stepped inside the wide entry. Flanking the high-ceilinged hall were the two front parlors whose pocket doors opened to the back rooms creating two large open spaces filled with stunning artwork. On the right side of the entryway past a huge carved ivory arch, a staircase rose against the wall and turned into a balcony across the high open space before rising a few more steps to the second-floor rooms. Ruby, Mallory, and Jake stopped and stared at the balcony railing and the space below it. None of them needed to say a word about where their thoughts all were.

From a room in the back of the house that had been added on more recently, a man approached and greeted Ruby warmly. "Out in the daytime, I see?" he joked as he smiled at her.

"Can't always just stand in the front yard at night talking about the place," she returned. "Sometimes, I have to come in and see it in all its spooky glory." Turning to the Winters, Ruby made the introductions. "Jake and Mallory Winters, this is Matt Kelly, one of the owners of the gallery."

Pleasantries exchanged, Matt turned his attention back to Ruby. "Something tells me you aren't here to buy art. Knowing you, there's something less tangible that's brought you by."

"You could say that," Ruby answered. "Rather than taking something out of the gallery, I have something to bring in. Something owned by Caroline Clouston. A silver hand mirror Mallory got from an antique shop in town."

Matt let out a low whistle. "That *is* something. How did you figure out it was hers?"

Ruby smiled sheepishly. "She told me."

Matt looked at Mallory. "How did you know?"

Mallory put her hands up in front of her. "No, no, not me. Caroline told her."

A long pause hung between the trio and Matt before he finally replied, "Well, then. That is *really* something."

"You don't seem surprised, Matt," Jake said.

Matt chuckled. "Not at all. If you spend any time here, you'd understand. Not that there's anything too terrible that happens, but we are definitely never alone. Whoever's here is protecting the house. Mostly, they all just want to be noticed, it seems."

"'They all'?" Mallory asked.

Matt grinned. "How 'bout a tour? Then, you'll see what I mean."

The gallery owner led them into the front room and showed them the cannonball dent Ruby had mentioned and then led them through the pocket doors to the back room that had a large painted grand piano. "Only a couple of people have picked up on it, but there is a man that seems to be laying on the floor. Or, in it rather. Seems he's stuck between the floor and the basement. Don't ask to go down there. I won't be doing that again."

"Why not?" Jake asked.

Matt shivered. "I went down there with some ghost hunters a while back. They had one of those things where spirits can talk through it. Mostly just got static in the house, but down there we picked up something. I would have thought it was bunk, but something touched my shoulder right when they picked up the words. After that, I never went down there again."

Mallory's eyes were wide. "What did it say?"

Matt shivered again. "It said 'not dead'."

Jake, Mallory, and Ruby stared at Matt and then each other, their mouths gaping open. Their thoughts flew back to the first séance Ruby attempted and the words whispered in her ear in the midst of the cacophony: 'Not dead.'

Matt looked back at them, confused. "Does that mean something to you?"

"Actually, yes," Ruby answered. "It means we might have more than one mirror for you."

Mallory nodded, pleased with herself. "I knew it. I knew there had to be more than just Caroline."

"Caroline?" Matt asked. "I'm not sure I'm following you."

Ruby put a hand lightly on Matt's arm. "I think we should sit down for this."

Over the next few minutes, Ruby, Mallory, and Jake summed up the mirrors and Ruby's encounter with Caroline Clouston. Matt interrupted once in a while to ask questions as the three filled in details. Finally, he sat back in his chair and let their story sink in.

"So, you don't know who all you have in those mirrors yet? Other than the ones you've already released. Just an idea from the séance and the chaos of people that brought out?"

Ruby nodded. "Right. We decided to try more of a rifle approach since the shotgun approach was a disaster. Most of the dead seemed to be from the time of the Civil War. Others seemed to be a bit later or earlier. None of them were more modern than the late 1800s, though. So far, all the ones we've met have some tie to the Battle of Franklin. Since Caroline died before the war, her tie seems to be her house's role in the battle aftermath."

Matt rubbed his chin as he thought. "So, we're looking at antebellum, Civil War, and Reconstruction eras. Tumultuous times. How did you get the Trust to take the Carter mirror? Surely, they didn't believe any of this."

Jake's face darkened as he spoke about his new-found nemesis. "Yeah, that's a story of its own. Ruby didn't exactly tell them about Tod Carter in the mirror that time. It wasn't until she developed a sense of moral obligation to the whole truth and nothing but the truth that Bob found out. Ruby tried to show him a spirit in a Carnton mirror, but now he thinks Ruby is a heathen witch and that Mallory poisoned his tea making him hallucinate."

For a moment, Matt sat in stunned silence, then burst out laughing. Ruby and the Winters could only stare at him until he caught his breath. "I'm so sorry," Matt said. "I know it's not funny and he could certainly damage your reputation if he had a mind to, but I would have given anything to see Bob's expression when he came face-to-face with a ghost!"

Ruby chuckled. "It *was* ridiculous. It would have been hysterical if he wasn't out to get me as a result."

Matt shook his head. "No, I can see how it wouldn't be funny from where you're standing. Look," he said patting Ruby's arm, "I know Bob. He's a lot of hot air, but he's basically harmless. Besides, I know as many people in this town as he does and no one will write you off just because Bob spouts off about ghosts and witchcraft. I mean, who would believe him? He's more likely to come off as the nutcase than you are."

Jake shrugged. "That's actually a good point. Hadn't thought about it that way."

"You just keep on doing your thing under the radar and let Bob's hissy fit cool off. Who knows? Maybe he'll even come around."

"I hope so," Ruby said. "Otherwise, I have one soldier who can never go home if we can't get him back to Carnton."

Matt winked. "At least not through the usual channels. We could always go the *Mission Impossible* route."

"Let's hope it doesn't come to that," Ruby said wincing.

He chuckled and rose from his chair. "Now, what's the plan with Caroline's mirror?"

"Well," Ruby began, "I'll need to get it in inside the house first, which is the easy part thanks to you. Then, I have to get her to willingly leave the mirror. That's the tricky part this time. She needs me to connect her to the energy of the house and the other side, sort of like completing an electric circuit, but she has to want to go. The last time I spoke to her she seemed reluctantly willing. She's afraid she's going to Hell for her sin of suicide. Hopefully, fire and brimstone hasn't scared her out of it again."

"I have faith in you, Ruby," Matt said with a smile. "You can talk her into facing her fate. I can't imagine this sort of thing is what you had in mind for your own fate, but here you are doing it."

"Good point," Ruby said flatly. "Definitely not what I imagined. I'm still not sure what I'm doing here with all this."

"A damn good job, I'd say. Bring the mirror at closing tonight and we'll set Caroline Clouston free."

"Thanks, Matt," Ruby said letting her friend wrap her in a hug. "For everything."

"No problem, kiddo," Matt said patting her back before letting her go. "Anytime. Mallory, Jake, it's been a pleasure meeting you. See ya'll tonight."

Twenty-Three

Clouston Hall was beautiful and serene at night despite the spirits that roamed the home. Warm lights accented the striking fireplaces and lit unique paintings and sculptures. The warm wood floors and soft golden and taupe walls kept the lights from being too harsh. Ruby had seen enough pictures of spirits that showed up in photos, some taken by Matt himself as he photographed items for insurance purposes, to discount the energy that filled the house. The ghost of Caroline seen dangling from the balcony rail. Miss Ninny Cliffe who used to sit in the front windows and shoot at passing Union soldiers, and whose ghost took to spooking guests by sitting on the foot of the bed when the Hall was a boarding house. There were also many spectral images of screaming faces in the windows or near other objects in places and positions that would have been impossible to stage. As elegant as the space was the night the four gathered with Caroline's mirror, it clung to its dark history with a vengeance.

"Let me turn some of these lights down," Matt said. "More to keep the lookie-loos outside from seeing in so easily. I'm figuring you prefer your ghost encounters to not be a spectator sport."

"Thanks, Matt."

Ruby and the Winters wandered the gallery trailing along as Matt went through the house turning the larger lights off and leaving on a select few lamps to keep from submerging them in total darkness. Once he was satisfied that they weren't on display to the passing public, they gathered in the main entry hall. "So, this is your specialty, Ruby. Where do you think we should be for this?"

Ruby had felt the mirror hum in her hand every time she passed under the balcony or near it as they walked through the house turning the lights off. "I think the balcony is the best place. She made her decision to die there before. Maybe she will choose to make the decision to pass on there again."

Jake nodded. "Makes sense to me," Jake said clearly appreciating the logic of the choice.

Mallory took Ruby's free hand and gave it a gentle squeeze. "Need anything before we get started? Water? Time to get your thoughts together?"

Ruby smiled at Mallory. "I appreciate it, but I'm good."

"Okay, then. Just checking."

"Shall we?" Matt asked as he stood at the bottom of the staircase with his arm out gesturing the ladies on ahead.

Ruby led the way, feeling the mirror in her hand thrum harder with every step toward the balcony space. By the time she had reached the top step, it was almost pulsing with Caroline's energy. It wasn't the hopeful tingle she had sensed with Tod and the Lotz children. This was more anxious and made Ruby fear Caroline was backing out. "This is good," Ruby said stopping on the landing.

The four sat in a semicircle facing the spindles and railing Caroline tied the curtain cord to. Matt sat on Ruby's right and the Winters on her left. Once everyone was settled, Ruby took a long slow breath in and released it. She had no idea what she would say to Caroline if she was reluctant to go, but held the mirror in one hand and rested her fingertips of her other on the glass. Holding it up in front of her face, she watched as Caroline shimmered into focus.

"I'm back home, aren't I?" Caroline asked.

"Yes. Matt is a good friend and owns the house. He's welcomed you back here."

Caroline lowered her eyes. "I'm grateful."

"I'll tell him for you. Are you ready?"

Tears welled up in Caroline's eyes and began to trickle down her cheeks. "I'm afraid."

"Understandable," Ruby replied. "I would be, too. This isn't an easy decision to make, but it must be your choice."

She gave the girl in the mirror time to sit with her thoughts. Ruby had no idea what she would do if she was in Caroline's place. She wasn't a huge believer in the spiritual constructs of Heaven and Hell herself, but Caroline was. Choosing the possibility of eternal damnation or eternal prison alone in a mirror seemed like the mirror would be the better choice. But there was also the possibility of forgiveness and penance paid and the chance to find eternal rest and peace. It was a choice people made every day with every action and every spiritual belief. Imperfect people who make mistakes or deliberate choices, weighing the punishment against the action. In Caroline's case, the action was already done, but the choice still remained. Would she choose the lonely safety of the mirror, or risk Hell for happiness?

After several long moments, Caroline finally looked up at Ruby. "I've made my choice. I made it long ago, right here on this balcony. I wasn't thinking about the price of that choice then. Most people don't get a chance to atone for such a sin. It's not fair that I should get that opportunity when others don't. I can only hope remorse and time imprisoned alone will soften the blow of my punishment."

"You are so strong, Caroline. Stronger than you give yourself credit for."

The ghost shook her head. "No, I'm weak. I chose death over fighting through the tough things in life. It wasn't worth dying for."

"I disagree," Ruby said gently. "You *were* weak. Not anymore. The choice you've made shows immense strength of character. I hope whoever or whatever determines our eternity realizes that, too."

Caroline smiled through her tears. "Thank you, Ruby. I hope so, too." Straightening her shoulders with a calm and determination Ruby hadn't seen in Caroline since she walked out of her bedroom with the mirror and curtain cord, she nodded. "It's time. I'm ready. But you must promise me one thing."

"If it's in my ability, anything."

"Help the others in this house. Miss Ninny wants to stay in the home she loved and protected, but the others, the soldiers, want to go home. They've sacrificed too much already."

"I promise," Ruby said as tears streamed down her face at Caroline's new-found selflessness. "Gladly."

With an apprehensive but resolute nod, Caroline placed her fingertips on Ruby's and closed her eyes. Ruby watched her expression intently to see if she could tell where Caroline's choice was taking her. At first, her expression was strained, but soon it relaxed into a peaceful sigh.

"Oh, thank god," Ruby whispered as Caroline Clouston faded from the mirror and found her eternal rest.

The Five Bloodiest Hours

Rifle cracks of skirmishes peppered the quiet countryside all day to the point where they had become unnoticed, but as the afternoon sun began to make its way further west, a quiet settled over the town. Apprehension hung thick in the air in town and the surrounding hills. Voices were reduced to hushed whispers as ears strained to hear anything that could signal the start of hostilities.

In the ranks surrounding Carter House, men held their positions in the trenches and kept their eyes trained on the hillside in the distance. Officers with field glasses scanned for movement with slow sweeps. Most men had taken turns resting and standing watch during the day, their extreme exhaustion overcoming their nervous fears. Silence reigned for ages before it became too much for some.

A lone piper began a slow rendition of "Battle Hymn of the Republic." Clear notes floated over the ranks as men tore their attention from the vacant hills to search for the location of the piper. As the piper began the second verse, a drum joined and the song picked up pace. One by one, other regimental bands joined in. Where silence had held court, song now reigned. War-weary soldiers began to regain some of their determination and spirit as hands worked faster moving ammunition to the trenches and hauling heavy armament into position around the cotton gin. A few men even sang along, thoughts wandering back home where they hoped to be going soon.

In the far distance, a staccato disrupted the rhythm of the anthem. Drums over a mile away beat a marching cadence. Eyes flew to the top of Winstead Hill where shadows began to crest. The song faded as more troops noticed the movement. A collective breath was held as every man listened for orders.

Officer's horses thundered past the soldiers who scrambled for position in the entrenchments. Hood was on the move, but Schofield had yet to give orders. Perhaps he was waiting to see if Hood would retreat at the sight of the fortification of the town and river. Perhaps he hadn't seen from his position at Fort Granger the spectral shadows advancing. Scrambling, officers relayed their positions to the commanders stationed at Carter House. Soon, word of the advance trickled along the trenches as men steeled themselves for battle. Hearts pounded, heads bowed, mouths prayed, and fingers loaded muskets. Their efforts were premature. They would not be the first called to action. Instead, a single regiment would be sent to the slaughter.

Above the heads of men seated on the front steps of Carter House came a deafening screech as a cannonball hit the front portico taking a chunk of the woodwork with it before exploding some thirty yards away. Men jumped to their feet and raced to their horses. Riding hard toward the men climbing into their saddles was a staff officer coming back from the front line. He rode straight to the place where General Wagner sat calmly astride his horse watching the advance of the Confederate columns.

The staff officer demanded orders from the general, who rocked loosely in his saddle. It wasn't unusual for men to steel their nerves with whiskey, but the general seemed to have taken this tradition further than most. Slurred words responded to the staff officer who requested he repeat them, not because the words were unintelligible, but because they were incomprehensible. Wagner ordered his regiment to march out to meet the advancing horde in front of the entrenchments and face them in the open field. The inebriated man would hear no objections to his direct defiance of Schofield's orders to stand against Hood at Carter House and not advance to meet the Confederates.

Hearts skipped beats as Wagner's orders and the repercussions of them hit home with the men. Murder. There was no other word for it. Facing Hood's thousands in open combat could be described as nothing else. Still, Wagner would hear no objection. Repeating his orders for the men to fight like hell, the general sent them straight in to the arms of Death itself. Any man who retreated or refused was to be shot by their commanding officer.

As the battalion of Wagner's sacrificial lambs marched through the opening at the pike, Union cannons sent return fire toward the hillside filling the air with thunder and smoke. The Battle of Franklin had begun.

Twenty-Four

After witnessing Ruby's abilities for himself, Matt Kelly promised his support of her efforts to return the souls of the past to their rightful places and head off any of Bob Lawrence's slander. Grateful for his help, Ruby focused her attention on finding out what mirrors contained spirits from the places on Main Street that might welcome a ghost story or two. To do that, she needed to meet more of the ghostly inhabitants.

Using Mallory's knowledge of the details of the mirrors and mirrored furniture along with Jake's love of the logical and systematic, the three set about creating a who's who of the Bennett House ghosts.

Several of the mirrors had common threads that made sense with the era they came from. One dressing table with an attached oval mirror contained the spirit of a young mother who died in childbirth. She chose the mirror so she wouldn't have to leave her baby. Another small mirror contained the ghost of a child who died of consumption who couldn't bear to leave his mother's side. Another larger one was home to three brothers who died together after the battle in a house that was used as a hospital. So much sorrow and loss in one short period of time.

As Ruby discovered their stories, Mallory kept detailed notes of specific features that could help them determine where each mirror belonged. Every new encounter wore Ruby down more and took longer for her to recover from than the last, which meant she could only handle one or two a day. More than a little concerned for Ruby's well-being, the Winters refused to let her tackle the entire house at once like she wanted to. Instead, they decided to focus on the first few with the mother, child, and brothers and get those mirrors and their inhabitants back where they belonged. This would give Ruby time to recover from the drain of energy from frequent and deep contact with the ghosts as they spent time away from the house and mirrors talking to the shop owners.

The first mirror they decided to go deeper with was the one with the brothers in arms. Ruby's heart broke as they spoke of the mother and sisters they wanted so desperately to see again and young loves that gave them strength to carry on in battle. She knew there were so many stories of mothers losing sons to the war, but to lose all three must have crushed the poor woman. How had she found the strength to go on after getting news that they were lost to the bloody Battle of Franklin?

Knowing she would need to see their final hours to discover how to get them back into the arms of their mother, Ruby reached out to the glass as all three placed their hands on part of hers. As she stepped into their reality the night of the battle, she watched as the two older brothers climbed weakly from the wagon that brought them from the battle field. Their uniforms were covered in mud and soaked in blood that oozed through grimy make-shift bandages hurriedly done on the battlefield. Pushing others out of their way, they found the barely-conscious body of their youngest brother. Blood poured profusely from a gash in his head, covering his eyes in slick crimson. His coat was drenched in blood at his chest where a musket ball had ripped into him. With a brother on each side under his arms, he was walked, if you could call it walking, to the front porch of a large home.

Ruby scanned the large double porch and thin columns. She recognized the place as the Pope-Moran house on 3rd Avenue. What she knew as attorney's offices was now filled with the dead and dying as surgeons rushed to stem the bleeding and remove bullets from as many as they could.

A woman hurried out to meet the wagon of wounded carrying a lamp high so she could light the way as best she could. Calling to other soldiers in better shape than the brothers to take the youngest straight to surgery, she cleared a space for the older two to rest as she cleaned and bandaged their wounds with pieces of ripped linens from her own bed. Tirelessly, Mrs. Campbell, the wife of a prominent attorney and judge, worked through the night helping those she could and praying over those who were beyond the help the surgeons could provide. After some time, a surgeon, aided by a nurse, brought the youngest brother into the room where the older two lay bleeding through the bandages that Mrs. Campbell had ceased changing. The woman's face paled as the youngest was laid beside his brothers. Her cheeks, that were smeared with blood and sweat became streaked with tears as her heart, the heart of a mother, shattered for the mother of the three who lay dying together on her parlor floor. Kneeling at their feet, she prayed for their souls and for their mother before leaning over them, one by one, closing their eyes in death. Over the mantle, candlelight glinted in the mirror.

"You'll see your mother again," Ruby said as the vision faded and the soldiers' reflections reappeared. "I know where you belong and will take you home. I just need a little time."

All three nodded and thanked her before fading away leaving only Ruby's reflection in their place.

Ruby turned to Mallory who waited for the details. "They died at the Pope-Moran House on 3rd. It's offices now, mostly attorneys. Pawpaw worked with a few of them on some projects and I think they'll be open to the mirror. One of the paralegals there showed me a video she took one night of whistling on a staircase when there was no one but her in the building. They won't have a problem believing me as long as Bob Lawrence hasn't gotten to them first."

"That man is a thorn in our side," Jake grumbled.

Mallory shook her head. "If we need to get Matt to vouch for Ruby, we can. If they already believe the place is haunted, Bob's accusations of witchcraft might actually make the mirror that much more interesting."

Jake chuckled and kissed Mallory on her forehead. "Always an optimist. I love that about you."

"Not always," Mallory said with a smile up at her husband. "But sometimes it comes in handy."

Mallory's optimism was well-founded in the case of the Pope-Moran mirror. One of the attorneys had talked to Bob Lawrence, as it turned out, but dismissed his accusations on the grounds that they were 'idiotically ridiculous.' The lawyer laughed that those grounds wouldn't hold up in court, but did the job of shutting Bob up, which he considered a win. After locating the room that Ruby had seen in the brothers' vision, the attorney and the Winters gave her space and time to explain to the soldiers that they could finally go home. As the mirror shimmered under her touch when the brothers found their rest, the attorney let out a low whistle.

Ruby turned to him and said grinning through the emotional exhaustion, "Are you sure it wasn't you whistling on the stairs in that video?"

The attorney chuckled and waved a dismissive hand. "I promise it wasn't me! Think it was our soldier boys?"

Ruby shook her head. "Not likely. I'd say your whistler is most likely Miss Mary Pope, and she must be pretty content here." Mary Pope had been the daughter of Dr. Thomas A. Pope who owned the Pope-Moran House and saw his patients in the small brick office next door. Congenial and well-liked, the widower doctor raised his daughter Mary on his own from when the child was three years old. A doting father, Dr. Pope sent her to the finest music schools in Georgia and Massachusetts so she could follow her passion. Eventually, Mary returned home and happily shared her gift of music with the town through lessons until she died in 1984.

Twenty-Five

After some coaxing, Ruby finally got the Winters to agree to let her tackle two of the mirrors at once – the one with the mother and the one with the child.

"I still don't understand why you want to put yourself through so much at once, Ruby," Mallory said shaking her head. "It can't be good for you."

Ruby shrugged. "Probably not, but I can't help feeling that there is something connecting them. I don't know why, but I do."

Jake patted Ruby on the shoulder as he got up from the kitchen table to pour himself another cup of coffee. "Sometimes you have to go with your gut."

Mallory laughed. "That's rich, coming from Mr. Logical."

"Hey, now," Jake said good-naturedly. "I resemble that remark."

Ruby leaned back in her chair and grinned. "That's such a dad joke thing to say."

"Now you're just ganging up on me," he said as he sat back down. "And here I was supporting you and your lunacy of working on two mirrors. I might just have to change my tune."

"I didn't say dad jokes were bad," Ruby said quickly.

"Nice recovery," Jake laughed. "Alright. Two mirrors it is."

Coffee cups put in the dishwasher, the three made their way upstairs to the other guest bedroom next to the one the Lotz mirror had been in. Across from the antique brass bed sat the delicate wooden dressing table with an oval mirror attached to the back. In front of it was a small slipper chair. Ruby walked over to the dresser and picked up the small silver stand mirror and brought it over to the dressing table before sitting down where she could see her reflection in both and putting her fingertips on each.

As she did, two reflections took the place of hers. In one was the mother, who couldn't have been more than twenty-five, and in the other a little boy of about three years old. The mother spoke first as the little boy looked at Ruby confused to see her again.

"Hello, Amanda," Ruby said softly.

"Have you come to take me home now, Ruby?" Amanda asked.

Ruby nodded. "If I can figure out where your home is, yes."

"Main Street," she said. "We lived on Main Street."

The child looked for where the other voice was coming from. In his eyes was an odd mixture of hope and panic. "Mama?" he cried out.

Amanda's face paled as tears rushed to her eyes. "It can't be," she breathed. "It just *can't* be." A sob choked any other words she might have said.

"Mama!" the boy said again. He craned his little neck trying to see the woman in the other mirror.

"My god," Ruby said. "This can't be happening."

The woman in the mirror found her voice once more. "Let me see him. Let me see my baby boy!" she insisted suddenly in a panic.

Knowing she couldn't release the mirror to turn it to face the other, Ruby glanced at Mallory who was standing beside her. "Turn the small mirror to face the other one."

"W-what? Why?" Mallory stammered. All she ever heard of Ruby's encounters with the mirror spirits was one-sided. Ruby had to fill them in on anything the spirits said afterwards. Never before had Ruby broken her conversation in the middle to say anything to her or Jake.

"Trust me. Just do it."

Mallory did as she was told being careful not to move it too fast for

Ruby to keep her fingers on the glass as she adjusted her seat on the slipper chair.

As the small mirror faced the larger one, Amanda's hand flew to her mouth as tears of joy puddled at her fingers. "My God! It is! Calvin! It *is* you!" As Amanda cried, the little boy tried to reach out to her, but couldn't get through the glass. Frustrated, little Calvin began to cry, too. "It's alright, my precious boy. Mama's here."

As Amanda tried to calm her frantic child, Ruby searched both mirror scenes for clues to where they belonged, but couldn't recognize anything. All she could do was hope the woman remembered where on Main Street she lived and died. Given the panic of her child, Ruby wanted to get them back to where they belonged as soon as possible. She was going to need a bit more information.

"I don't understand," Ruby began. "I thought you died in childbirth. His mother was alive when he died of consumption."

The woman kept her eyes on little Calvin as she answered Ruby. "Cal was my first child. We were devastated when we lost him. It's horrible watching your baby suffer and fade away. I prayed to take his illness on myself, but there was nothing to be done for him. He grew so pale, so weak. Blood dripped from his little mouth with every wracking cough. Until—" Amanda's eyes broke her intense gaze at Calvin and were looking well past Ruby as she talked. Her thoughts were with her dying child. "There is nothing worse than the helplessness a mother feels watching her child die and not being able to do anything to stop it. I'm not sure I ever recovered from it, but was hopeful for a second child to take some of the pain of his loss away. I didn't know Cal had stayed behind for me. If I had, I don't know that I would have stayed behind to watch over Anna."

"Anna?" Calvin asked, slowing his sobbing for the moment.

Amanda smiled at him. "Yes, little one. You had a sister. A beautiful little sister."

"Anna!" Calvin said excitedly trying to look for his sister.

"No, no, Cal. She's not here right now. She's—" her voice broke as she struggled to find a way to tell the child his sister had died over a century ago.

"She's waiting for you," Ruby jumped in. The woman smiled gratefully. "In fact, I'm going to help you to meet her and lots of other family." Turning her attention from the child to his mother, Ruby said, "I hate to do this, but I'm going to have to ask you to wait a little longer. We'll need time to get the mirrors back to your home." Amanda's eyes filled with heartbroken tears at the thought of having to let her little boy go again, but nodded slowly as Ruby continued. "Do you remember where you lived when you both died? I can't recognize it."

"Yes," the young mother answered. "We lived on Main Street in lodgings above my husband's blacksmith's shop. He did the best work in town," she said with pride. "He was the only one the Union officers would have shoe their horses. He was proud of his work, even if it was for the occupiers."

"I'll need you to help me narrow it down a bit more. There would have been more than one blacksmith shop at that time. What was across the street?"

Amanda thought for a moment, seeming to struggle with a memory that old before she spoke. "Brigg's. Brigg's Corner. It was Dolly Brigg's place. Does that help you?"

Ruby smiled. "Immensely."

Amanda glanced back at her son, then back to Ruby. "Please, hurry. I can't lose him again."

"You won't. I promise." Ruby smiled at little Calvin. "Cal, I'm going to need you to wait for me, okay? It won't be long."

Calvin's frightened eyes widened. "Mama?" he said with quivering lips.

"She'll be right here waiting, too. It's going to be alright."

Through his tears, Calvin nodded and took another long look at his mother, who smiled and nodded at him. Ruby took a deep breath as she reluctantly pulled her hands away from the mirrors, separating mother and child once more.

Twenty-Six

The unseasonable warmth brought out the shoppers in full force the afternoon than Ruby and the Winters headed down Main to find the location of the original home of the two mirrors. The narrow sidewalks made narrower by the occasional ornamental tree planted in them turned the short walk from Onyx and Alabaster on Public Square to 4th Avenue behind throngs of strolling day-trippers a mincing one.

As the trio made their way closer to the corner, they stopped as a group stepped out of Gray's restaurant and attempted an awkward merge into the foot traffic. Looking to find an opening, one of the men grinned at Ruby. "Well, it's been a while, hasn't it?"

Ruby smiled but inside was grateful Tilly wasn't with them to insist she ask about the job with his restoration company. "James, good to see you."

James Cavanaugh flashed a warm smile at Mallory and Jake as his blue eyes sparkled in the autumn sunshine. "You must be the Winters," he said holding a hand out to Jake. "Tilly's told me a lot about you. I'm James Cavanaugh."

Mallory nudged Ruby in the side with her elbow and grinned. Ruby rolled her eyes. "Nice to meet you, James. It's good to finally meet the one who put the finishing touches on our house. Excellent work, by the way."

James gave a slight bow of his head in thanks. "I'd like to take credit for the Bennett House, but I'm afraid I only put the jewelry on it. The real craftsmanship goes to Mitch Baxter. There'll never be another one like him."

Mallory, who Ruby made a mental note to throttle later, said, "We'll let you two catch up for a few minutes. We're going to go in this little shop and see if we can find a—something."

"We are?" Jake asked as Mallory looped her arm through his and tugged him into the doorway.

Ruby sighed. "Sorry about that."

James laughed. "No problem. I'm glad we get a minute to talk, though. I've been meaning to see how you've been after, well," he paused then abandoned the sentence. "But I hear you've been busy rehoming antiques."

"And how did you know that?" she asked.

"Bob Lawrence."

"Oh, god."

"Don't worry, I don't think you're a witch."

"Oh, good."

James smiled again. There was mischief in his expression. "I have to say, though, that trick of touching things and knowing all about them could come in handy. Especially in restoration work."

"Well, only if you're restoring mirrors. Not sure it works on anything else."

James' eyebrows went up in surprise. "Wait, you mean you can really do that?"

Ruby kicked herself for saying it. Now she had a hole to dig out of. At least Tilly could stop hounding her about working for James. He wasn't likely to hire a lunatic. "Um, yeah, I can, actually. Weird, I know."

"Not weird. Fascinating."

"You sound just like Andrew McHale."

"But only with mirrors?" James asked with genuine curiosity. "You really haven't tried it with anything else?"

Ruby shook her head, relieved that James wasn't looking at her like she had three heads or running away screaming. "I've been a little busy with the mirrors."

James glanced back at the group he had been with who were dawdling at the corner. "I guess I should go. Hey, if you find some time, I'd like to talk to you about something."

"Sure," Ruby said knowing exactly what he wanted to talk about. Tilly must have gotten to him, too. "I just need to take care of a few more things for the Winters first."

"No problem," Jake said smiling. "Speak of the devil. We'll talk soon. Glad to see you, Ruby." With a wave to Jake and Mallory who came out of the shop empty-handed, James trotted off to catch up with his group.

Mallory grinned at Ruby like a schoolgirl with a crush.

"Stop it," Ruby said flatly.

Mallory held up her hands. "Okay, okay. I won't say another word."

"Good." Ruby steered them through the crowd toward the corner of 4th Avenue and Main Street. Pointing over at what was now the restaurant 55 South, she said, "That's Brigg's Corner. Or it was. This," she said turning around to face the sleeker building on the corner, that housed a women's clothing boutique "wasn't built until a while after the time of the mirrors. That leaves," she said taking a few more steps down the sidewalk and stopping in front of a white brick storefront, "The Heirloom Shop. According to the bicentennial book, it used to be a blacksmith's shop before this building was built here. This must be it."

Jake and Mallory looked up at the building and into the large storefront windows. "And what are the odds they're up for a ghost story?" Jake asked.

"Not sure. The owner goes to church with your new best friend," Ruby said with a grin at Jake.

"Well, that doesn't bode well."

"Not necessarily," Ruby said with a wink. "She also is a good friend of Miss Dot." Bob and the church might hold sway over a lot of the town when it came to history, but Miss Dot held sway over everything else. Ruby was counting on that fact to be her foot in the door with the mirrors.

Mallory grinned. "Optimism, it is, then!"

A tiny bell tinkled as Ruby opened the door to The Heirloom Shop. Behind the counter, a smiling teenager greeted them. "Welcome in! Let me know if I can help you with anything."

"Thanks," Ruby said. "Actually, is Miss Faye in today?"

"She sure is," the cashier answered. "She's just gone upstairs to pull a few things out of storage. If you want to take a look around, I'll tell her you're here when she comes down."

"Perfect, thanks."

Ruby and the Winters wandered the shop that was filled with a variety of local novelty items like Jack Daniels syrups and roasted nuts, GooGoo Clusters, and watercolors of various parts of town printed on throw pillows. Other sections had insulated mugs, tote bags, tea towels, candles, and kitchen knick-knacks. In the back of the store was a section of lounge wear. If you needed a gift for anybody, this was the place you'd find it. It seemed like Miss Faye hadn't decided what sort of shop she wanted it to be, so she had a little of everything. Given that The Heirloom Shop had been on Main Street for years, it seemed to be working for her.

By the time Mallory had almost decided she had a use for a set of specialty flavored honeys, Miss Faye appeared from behind a rack of t-shirts with southern sayings on them like 'Kiss my grits' and 'Bless your heart'. Beaming at Ruby with lips a shade too hot pink and eyeshadow a shade too light blue, Miss Faye reached her arms out for a hug. "Oh, Ruby, honey, it's so good to see you. I tell you, I was so sad to hear about your pawpaw's passin'. Good man, that one. Good man. But how're *you* doin'?"

Finally released from the bear hug, Ruby answered, "I'm fine, Miss Faye. Keeping busy." Miss Faye tutted as though she wasn't buying Ruby's being fine. Deflecting the conversation away from her grandfather's death, Ruby turned to the Winters. "Can I introduce you to some friends of mine? Jake and Mallory Winters."

"Oh!" Miss Faye exclaimed merrily. "The ones who bought the Bennett House! I wondered when I'd see you two in the shop. Glad to have you!"

Mallory smiled and held out her hand to shake Miss Faye's, realized she was still holding the honeys, and switched them with a chuckle. "Sorry about that. So good to meet you. I love your store. It's adorable."

"Thank you! Means a lot comin' from an interior designer like yourself. Jake, nice to know you."

Jake shook hands and exchanged greetings.

"Actually, Miss Faye, I wanted to talk to you about something," Ruby said deciding to just get to the point of their visit.

Miss Faye's penciled on eyebrows came together as her expression darkened. "Somethin' to do with Bob Lawrence, I'd imagine."

Ruby sighed. "Yes, I'm afraid it is," she admitted. "I see he's already gotten to you."

"That man wastes no time spreadin' tales," Miss Faye said with a shake of her head. Her highlighted-to-hide-the-gray hair didn't move an inch with all the spray holding it in place. She reached out and patted Ruby's arm. "But, darlin', that's all they are. Anybody with any sense knows to ignore half of what the man says." She laughed. "Imagine sayin' you're up to some witchcraft! And, now, I know I've just met her, but I can't see this lovely woman poisonin' anybody."

Ruby let out the breath she'd been holding and relaxed. "Well, to be honest, he wasn't all wrong. No witchcraft and poisoning, but the ghosts in the mirrors are certainly real."

"And Ruby's the only one who can help them find peace," Jake added.

Miss Faye clicked her tongue and nodded slowly. "Well, then. I can see why Bob might've been a little spooked. He's not the type to admit to being afraid of anythin', so of course he'd be puttin' that off on someone else. Guess that someone was you, darlin'."

"Guess so," Ruby said.

"I know you didn't come just to see if I thought you were a loony. What can I do for you?"

Ruby explained about the mother and son in the mirrors. As she told the tale of their deaths, Miss Faye's eyes got misty and she blinked her blue eyelids quickly to keep tears back. Once Ruby finished and explained that the mirrors needed to be in the building to set the mother and child free, Miss Faye was completely engrossed.

"Well," she said as she let the story sink in. "We've always said there was something making mischief in this place. Frames'll fall off with no one bein' near 'em all day. Once I came in and found all the shirts on that rack on the floor," she said pointing to the rack of t-shirts she'd appeared from behind earlier. "Could've accepted they fell off their hangers if they hadn't been folded and stacked."

"So, whatever Bob came in here spewing," Jake began, "you already knew it was nonsense. You've believed in the ghosts all along."

Miss Faye smiled and nodded. "Now, understand it's not somethin' we go around talkin' about here, but you'll find more people than you might think believe this town's haunted. For the most part, the haints don't do much more than mischief, but once in a while, somebody'll get a good fright. I'm not going to go hangin' a sign in my front window sayin' the place is haunted like they do down in New Orleans, but it's haunted all the same."

"So, you'll help us with the mirrors?" Ruby asked hopefully.

"Of course, I will, Ruby. Give yourself some credit, young lady. If you say somethin' is so, it's so. You've always had a good head on your shoulders. A far more sound one than that blow-hard Bob Lawrence. Don't worry, hon, he'll come 'round."

Ruby sighed. "I hope you're right. We need to get a mirror into Carnton."

Miss Faye whistled. "That's a tall order. Does it have to actually be *in* the house to set the soul free?"

"I'm not entirely certain. Why do you ask?"

"There's a lot of grounds around that house that might be easier to get to undercover. Not to mention the cemetery that's far enough from the house and visitor's center not to be seen too easily. If all you need is the property, you don't need Bob Lawrence to cooperate at all. Bottom line is, don't let one man keep you from doin' what you know's right."

Ruby smiled and hugged Miss Faye. "I needed that. Thank you."

"Of course," Miss Faye said patting Ruby on the cheek. "Now, tell me what you need me to do."

Mallory explained that one mirror was part of a dressing table and the other was a small stand mirror. "Maybe the table could be a display piece and the small one sit somewhere else in the shop? By the register?"

Miss Faye scanned the store looking for a spot for the dressing table.

"I think I can find a good place for it. Certainly not gonna to stand between a mother and her baby just because of space in a gift shop. We'll make it work."

Jake nodded. "Thanks, Miss Faye. When would be a good time to bring them?"

"Might as well do it tonight. We close at five, so if you want to meet me in the lot behind the building around then, we can bring it in the back door. I'll make some space for it in the meantime."

With the plan in place, Ruby hugged Miss Faye once again and walked out with Mallory and Jake feeling better about the whole Bob Lawrence mess than she had in a while.

Twenty-Seven

"I don't know when you're gonna start believin' in the gifts you've been given, Ruby," Miss Dot said with a shake of her gray head. "How many of your so-called coincidences is it gonna take?"

Ruby poked her fork at the slice of apple pie on her plate as she sat in Miss Dot's living room. Stanley the cat had been unenthusiastic as usual with her stopping by, but Miss Dot greeted her with a hug and pie. "I don't know." She really didn't.

"You mean to say that seeing James Cavanaugh and Faye on the same day sayin' that Bob Lawrence was full of hot air wasn't a sign?"

"A sign from where? Who?"

"Young lady, stop resistin' this. You're a pathetic martyr."

Ruby rolled her eyes. "I'm not trying to be a martyr. That's so dramatic."

"Then, stop bein' dramatic. It doesn't suit you."

"I'm not sure being a medium suits me, either."

Miss Dot laughed. "Maybe not, but it's what you are. The sooner you accept that, the better. Seems the folks in town aren't havin' as hard a time with it as you are. Well, except Bob Lawrence, and I stopped carin' about what that man thinks ages ago."

Ruby put another bite of pie in her mouth as she thought back to her first encounter with Bob. Jovial and kind, he seemed genuine about his enthusiasm for the mirror and his faith in her knowledge that it came from Carter House. Never questioned her about how she knew. Now, he'd lost his faith in her. "I don't get it. The folks in town believed me because they know what kind of person I am. They know I'm not one for theatrics, and if I say the mirrors are haunted, then they must be. Bob knew that about me, too, but went off the deep end about it all."

Miss Dot set her pie on the side table. "Look, Ruby, there've been a lot of other people besides you that've tried to bring the idea of hauntings to Carter House and Carnton. From the start, Bob's been against it and pretty loudly so. You're just a victim of his need to protect his stance on the issue. The goin' off the deep end part came more from havin' to face somethin' he can't deny anymore. That's a lot for someone to handle that's spent a couple decades pooh-poohin' it."

"And he's not the kind of man to do an about-face and admit he was wrong," Ruby added.

"Exactly," Miss Dot said picking her pie plate up again and taking a bite. "When he sees the town isn't turnin' against you and your ghosts, that they're willin' to face their own history which includes the spirits who are part of it, then he'll come around."

"For Jasper's sake, I hope you're right."

"Trust me. I know things," Miss Dot said with a wink. "You just get little Calvin back to his mama and leave the Carnton mirror to work itself out. Or, sneak it onto the property if you have to. His loss if he doesn't want the mirror in the house."

Ruby sighed. "That seems to be the consensus as a Plan B. Not sure I'm up to sneaking around the place."

"Nonsense," Miss Dot answered with a dismissive wave of her wrinkled hand. "You weren't sure you were up to bein' a medium, but here you are. Besides," she added with a mischievous chuckle, "a clandestine mission under the cover of darkness to release a trapped soldier sounds way more excitin' to me."

Ruby grinned. "Of course, it would," she answered.

Finishing her pie, Ruby rose to head back to the Bennett House to get ready for the evening's mirror mission grateful for the counsel of the one person who could truly appreciate the feeling of not being accepted for who she truly is. Maybe, just maybe, times were changing in Franklin.

Twenty-Eight

Darkness came early in October. As night fell in what was really mid-afternoon, it seemed to make sense that the shops were closing at five. In the long days of summer, it seemed silly. The unseasonable warmth quickly became chilly as the sunshine faded into long shadows and finally darkness. It was that time of year in the south where no one knew what to wear. Short sleeves in the daytime, a sweater at night. Layers were the key, but no one wanted to carry the extra layers around all day. Including Ruby, who was regretting leaving her sweatshirt at home as they brought the dressing table out the front door of the Bennett House.

Getting the table down the steep stairs was the most difficult part of the whole process. With delicate thin legs, they had to be extra careful not to catch them on the steps as they descended. Once they were down, Mallory put the small silver stand mirror in one of the drawers and held the front door open for Jake and Ruby to carry the dressing table out. It wasn't particularly heavy, so rather than loading it up in the truck and driving over, it seemed like less effort to just carry it across the street and through the back parking lot to the rear of the store.

With slow steps to keep from snagging the table legs on curbs and broken asphalt in the parking lot, they made their way to The Heirloom

Shop. Miss Faye met them at the back door, grinning with her hot pink lips. Even at the end of the day, she was freshly made-up.

"What a darlin' little table!" she exclaimed as Ruby and Jake set it down outside the door.

I've got a perfect spot for it all ready to go." She ran a finger along the wooden frame of the mirror and said, "Hang on, mama. We're gonna get you outta there."

Mallory opened the drawer in the front and added, "We've got Calvin's mirror here, too."

"Good, good. Let's go reunite a family!" Miss Faye held the door wide open for them as Ruby and Jake lifted the table and carried it inside.

In the front of the shop, Miss Faye had cleared a space where a small nondescript table had been before holding some seasonal items. Now, the space was meant for the dressing table. Ruby had to admit that the mirror reflecting the candles and ornaments for Christmas would be beautiful as customers walked in. A fitting place for a happy ending to a beautifully sad story.

Setting the table down, Ruby opened the drawer and took Calvin's mirror out. She placed it on the dressing table close to Amanda's mirror. "Well, this is going to be another first among many. I'm not sure how to release both of them together from separate mirrors."

Miss Faye smiled, creases forming along her ice blue eyelids. "You'll know what to do in the moment. Trust yourself, Ruby."

With a nod, Ruby positioned herself in front of the dressing table where her reflection could be seen in both mirrors. Before she began, she explained to Miss Faye. "You won't be able to hear them, just me. If you see anything, it would just be shimmering in the mirrors. It gets pretty emotional sometimes, too. It takes a lot out of me physically and emotionally, but I'll be okay."

Miss Faye nodded and seemed grateful for the warning. "Anything you need, you let us know."

"I will. Are you ready? You might not see me the same way after this."

Miss Faye chuckled. "I'm no Bob Lawrence, honey."

Ruby smiled and nodded. Turning to the dressing table, she moved closer to see her reflection in each one. As she did, hers faded as Amanda and Calvin came into view. Reaching both hands out, she laid her fingertips on each of the mirrors.

"Ruby," Amanda whispered as though she was afraid to get her hopes up. "Where are we?"

"You're in a shop on Main Street. Before this building was here, it was your home and the blacksmith shop."

"Will it work not being the same building?"

"I think so. There are places in town haunted by people that were alive before the building was in place. From what I can gather, it seems to be the land as much as the actual structure."

Amanda nodded. "I trust you, Ruby. Can I see Calvin?"

Ruby smiled and pushed the smaller mirror so the mother and child could see each other.

"Mama!" Calvin squealed happily.

"Hello, sweet boy," Amanda said beaming at him. "Ruby's going to help us. We need you to listen to what she tells you to do. Can you do that for me?"

Calvin nodded with a glance at Ruby.

"Good boy. Are you ready?" his mother asked.

Calvin's joy at seeing his mother faded a little as nervousness set in. Still, he nodded again.

Amanda turned her attention to Ruby. "What do you need us to do?"

"I have to be honest with you, Amanda," Ruby said with a sigh. "I've never tried to do this with two mirrors at once. Usually, once we are in the space with the energy the spirits need, they are able to let go of the earthly world and release themselves to the other side."

"But, if I let go, how can I know Calvin will be able to find me?"

"That was my concern, too," Ruby replied. "And if he goes first, which could be terrifying for him and he may not do it anyway, how would you find him?"

Amanda and Ruby thought in silence for a moment as they tried to figure out the best way to do what needed to be done without the two souls losing each other again. "I wonder," Amanda said quietly at last.

"What?"

"Well," Amanda began, "I can see Calvin because of you. You're the link between us just like you're the link between the mirrors and the spirits."

"What are you suggesting?" Ruby asked.

Amanda's forehead wrinkled as if she wasn't entirely confident in her plan, but explained anyway. "What if you could be a link between the two of us more physically than just touching the glass? What if you could bring us together before we leave the mirrors?"

Ruby nodded slowly as she began to understand what Amanda was thinking. "You mean using me as a channel for Calvin to come to you? Like a bridge?"

"Right. I'd go across to him, but if I don't make it, he might be too afraid to leave his mirror without me."

"It wouldn't hurt to try, I guess." Ruby conceded. "But I don't know if it will work and there are so many things that could go wrong."

"Nothing could be worse than being in separate mirrors for eternity," Amanda said darkly. "I'm willing to risk it if you are."

Ruby had to admit that Amanda had a point. Best case scenario Calvin would make it into her mirror and they could go home. Worst case, they would remain separated and they would have to try something else. She hoped that was truly the only worst-case scenario. "I'm willing. Let's try it. Calvin, I need you to do something for me, alright?" she asked the little boy who was listening to Ruby and his mother but had no idea what was going on.

"Alright. What do I do?" he asked. His little voice was shaking with his nerves.

"I want you to pretend that my arms are a bridge," she explained. His eyes narrowed as he thought, but he said nothing. "Do you see how my arms reach from you to your mama?" Calvin nodded. "I want you to use my bridge to go to her mirror, okay? Can you try that for us?"

Calvin hesitated and looked at his mother for reassurance.

"You can do it, Calvin. I know you can," Amanda said smiling warmly at him.

"Close your eyes, Cal, and imagine you are walking along my arms like a bridge to your mama."

Calvin did as Ruby instructed. He closed his eyes tightly. Ruby closed hers as well trying to visualize the little boy walking toward her and then past her to his mother. She could see him taking tentative steps and felt a tingling along her hand and up her arm. "You're doing a great job, Calvin. Keep going."

Calvin looked around him to see where her voice was coming from, then continued to walk on. The tingle moved up her arm to her shoulder. When it reached the middle of her back, Calvin stopped and looked around in a panic. He couldn't find the way to the other side. In her mind the frightened child began to cry.

Ruby began to panic, too, but tried not to let the little boy sense it. He had to get past the middle of her bridge, but how could he if he couldn't find the other side? Ruby refused to give up and send him back down into the mirror, but certainly didn't want him stuck in her head either. "Amanda!" she called out. "We need your help. Cal can't find the other side of the bridge. Call to him. See if you can use me to find him and guide him across." Ruby was regretting her choice to send Calvin instead of sending Amanda, but then again, if Amanda had gotten lost crossing over, would Calvin have been able to help reach her?

"Calvin? Can you hear me?" Amanda called to her son.

Calvin stopped his sobbing and listened.

"He can hear you," Ruby said. "Keep calling him."

Amanda did as Ruby instructed and Calvin began to follow the sound of her voice. The tingle that signaled his progress began to move to Ruby's other shoulder and down her arm toward Amanda's mirror. Finally, she felt it in her fingertips and opened her eyes. In Amanda's mirror, the young mother was sobbing and holding her child tightly in her arms for the first time in over one hundred and fifty years.

"You made it, my sweet boy!" she said kissing his little chubby cheeks. "You brave, brave boy."

Tears of relief filled Ruby's eyes and ran down her face. "I'm going to release his mirror now," she said to Amanda. "Hold onto him." Amanda nodded and Ruby pulled her fingertips away from the small stand mirror. As she did, she kept her eyes on Calvin to make sure he stayed in Amanda's. To her relief, he did. She took a deep breath and relaxed a little.

"What do we do now, Ruby?" Amanda asked. She held Calvin tightly in her arms as though she was afraid to let him go.

"You'll need to both release what holds you to the earth. You're together now, so that should be easy enough."

Amanda smiled. "Together. I never thought I'd see the day. Thank you, Ruby."

"You're welcome, Amanda. I'm glad it worked."

"I knew you could do it. You just needed to know you could," Amanda said in the gentle voice of a mother. "I wish you could see yourself how I see you. Strong, wise, and with a special gift. You spend a lot of time with mirrors, but I don't know that you've really taken a look at yourself in one."

Ruby smiled through her tears. "That's kind of you, Amanda, but I don't see myself that way."

"It's who you are, Ruby," Amanda replied. "I hope someday you see it, too."

"One day," Ruby whispered.

"Thank you, again, Ruby." Amanda ruffled the hair of her happily squirming little boy. "Cal, tell Ruby thank you."

Calvin grinned and waved at Ruby with a dimpled little hand. "Thank you, Ruby!"

Ruby waved back and smiled as Amanda looked down at her son. "It's time to go home now. Are you ready?" she asked him. He nodded and held onto her a little tighter. "Me, too."

Ruby gave them another wave and wiped at her tears with her free hand. Amanda smiled back at her as she and little Calvin faded away. Once they were gone, Ruby pulled her hand back and sank to the floor, exhausted.

Miss Faye knelt beside Ruby and gathered her into her arms. For a while, they sat there on the floor together as Miss Faye rocked slowly back and forth letting Ruby cry.

The Five Bloodiest Hours

Atop Winstead Hill, officers could provide no answers to their men who pled for reasons for the charge against the entrenched forces below them. In truth, the officers had no reasons to give. Nothing could justify what they were ordering their men to do.

Questions turned to surprise as orders that had never been issued to them on a battlefield before were relayed through the regiments. Parade formation. Was it a show of Hood's arrogance or confidence that possessed him to order such a thing? It was no use questioning the formation any more than questioning the destination. Men filed into ranks and columns. Officers on horses rode alongside. Generals called out to their men to hoist the colors. Along the ridge, regimental flags began to rise up and ripple in the breeze under the afternoon sun.

Another shout signaled the bands. First the drummers began a staccato rhythm as men marched in place to the beat. Behind the ranks, a piper struck up his song with clear notes that sailed over the heads of the men in front. "Dixie." As the anthem played, men stood taller, war-weary spines straightening with pride for their homes and those they joined the army to fight to protect. If they were going to die, they would die like men. As "Dixie" ended, another regimental band struck up "The Bonnie Blue Flag" and the parade march began in earnest. Confident, slow, and deliberate. The infantry moved in long columns down the hill toward the open fields two miles from the Union trenches and artillery at the Carter cotton gin.

Perhaps it was the martial music that spurred the men onwards to fight. Perhaps it was the sense of duty. Perhaps it was the embracing of the inevitable. Whatever the reasons, the feet of the men carried them forward, closer and closer to the yawning mouth of Hell.

At the front, a cannon stopped and men scrambled to load it. With a deafening roar over the music of the band, the cannonball ripped through the sky toward the Union forces. Hood had made the first move in a deadly game.

In response to the shot, men below the hill surged into motion. A battalion of Union men broke through the front line and surged toward the open fields. Men in the gray ranks watched in disbelief as the men in blue rushed headlong toward them. There was something both brave and insane in the suicidal action. With a shout, one of the Confederate generals sent forth an infantry regiment to meet them. Guns fired and orders to break parade formation were called out. The men rushed into long lines parallel to the trenches to take the Union fortifications. Chills raced along the spines of the men in blue as a terrifying Rebel yell erupted from the full force of the Confederate troops who surged as one down the hill to certain death.

Twenty-Nine

After Ruby's orders to the horde of spirits in the Bennett House to leave the Winters alone, things had been fairly quiet. However, as time passed with the methodical removal of the mirrors, some seemed to get restless waiting on their turn. Objects were moved during the night, lights flickered, and doors opened and closed on their own. Mallory and Jake did their best to ignore the antics of the ghosts in the mirrors since they were clearly just trying to get their attention. Once in a while, one of them would tell a flickering chandelier or a slammed door that they hadn't forgotten about them, but it wasn't enough to stop the haunting.

"I never thought I could get used to this kind of thing," Mallory said as she knelt in the middle of the kitchen floor to clean up the latest in spiritual messages. Overnight one of the ghosts had spelled out the word 'help' in flatware on the kitchen fireplace hearth.

"Me either," Jake replied as he poured two cups of coffee. "It's like having naughty invisible children."

Mallory chuckled. "It is, isn't it? At least they're letting us sleep now."

"Definite improvement," Jake said blowing across his coffee cup.

In the entryway, the doorbell chimed. "That'll be Ruby," Mallory said standing and putting the flatware in the kitchen sink to be washed. "I'm getting a little worried about her. This is a lot harder on her than I expected."

Jake nodded and handed Mallory her coffee cup. "Mm-hm. I don't think any of us were prepared for the toll this would take. They make it seem so simple and painless on reality tv."

"This is *reality*, not reality tv," Mallory said flatly. She paused in her walking to the front door. "I can't believe I just said that *this* is reality. Ghosts, mirrors, and a reluctant medium is our actual reality. Weird."

"Indeed," Jake replied with a shrug and a shake of his head.

The soft rays of early morning sunshine poured into the entry hall as Mallory opened the door for Ruby. Backlit against the morning, Ruby looked especially worn out. Dark circles under her eyes made her look like she had aged years in the last week. Her smile seemed forced as she greeted Jake and Mallory with a half-hearted 'good morning.'

Mallory gave her a hug and tucked Ruby's arm in hers as she led her back to the kitchen. "You just missed the morning message," she said trying to perk Ruby up.

"Oh? Someone writing in the steam on the bathroom mirror again?" Ruby asked.

Jake shuddered. "That was weird. Thankfully, it seems they've gotten tired of us and our showers."

"Flatware is the new method of communication now," Mallory explained.

"Like spoons and forks?" Ruby asked.

"Uh huh," Jake answered. "They do struggle a little with rounded letters. They end up looking a bit Greek."

Ruby ran her fingers through her hair and leaned back in her chair as Mallory poured her a coffee. "At least it's entertaining instead of scary."

Mallory set the cup down in front of Ruby and sat across from her. "Ruby," she began growing more serious, "we're worried about you. Maybe you should take a break from all of this for a while. Jake and I can handle what they're doing now."

Ruby took a sip of coffee and felt the warmth spread through her. As exhausted as she was, and as much as she wanted to step away from the new madness of the mirrors, she couldn't bring herself to do it. "I appreciate the concern, really I do, but I can't. I can't stand to leave them trapped in there longer than we have to. Besides, we don't know that they won't step up their mischief if they think we're not working on helping them."

"And we don't know that they *will*, either, Ruby," Jake said.

Ruby's weary gaze went from Mallory to Jake, then to her coffee as she thought. "I need to do this," she said at last. "It's as much for me as it is for you or them. I need a purpose to take my mind off of, well,...everything. Bob Lawrence, Pawpaw...everything."

Mallory's smile was genuine and warm as she squeezed Ruby's hand. "I understand. We just don't want this to become too much, and we're afraid it's close."

"It's a lot. I'll give you that," Ruby admitted. She took a deep breath and let it out slowly. "I promise I'll tell you if it's ever too much."

Mallory released her hand and sat back. "You better."

"We'll say no more about it and let you decide when you need a break," Jake said.

Ruby knew the Winters well enough to know that they might say that, but they would be keeping a close eye on her anyway. As independent as she was, Ruby had to admit she liked having someone care about her well-being and watching over her. It was an interesting cross between friends and parents, and it was nice.

Turning the focus away from herself, Ruby asked, "So, what mirror do we want to take on next?"

Jake scratched at the whiskers on his cheek as he considered their options. "Any particular mirror calling to you, Ruby?"

From the living room, there was a loud crash and the tinkling sound of breaking glass. Jumping up, all three raced from the kitchen to see what had happened. On the far wall, one of the mirrors was cracked badly and shards of glass lay on the floor next to a broken vase.

"What the hell?" Ruby exclaimed as she took in the scene.

Mallory gasped. "That vase was on the table under *that* mirror," she said pointing directly across the room from the broken mirror.

Ruby scowled. "Wonder how Bob Lawrence would explain that one?"

"Smoke and mirrors?" Mallory joked feebly.

"Why would one of the spirits want to break one of the other mirrors?" Jake asked. "Don't they know they don't stay broken?" As if on cue, the shards rose up and slid silently back into place and the seams faded into a solid sheet of mirrored glass. With everything they had seen lately, the trio watching it all happen were relatively unphased.

Ruby shrugged. "I guess we have a bit of a feud going on here. I'd say whoever is in these two mirrors don't like each other much."

"Well," Mallory said with her hands on her hips, "I guess we know what the next two mirrors are. Eenie meenie miney mo to pick which one?"

"Maybe we start with our vase thrower?" Jake suggested. The words were hardly out of his mouth before the vase reconstructed itself and flew back across the room missing the other mirror by mere inches before crashing to the floor. "Or eenie meenie miney mo."

Ruby looked from one mirror to the other. "Something tells me we have a another two-for-one situation here. Maybe it's time we bring these two out and see what the fight's about."

"What do you suggest? Should we take them off the walls and put them together? Or do you want to tackle one at a time to start with?" Jake asked.

"Ruby, I don't know that taking them on together is a good idea," Mallory cautioned. "I don't want you caught in the cross-fire if those two come out fighting."

Ruby nodded. "Good point. One at a time it is, then."

Thirty

For no reason whatsoever, Ruby chose to work with the mirror that received the first blow in the fight in the living room. The mirror was similar to the Carter House mirror in that it was long and horizontal as though it was intended to be mounted above another piece. In the Winters living room, it was hung above a sideboard with lamps on either end. In the evening, with the lamps lit, the mirror reflected the warm glow and created a sense of cozy space under the high ceilings. It was on an opposite wall from the other offending mirror, but not directly across to avoid the strange infinity reflection that would be created if it was. The frame was a single layer of simply carved molding. Whatever the mirror was originally made to reflect was clearly meant to be featured more than the mirror itself.

"Alright, let's see what all the vase throwing is about."

Ruby stepped in front of the mirror and saw her reflection fade and be replaced by that of a man older by several years than Tod and Jasper had been. He also wasn't in uniform. Instead, he had on a dress shirt, vest, and topcoat and his hair was neatly combed and oiled. The man's mustache and beard completely hid his mouth while his clean-shaven cheeks revealed a sharp and set jaw. "Well," he said with a twitch of his mustache, "you're as pretty as a picture, aren't you? What's your name, miss?"

Dismissing the obvious flattery, she replied, "Ruby. And you are?"

With a slight bow, the man answered, "Colonel John House. Pleasure to meet you."

"Likewise," Ruby said not getting caught up in the man's attempt at charm or manners, whichever it was. Either one was annoying given the fact that he had just been throwing knick-knacks across the room. Ruby narrowed her eyes as she scanned the man's clothes. "Colonel, is it? You aren't in uniform."

House chuckled. "Miss, just because the war is over, an officer isn't stripped of his rank."

"Which side were you on?" Ruby asked, unimpressed.

House seemed to take offense at the question but worked hard to maintain his manners as he answered, "I, Miss Ruby, was a colonel in the Confederate army."

The pride wasn't hidden in his answer. "I see. Are you going to tell me that the person in that mirror across the room is a Union soldier? You know, the one you threw the vase at?"

House scowled. "I was simply returning fire unleashed upon myself, miss. And, no, that scoundrel is no Yank. In fact, he served the Confederacy as well. Pity he didn't maintain his honor after the war. Instead, he became corrupt and power mad."

"Who is he?"

"Griff." The colonel smiled sarcastically. "Apologies. Marshal Daniel Griffin."

"So, you're telling me a colonel and a lawman are throwing vases at each other? Seems a bit childish, if you ask me."

"With all due respect, Miss Ruby, no one asked you. You'd do well to stay out of this fight, young lady. Griff's a hot-head and a drunk."

Ruby raised an eyebrow. "And what would he say about you?"

A wry chuckle came from beneath the heavy mustache. "Likely the same thing."

Ruby stared hard at the colonel. "You want to tell me what this is all about so we can put an end to it before you and Griff ruin all of Mallory's vases? Honestly, I'm exhausted and I don't really have the energy or the patience for childish crap from grown men who should know better."

"I'll do more than tell you," Colonel House said with an air of confidence befitting his rank. "I'll show you. Then you can see that the rat deserves to have things thrown at him. And a damn sight more than a vase." The former soldier held his palm against the glass and cocked his head to one side waiting to see if Ruby had the guts to take him up on it.

Clearly this man had been so wrapped up in his own tantrum that he didn't know what Ruby was capable of. Steeling her expression to not give him any satisfaction of intimidating her, she placed her hand flat against the glass.

As her surroundings solidified and she faded into the spirit in the colonel's reality, she didn't find herself in the middle of a battle. Instead, she was in the middle of Main Street. The dirt road was rutted from carts and carriages. Hoof prints dried into what had been mud a few days before created a rhythm of potholes down each side of the street. Turning in a slow circle, Ruby marveled at how many buildings were familiar from her own time. The signs and colors, to a certain extent, were different, but the architecture was the same.

Faces were pressed against familiar shop windows as a commotion rose on Public Square around the courthouse and a large dry goods store. It seemed the town knew what was happening and Ruby was coming into the scene a little late. She made a mental note to find out why she hadn't been privileged to what started all the fuss. Something told her there was more to the situation than the colonel was willing to show her.

As she stood on the opposite side of the street from the scuffling, she watched a man drag another out of a door on the side of Carother's dry goods store. A man Ruby assumed was Marshall Griffin had Colonel House by the collar and his revolver in the colonel's ribcage. Behind them trailed another man. Griffin called back to the man, Will, to keep an eye on the colonel's son, Manse. House seemed to be cooperating and even attempting to calm the enraged Marshall as he was marched into the street.

However, Will Allison had been paying too much attention to what Griffin was doing and hadn't noticed a young man, apparently Manse, running out of the store behind them with a pistol in his hand. Griffin pulled House into a headlock and pointed his gun over his shoulder at the young man, demanding to know if he was going to take his shot. Manse's hands went up and he loosened his grip on the pistol letting it dangle from his fingers and said calmly that he wasn't going to shoot. With the marshal distracted, Colonel House wrenched himself free and pulled his own gun on Griffin declaring that if Manse wouldn't take the shot, he would.

Before he got the shot off, Griffin dropped him in the middle of the dirt street with a single shot and all hell broke loose. Manse House began to try to get a grip on his pistol again, and Marshall Griffin shot him for it. Falling to the ground, young Manse began to beg the Marshall not to shoot him again. Gasping and straining with the pain of his gunshot wound, Colonel House managed to pull himself up to his knees and raise his weapon to take another shot at Griffin. Before he could pull the trigger, a shot rang out from somewhere else. Colonel House looked down at his gun, perplexed, realizing his gun had misfired. At that moment, another shot went through the colonel's chest by way of his lung sending his body back down into the street. As House choked out his last breaths, the marshal spun around and fired two more shots into him for good measure.

Once more, Ruby found herself back in her own reality as the colonel's reflection took its place once more. "Bastard shot my son. I had no choice but to try to shoot him. Damn gun. Goddamn gun!" the colonel fumed. "Then out of spite, he shot me twice as I lay dying in the street. Goddamn bastard," Colonel House snarled. Ruby cleared her throat and raised an eyebrow at the man who seemed to have forgotten a lady was present. "Apologies, miss, forgive my language."

Ignoring both the outburst and the apology, Ruby asked, "What happened to Manse?"

The colonel's rage at the marshal ebbed for a moment as he spoke about his son. "He lived, thank God. Took a few months to recover from the bullet wound, but he lived."

"And Griffin?"

"Walked as a free man. Self-defense," House scoffed. "The boy didn't even have his gun aimed at him and I was dead, for God's sake. Self-defense, my ass. Sorry, miss."

"So, all this vase throwing is about getting away with shooting your son and your dead body?" Ruby asked. "It's not like he actually killed you."

"He was certainly going to!" the colonel exclaimed.

"And you were going to kill him. I'm not sure how this became a feud to last one hundred and fifty years. Or how you ended up in this mirror, as a matter of fact."

The colonel scowled. "You don't think I was going to leave without seeing that Griff got what he deserved, do you? And someone had to keep an eye on Manse. Wasn't going to have the marshal picking a fight with the boy again."

"What exactly was your plan if he had?" Ruby said sternly.

Colonel House, for the first time, had nothing to say for a few moments. "Well," he said at last, "I don't rightly know. Hadn't thought that far when I decided to stick around."

"And this particular mirror? You died in the street. How did you get here?"

"Not sure about that either."

"Do you know where the mirror was when you died?" Ruby asked trying to get something out of the colonel that was remotely useful.

Colonel House nodded. "It was across the street. Hung over one of the display cabinets at Cayce's Jewelers. You could see it through the window from where I was."

"I see," Ruby said. It was something to work with anyway. She had been watching the scene from near the jewelry shop so she knew where it was to get the mirror back. Something else was bothering her that she wanted answers to first. "I think you left off some important parts of that little trip down memory lane, Colonel."

"Oh?"

"Yes. Like what started the fight. Tell me, Colonel House, what was worth killing or dying for?"

"Griff was a nasty drunk. He started it at the saloon. Bastard hit me with a glass of beer."

"A glass of beer," Ruby repeated flatly. "Let me get this straight.

You're telling me that you and Griff both fought in and survived The Battle of Franklin, The Five Bloodiest Hours of the Civil War, only to try to kill each other over a glass of beer? Does that sound as ridiculous to you as it does to me when you hear it out loud?

"Are you always this mouthy, young lady?" the colonel asked irritated at Ruby making him look foolish.

"Let's just say I have no patience for arrogance and stupidity, dead or alive. I also have no patience with half-truths, so you'll just have to stay put in there while I see what Griff has to say."

The colonel opened his mouth to protest, but a withering look from Ruby made him rethink it. "If you must."

"I must." With a warning look at the colonel to behave himself in the meantime, Ruby pulled her hand away from the glass and watched as the man and the mustache faded away.

Ruby sighed in exasperation and turned to the Winters. "Of all the childish nonsense!" she said and flopped into the armchair to get her strength back before talking to the marshal. "Poor Jasper stuck in his mirror wanting so badly to go home and I've got to deal with these two idiots because Bob Lawrence is being as petty as they are!" Ruby pushed her hands through her hair and pulled at it in frustration. "I have a half a mind to leave those two where they are, except I'm not sure your knickknacks can take the beating," she groaned at Mallory.

"I appreciate that," Mallory replied. "Coffee?"

"Thanks."

As she blew across her cup a few minutes later, Ruby decided it was good that Mallory's cure-all was coffee and not booze. If it was wine or something, Ruby would probably need to be checked in somewhere by the time the mirrors were all taken care of.

Thirty-One

After a break that was long enough for Ruby but not nearly long enough to make the Winters happy, Ruby stood in front but off to the side of the second vase-throwing mirror. This one was a stark contrast to the sedate one that Colonel House inhabited. Rather it had a touch of the gaudy about it. Silver gilt surrounded the slight curves of the square piece. Corners had mermaids in playfully seductive poses made of plaster and covered in more silver gilt. While this one didn't particularly look like a mirror Mallory Winters, interior designer, would be drawn to, Ruby figured that after the weird gold bubble mirror she really didn't know Mallory's style as well as she thought.

"Well, let's see what the marshal has to say for himself." Ruby stepped in front of the glass and saw her own faded reflection in the speckled glass before it faded and revealed Marshal Daniel Griffin. Close in age to the colonel, Griff sported a similar over-sized mustache that mostly hid his mouth. His wavy hair wasn't slicked like House's was. Instead, it was longer and had a sense of the unkempt about it. In fact, all of him did. His clothes and carriage were both in stark contrast to the rigidness of Colonel House. His temperament, however, proved to be nearly identical.

"Marshal Griffin, my name is Ruby and I'd like to talk to you if that's alright," Ruby said with as much no-nonsense as she could muster.

Griff gave a quick bow of his head and replied, "Been a long time since I had a chance to talk to a beautiful young lady. Happy to talk to you as long as you like."

Ruby did her best not to roll her eyes at the lawman who was as much a flirt as his enemy in the other mirror. "Thank you," she said coolly. "Seems you've been keeping yourself busy throwing Mallory's vases at other mirrors."

"My apologies to Mallory. If she had more substantial things sitting around, I could have finished all this in one throw."

"Or none at all," Ruby shot back.

"Apologies again, miss. Don't tell me all you wanted to talk about was vases."

"No, actually, I wanted to talk to you about your target. Colonel House."

Griff's expression darkened. "Bastard. Apologies, Ruby."

"You and the colonel share a similar vocabulary. Something tells me your stories aren't quite as similar. I'm hoping you can give me your side of things. But, please start at the beginning. The colonel neglected to show me how the fight began."

The marshal threw his head back with a hearty laugh. "I expect not, the coward. He always did spin things to make himself look like a victim. He got what he deserved from the beginning to the end."

"Let's start at the beginning," Ruby instructed.

"Best I show you," Griffin said as he placed the palm of his hand on the speckled glass.

Ruby nodded and placed hers on his. In a moment, she was a shadow standing upstairs in a dark smoke-filled saloon. Men stood around her smoking cigars and cigarettes as they drank deeply from large glasses of beer and smaller glasses of whiskey. The inebriated clientele, with their boisterous laughter and foul language, reminded Ruby of a college frat party. As she scanned the room, she noticed the silver mirror hanging on a wall across from the bar. Apparently, the beginning of Griff's fight with House was in the same place that he met his final end.

In one corner, several unsteady men stood around the marshal getting louder and more vehement as they talked and drank. Griff seemed in more command of his senses than the others, with the exception of a man who stood next to him that Ruby recognized as William Allison. Slipping through the crowd unnoticed, Ruby made her way within earshot of the group. The heated discussion was, of course, about Colonel House. Each of the men told a tale of how they heard House saying that the marshal loaned his gun to someone who then used it in a shooting. The more the men told their tales, the darker the marshal's face became. He insisted that he hadn't loaned the gun and was insulted that anyone would think a lawman would do such a thing. The men continued to insist that the rumor was all through town and if Griffin wanted to keep the respect he had as marshal, then he better put a stop to it.

It was at that moment that Colonel House weaved and swayed his way over to the corner. Griffin confronted the colonel who squared off with the marshal to insist that what he said was the truth. He added that if the marshal was a man, he would own up to doing it. Griffin took extreme exception to the taunting and let his anger get the better of him. Without warning, the marshal swung the heavy beer glass in his hand and shattered it on the colonel's head, sending him to the floor with a nasty gash on his scalp. Scrambling to his feet, House lunged at Griffin and the two were soon locked in a brawl. As things began to get out of hand, the barman called for Judge Cook who was on the other side of the room to come break them up. Cook and some others managed to drag the men apart and gave them a stern warning that, if they didn't cool their heads, they would both find themselves in front of his bench in the morning. With that admonition, the judge stormed out of the bar.

House began to grow pale as blood ran down his neck. His friends pushed their way through the crowd to get to him. With some more angry words and insults thrown at the marshal's group, they helped the wounded colonel outside. Ruby assumed from House's story that they had taken him to Carother's Dry Goods next door to tend to the wound.

High on adrenaline from sending the colonel to the floor in a heap, Griffin stood a little taller and accepted handshakes and pats on the back from those in the bar that were glad to see House shut up in such a dramatic fashion. Will Allison pulled Griffin aside and began to insist that the marshal arrest House on assault charges. Griffin hesitated saying he didn't want to risk getting shot by the colonel's son, Manse, or any of House's friends who may be waiting on him to do just that. Allison insisted he would come with Griffin to keep a gun on anyone who tried anything. Finally, the marshal agreed and strode out of the bar with Allison and cheers from his friends trailing behind him.

From that point forward, the story was remarkably close to that of the colonel's. Ruby's vantage point had changed to the opposite side of the street from where she had been before. This time, she was on the same side as the bar and Carother's Dry Goods. This proved to be extremely helpful as the shots rang out. Griffin shot Manse as before and House wrestled himself loose and took aim at Griffin. The gun misfired and two shots rang out from across the street. Ruby's head whipped around to see E.B. Cayce in the doorway of his jewelry store with a gun in his hand as she heard Griffin put his two bullets in the colonel's body. Cayce was the one who shot and killed House, but House didn't know that. Looking past Cayce, she caught a glint through the window. The colonel's mirror in the jewelry shop.

From every door way, people flooded into the street to see what was happening. Ruby thought for a moment that this was an idiotic thing to do given the fact that there were still guns out and could be more shooting, but she couldn't say anything to any of them. A young man rushed over to Manse House who stood staring wide-eyed at his father's body in the street and Griffin standing over it. The friend tried to give Manse a shotgun to avenge his father's death, but Manse refused to take it. Irritated by Manse's weakness, the young man stormed over to Marshal Griffin and pulled the trigger of the shotgun at point-blank range. Like the colonel's gun, the shotgun misfired leaving an angry marshal unscathed. Several men from the crowd rushed the young man and wrestled the shotgun away from him as the marshal shouted at the citizens to go home.

The episode over, Ruby watched Main Street fade away as Griff's reflection came into focus. "He started it. Makes sense he wouldn't want me to see that part."

Griff nodded. "Hot-head old fool."

"So, you didn't loan the gun that was used in the shooting?"

"Of course, I did, but that's not the point. He had no business rattling on about it."

Ruby sighed and allowed her eyes to roll. "Classy. House is still angry at you, but it was Cayce who shot him. Did Cayce fight in the Battle of Franklin, too?"

Griff's face darkened as his eyes narrowed with the mention of the battle. Ruby could have sworn she saw the arrogant lawman flinch. "He did," Griff replied. "Most every man in town old enough to fight was in that massacre. Didn't any of us come out of that the same as we went into it."

"And not for the better, I see."

A sadness came over him. "No," he said quietly. "We all lost family and friends. Some of 'em were on the other side, too. I never knew such horrors could exist until that night. The things we saw..." The marshal couldn't finish the sentence as his thoughts were far away. Ruby didn't need him to finish it. She'd seen the battle for herself. It had changed her, too. Both broke her heart and hardened it.

"You didn't die that day in the Square, did you?" Ruby asked.

"Part of me did," Griff answered. "My reputation was never the same. I resigned and went away for a while. Texas. Didn't like it much. After some time passed and I figured things had cooled off, I came back to town. Probably should've stayed away."

"What happened when you came back?"

Griffin sighed. "Folks still had their opinions, and I still had a quick temper. Then, John Wells mouthed off in the Square on day. I'd had too much to drink and so had he. I didn't shoot him, but that didn't stop him from coming after me."

Ruby pressed him a little further. "I saw the mirror in the saloon. He followed you there, didn't he?"

With a nod, Griff said, "Yeah. He wouldn't let it go and things got heated. He pulled the trigger and that was it for me."

"And, unlike the other guns, his actually worked."

"Figures."

"I believe that's called 'karma'," Ruby said with a wry grin.

"Karma?" Griff asked.

Realizing a man from the 1870's would have no concept of the word, she just shrugged. "Never mind. Why did you stay in the mirror? You didn't have a fight with House, and you said yourself your temper got the better of you."

"But I didn't kill anybody. I didn't deserve to die like that. Besides, I needed to see that Wells got what he deserved."

"Did he?"

Griffin scowled. "No. Bastard got off on self-defense."

"Sounds familiar," Ruby said sardonically. "Isn't that the same defense you and Will Allison used to get off for House's murder?"

"Yeah," Griffin answered, then narrowed his eyes at Ruby. "Karma?"

"Karma."

"That's why House is throwing vases at me. I shot his son and got off for his death. Not sure why I was even charged for that one. I didn't kill him, just shot his dead body."

"You did shoot him before that, though." Ruby remembered the jeweler who actually shot House. "What happened to Cayce?"

"Got off, too. Self-defense just like me and Allison." Griff gave a short laugh. "Judge saw it as 'a service to the community for preventing more bloodshed.'"

"No wonder House is pissed."

"I guess. He deserved what he got, though."

Ruby sighed. "Look, you two can't keep throwing things at each other. You have to let this fight go." The marshal opened his mouth to retort, but Ruby cut him off. "I'm not saying make peace with the man, just put the past behind you. And it *is* the past. Like a century and a half in the past. It's time to stop acting like children over all this. It's over and done. Fighting for eternity isn't changing a damn thing. It's just going to break Mallory's vases."

Griffin nodded as his shoulders slumped a little. "I'm tired. Tired of fighting, tired of being alone, tired of being in this damn mirror. Maybe you're right. Maybe it's time to let it go and just rest."

"That's the spirit," Ruby said before she realized what she'd said to a ghost. "Sorry. I can get you out of the mirror, but I can't guarantee where you'll end up. You have to go willingly, so you'll have to square with that unknown."

"Wherever it is, I'm sure it'll be karma," he answered quietly with a grin that didn't make it to his eyes to replace the sadness.

"Indeed. Now, I just need to convince Colonel House."

"Does he need to go for me to go?"

Ruby thought for a moment. "No, I don't think so." The colonel didn't seem as keen to relinquish the fight as the lawman was. If Ruby could get Marshal Griffin to leave first, it would be easier to convince House to leave. Manse was long dead, so he didn't need to stay to look after his son. His only reason for staying was the fight with Griff. With no one to fight with, there would be no reason to stay. "The saloon is a stationery store now. I'm pretty sure I can convince Rock Paper Scissors to take the mirror, which would mean I can release you if you're willing to go."

"Stationery store?" Griff asked with a chuckle. "Wonder what the ladies that go in there would think if they knew what went on in that place?"

Ruby grinned. "We ladies aren't as inclined to blush about those things as the women in your days. In fact," she said with a wink, "some even like a bad boy."

Griff returned her wink. "Maybe I'll stick around after all."

"Don't get any ideas," she said with a shake of her head. "I'll have to arrange things with the shop. Think you can keep from throwing anything at the colonel for a few days?"

"As long as he keeps his vases to himself."

"Griff," she warned.

"Alright. But only for you, Ruby."

Ruby smiled and pulled her hand away letting Griff fade into darkness for the time being.

Thirty-Two

Ruby's patience was wearing thin as she stood in front of the colonel's mirror. All of this nonsense was keeping her from figuring out what to do with Jasper and Bob Lawrence. If Colonel House refused to leave his mirror, she was just going to send Griff back and leave House there. It would serve him right for starting a bar fight that got his son shot. His own shooting was his own doing and Ruby struggled to find pity for that one.

"Colonel House, I need to speak with you," she said flatly to her own transparent reflection.

Almost instantly, the colonel appeared with a grin underneath his mustache crinkling the edges of his eyes. "Ruby, I knew you couldn't stay away long."

"Cut the crap, Colonel," she snapped. House's face fell into a pout at being rebuked by a lady, but kept quiet. "I know you started all this idiocy that ended up with you dead and Manse wounded. Couldn't stop yourself from stirring the pot, could you? Had to goad Griff about the gun."

House's expression darkened. "So, he showed you, did he? Nothing I said was untrue. He loaned that gun and it ended up with a man dead."

"And yet, Cayce didn't loan his to anyone and you ended up dead. What difference does it make if Griff loaned the gun? Your quarrel, and I really don't see how it's any of your concern, should be with the man that pulled the trigger."

"But—" House started.

"Don't talk," Ruby commanded. "Nothing you say is going to make this less stupid than it is. Shut up and listen for a change. Can you do that?"

The colonel studied her stern expression for a moment before nodding his head.

"Good. Now, Griff is as sick of all of this as I am and is ready to let it all go. He's tired of fighting and understandably tired of you. He's ready to go and I have every intention of helping him do that. Which leaves you with a choice. Do you stay in the mirror fuming for eternity without a foe to direct it at, or do you put the past in the past where it belongs and leave the mirror? I can't guarantee where you'll end up, though. That's between you and whatever higher power decides those things."

For once, House remained quiet as her words settled in the space between them. The choice wasn't an easy one given the life he'd led and Ruby knew it. The colonel was full of hot air and boasting, but that was only words. When it came time for the rubber to meet the road with his fate, there was no telling where his past would land him.

"Griff is going? Even though he could end up somewhere...bad?" he asked at last.

Ruby's gaze never wavered. "Yes," she replied holding her determined stare. "He's made his choice. And his choice doesn't have anything to do with yours, except you'll lose your playmate."

The colonel began to sputter indignantly. "Playmate?" he growled at her. "That man is no playmate. He's a crooked cop."

"And you're a crooked colonel. You're both acting like children, but Griff at least has the maturity to stop the nonsense. Do you?"

The comparison to the marshal was the direct hit to his machismo that Ruby was going for.

"Yes," he replied. "At least this time someone more qualified will pass judgment on me."

Ruby rolled her eyes at the colonel's final dig at the marshal, but said nothing about it. "Good. Your mirror belongs in what used to be Cayce's jewelry. He's the one that shot you, not Griff. The mirror hung behind him in the same sightline as your death in the street, so it reflected what happened and trapped you when you decided to stay." Ruby paused for a moment in case the colonel had questions about Cayce since his face tightened as she described his shooting death. As he stayed silent, she continued. "Now, it's a spice shop. I know the owner and I'm pretty sure she'll be fine with the mirror being back there as long as she doesn't have to deal with your crap. The only way I'm taking you back there is if you promise on your honor that you'll leave when I release the mirror's hold on you."

Colonel House gave a slight bow of his head and put a hand on his heart. "On my honor, Miss Ruby."

Ruby still harbored some doubts about the colonel's intentions, but knew Marshall Griffin was sincere in his. For that reason, she decided the only thing to do that would ensure the colonel's compliance was to release Griff first. "You'll have to wait here for a little while longer. I need to arrange for the mirrors to be placed back where they came from. In the meantime, leave Mallory's vases alone. Leave all of Mallory's things alone. Understood?"

"I promise not to start any trouble, but I can't guarantee I won't fight back if he starts some."

Playing on his machismo again, Ruby said as sweetly as she could muster in the midst of her annoyance, "Surely you can be the bigger man here, Colonel."

As expected, House took the bait. "Of course. I'll be the perfect gentleman, but for you, Ruby, not him."

Ruby nodded. "I'll take what I can get."

As expected, it wasn't difficult to get permission from either shop to return the mirrors, even though Bob Lawrence had, of course, put his two cents in with the owners. Savory was already part of her ghost tour with stories of something moving things around in the back storeroom and knocking cookbooks off shelves. Rock Paper Scissors seemed to care more about what the mirror looked like than what was contained inside it. It seemed to fit their aesthetic, so they were happy to have it. Since she was going to work with Griff first, she began with the stationery shop.

Like many of the shops on Main, Rock Paper Scissors had combined modern style with the historical features of the building to create a beautiful space. Inside was light and airy with cream-colored walls and wooden and glass shelving that showcased their paper and cards. It was clearly aimed at a female clientele with its decorative touches. The store was deep and narrow, but the light colors made it feel more open than it really was. Like The Heirloom Shoppe, a place had been cleared for the mirror once it was free of its ghostly resident.

Ruby, the Winters, and Marci, the store manager and former high school classmate of Ruby's, all sat on the floor of the shop after hours. Marci decided to make a party out of the whole thing and poured wine into some plastic wine glasses from her party supply stock. Marci insisted it was fitting since Griff died when the place was a bar. While Ruby wasn't sure about a haunted mirror party, she was happy to go along with pretty much anything that came with wine.

"So, how does this work?" Marci asked as she sat cross-legged on the wood floor with her wine glass in one hand balanced on her knee. "Do you have to do something or does the guy just go away on his own?"

"I have to do something," Ruby answered. "But it won't look like much to you."

Marci took a swig of her wine and chuckled. "I can't believe you can talk to dead people. Why didn't you tell me when we were in school?"

"I didn't know I could do it until recently. Still not sure why or how I can."

"Well, between your grandmother talking to ghosts all the time and living across the street from Miss Dot, you were bound to pick some of that up, weren't you?" Marci said grinning as if she solved the question of the meaning of life or something.

"Maybe," Ruby said with a shrug.

"Or," Jake chimed in, "Maybe she's special on her own merit."

Mallory winked at Ruby, who blushed but smiled gratefully. "Thanks," Ruby said softly.

"Shall we get this show on the road, Ruby?" Mallory asked.

"Might as well." With the mirror on the floor propped up against the register counter, Ruby scooted herself in front of it to where she could see her reflection. Marshall Daniel Griffin began to replace her reflection as she placed her hand on the glass to solidify her connection to him.

"Ruby," Griff said with a genuine smile at her. "This is a far cry from the saloon," he said looking around at the feminine stationery shop.

"Maybe. We have booze, though. Does that make it feel more like you belong here?" Ruby asked with a mischievous grin.

Griff chuckled. "It does. It sure does," he replied.

"Are you ready to go?" she asked as the smile faded.

The marshal nodded slowly. "It'll be interesting to see where I end up."

"It will. Maybe there's time to atone for your actions, if you're so inclined."

"Can't hurt to try," Griff said and closed his eyes. His face was drawn and tight. Exhaustion seemed to have aged him since their last encounter. It was as though deciding to reconcile with his past and let it go had aged him several years. Ruby gave him time with his thoughts and his confessor, whoever that may be, until Griff opened his eyes again. As he did, the strain seemed to melt away some as peace with his decision took its place. "I'm ready now. Whatever will be, will be."

Ruby nodded and placed her other hand on the mirror as Griff did the same. "There's nothing to hold you here anymore. Nothing to fight about, feel guilty about, or harbor anger about. What's done is done and it's time for you to release the past and release yourself."

"Thank you, Ruby, for helping me see what really matters. What's really worth dying for and what isn't. If I'd only seen it sooner."

"What matters is that you see it now," Ruby said gently.

"Goodbye, Ruby," Griff said as tears gathered on his lashes. "Wish me luck."

"Good luck, Griff. And goodbye." Ruby smiled warmly as Griff took a deep breath. What happened to him next was beyond her control. She hoped his moment of confession hadn't come too late.

With a nod, she watched the marshal begin to fade. She watched his face closely to see if there was any sign of where he was going, but his expression was nothing more than resolute. He would bravely face whatever awaited him, and for that, Ruby respected the wayward lawman.

With Griff's mirror removed, Colonel House had been well-behaved. No vase casualties at all. Even so, Ruby wondered if getting him out of the mirror was going to be as easy as setting Griff free. House was definitely the more obstinate of the two men.

As the little shop bell chimed as she opened the door to Savory, Ruby took a deep breath. Nothing smelled quite as delicious as the spice shop. There was something warm and inviting about the fragrance of all the herbs and spices blending in the air. It reminded Ruby of her grandmother's soups. She could make soup out of anything. No soup was ever like another because there was no recipe other than whatever she had in the vegetable drawer or pantry. No matter what went in the pot, the slow simmering soup always filled the house with delicious warmth.

Mallory and Jake did the same thing. A deep breath and a smile seemed to be how everyone entered Savory. Dawn, the owner, chuckled at the register counter. Streaks of gray showed in Dawn's dark hair, but her face certainly didn't show her age. With her kids being older teenagers, Ruby guessed Dawn was in her forties, but couldn't really say for sure. "That never gets old," Dawn said. "I know I'm doing something right when folks walk in and have to stop and smell the aroma."

"It's amazing," said Mallory. "What exactly am I smelling?"

"Nothing in particular. It's just what happens when you have all sorts of spices in one place." Dawn turned her attention to Jake and the mirror he was holding by the thick picture hanging wire. "Here, let's set that thing down before that picture wire takes a finger off."

Jake followed Dawn to the back of the store near the door to the storeroom. "That thing is heavier than you think after carrying it around a while," he said rubbing at the purple line across the middle of his fingers put there by the weight of the mirror on the wire.

"I imagine so," Dawn said taking a look at the mark. "Want some ice for that?"

"No, but thanks. I'm good."

Ruby crouched down by the mirror that was now leaning against the back wall of the shop. "I'm guessing you chose this particular spot for a reason?"

Dawn nodded. "I figured since most everything that happens in the shop seems to be concentrated in the storeroom, we might as well be close to the action."

"Makes sense to me," Mallory replied.

Dawn sat next to Ruby on the floor next to the mirror. "This Colonel House sounds like a piece of work."

"He was, is. Let's just hope he's bored without the marshal to mess with and wants to go. He was enough trouble alive. Can't have him making more trouble dead."

"Well," Dawn said slapping her hands down onto her knees. "Let's do it, then."

Ruby nodded and moved in front of the mirror. Her reflection faded and Colonel House came into view as Ruby's hand met the mirror.

He was smiling under his mustache again, and Ruby would have sworn there was mischief in his eyes. "Miss Ruby," he said genially. "Always a pleasure to see your pretty face."

"Take a good look, Colonel. This is your last chance."

The look of mischief became more sly than playful and made Ruby nervous that this wasn't going to go to plan. Something deep in her gut was warning her to tread lightly. "It certainly doesn't have to be the last time, you know," House said silkily. "There's really no rush, is there?"

"As a matter of fact, there is. Mallory and Jake would like their things left alone and Dawn here would like a mirror that doesn't cause trouble. So, yes, Colonel, I'm afraid the time has come."

"And how do I know you sent that mongrel of a marshal off to where he belongs? Maybe I should stick around and make sure he doesn't cause you any trouble. It's the gentlemanly thing to do, Miss Ruby."

"A gentleman would do what a lady asks him to do and leave when its polite to do so," Ruby returned.

House laughed. "You're a feisty one, aren't you? That's not making it any more appealing to leave, you know."

"You promised, remember?" Ruby shot back. "On you honor."

"Honor is for the living. There's no one but you who can call me out on my honor, or lack thereof."

"You can keep your promise, or I can leave you in the mirror. Regardless, this is the last time you and I will meet." Ruby was growing impatient and struggled to keep her temper in check.

"Now, now, missy, don't say that. Besides, I'd consider it an honor to defend yours from that snake of a lawman." Colonel House's mouth curled and his eyes crinkled. He was enjoying his flirtation with Ruby a little too much for her liking. She knew she wasn't the reason he was staying and it was starting to really piss her off.

"There's no one to defend me from, Colonel. Griff left."

Colonel House smoothed his mustache as he thought about his next move. "Griff was always a wily one. You can't be sure he's gone and neither can I. I'd hate to see him start trouble for you again."

"I know he's gone. I could feel him leave. It's, well, sort of what I do." Ruby still wasn't comfortable talking about what she could feel and see even though it was becoming more routine. It just sounded idiotic every time she said it out loud.

"While I hate to question your talents, Miss Ruby, it's going to take more than words of reassurance to convince me to leave this mirror."

"Fine," Ruby said exasperated. "I'll prove it. Come on, we're going across the street. Sit tight for a minute," she instructed as she released her hand and the Colonel's reflection vanished. Ruby stood up in a huff and swung around to look at Jake as the others all got to their feet.

"What's going on?" Mallory asked.

"Arrogance and defiance. The man's a petulant child!" Ruby tried to regain her composure for a moment. It irritated her that House was getting to her as much as his refusal to leave the mirror was.

"Why, exactly, are we going across the street?" Jake asked.

For a moment, Ruby hadn't thought about the fact that the Winters and Dawn couldn't hear the other side of the conversation. "He wants proof that Griff is gone. Says he can't leave me here defenseless against the marshal."

"Good grief," Jake said rolling his eyes. "Well, let's get this over with. I'm assuming we're taking his mirror over to Rock Paper Scissors?"

"Yep," Ruby said. "Wanna come along?" she asked Dawn.

"Absolutely!" she replied. "Just let me lock up first."

Moments later, the group were gathered on the sidewalk outside the spice shop. Jake carried the mirror by the wire with his other hand, apparently trying to balance out the pain. Almost directly across Main was the stationery store. Even though it was closed, lights were still on which meant Marci was still closing up.

Ruby knocked on the glass door of Rock Paper Scissors and startled Marci. Ruby mouthed 'sorry' and waved her over to the door. Marci grabbed the keys off the counter and unlocked the shop. "What's going on?" She looked down and saw the mirror Jake was balancing on the top of his foot to take some of the weight off his hand. "Another mirror that belongs here?"

"No, just a jerky spirit who wants proof the other one is gone. Mind if we take the marshal's mirror down so I can straighten the colonel out?" Ruby asked.

"Anything you need. I'll get the step ladder."

Jake set the colonel's mirror against the counter and climbed up to take the marshal's mirror off the wall and down the ladder. Once the two mirrors were down on the floor, he sat behind Griff's to hold it up facing the colonel's. "How's this?" he asked.

Ruby sat between the mirrors and held her hands out. "Perfect. Thanks. Time to set this man straight."

Positioning herself in front of the glass of both mirrors, she reached out and placed her palm on Colonel House's mirror. He shimmered into view with a wry grin on his face. "I told you I'd see you again," he said with a chuckle.

"You're splitting hairs, now, Colonel," Ruby retorted. "If thinking Griff is still in his mirror is what's keeping you here, let's get this over with."

House said nothing, but smirked as Ruby placed her hand on Griff's mirror. For an instant she feared the mirror wouldn't be empty. That maybe the marshal was sentenced to do penance trapped in it for his crimes. She held her breath and waited for several long moments. Nothing. The mirror was decidedly uninhabited.

"He's not here, Colonel." Ruby met House's eyes and saw a glimmer of something other than the smug defiance he was trying to project. It was fear.

"I told you, he can't be trusted. Just because you summon him doesn't mean he has to come forward."

"Could you resist it if I called you and you didn't want to come?"

"Now, why would I want to do that?" he asked, his smirk returning.

"Answer the question."

House sighed. "No. I couldn't. Part of the bargain with staying behind, I suppose."

"Then, you have to accept that Griff is gone and you have no reason to stay anymore." Ruby took her hand off the empty mirror and turned to face Colonel House. "Well?"

Defeated, the colonel's expression changed from defiant teasing to genuine sorrow. "That's not entirely true, Ruby."

"Explain."

House shook his head and lowered his eyes. "I've done some rotten things in my life. Things I'm not proud of. Things that hurt others for my own gain. I've killed men in battle. Even in the chaos, you don't forget the faces of the ones you cut down. Maybe not the ones at a distance. Those you can fool yourself into thinking someone else hit them. But the ones right in front of you – the ones you look in the eyes – those you never forget." He paused for a long moment as he fought back tears. When he finally continued, his voice was raspy and stilted. "You can't forget something like that. The fear. The horror. The battle ends, the war ends, but life goes on. But it's not the same. Every time you close your eyes, those faces are there. Horrors in the night. Terror for your immortal soul. What will your death be because of the ones you sent to theirs? Soldiers can't show the wounds on the inside. Missing limbs are a badge of honor. Broken men on the outside are revered or pitied. Broken men on the inside have to hide it as best they can and pray it doesn't shatter them completely."

Ruby let the words hang between them as she thought about what

House went through. His bravado was to cover his own brokenness. Mental and emotional anguish that couldn't be shared. Rage at having a normal existence without trauma ripped away from him was channeled into conflict with others because he couldn't deal with the conflict within.

"Griff isn't what kept you here, is it?" she whispered.

House shook his head. "No, it was my own demons that kept me here. Trouble I'd caused because I couldn't face what I'd become after the war. I needed to make peace with myself, but I couldn't face that. So, I took it out on others not thinking about what the ultimate consequence could be. There always seemed like there was so much time to make amends. And then, there wasn't."

"You and Griff have more in common than you realize, you know." Ruby's gaze softened along with her heart as she saw the bravado for what it really was. A mask that kept people from seeing him as he truly was, even himself after a while.

"The marshal was afraid of where he would end up?"

Ruby nodded. "He was, but he came to grips with the fact that he couldn't run forever and that maybe repentance could ease the consequence. He was tired, Colonel. Tired of fighting. Tired of hiding. I suspect you are, too."

"Never have truer words been spoken. I didn't want to admit it until now," said the colonel, his face beginning to show the strain of pretending to be something he wasn't for over a century and a half. "It's time, Ruby. Time to face what I've done and what I am. Time to face whatever the consequences may be."

Ruby nodded. "We'll take you back to Savory. You need the energy there to help you." House bowed his head and faded away a more reticent man than the one that appeared moments earlier.

Back in position at the spice shop, Ruby asked the colonel, "Do you want some time to make peace with the universe first? You aren't the same man you were when you decided to stay."

House nodded, and, once again, Ruby let the man in the mirror have some time with his own thoughts, soul, and creator. As he sat with his eyes closed, tears began to streak down his face and dampen his mustache. He didn't seem to notice or care. His mind was elsewhere.

After several long moments, his glistening eyes opened and he finally swept the tears from his face. "Thank you, Ruby," he said softly. For the first time, Ruby felt like the colonel was speaking from his heart. "It's time. Manse will be waiting for me."

"Of course, he is. Your son is a good man. This part of the process is all yours. I'm your channel for the energy of the place and the mirror, but you have to go on your own." She smiled warmly. "Whenever you're ready."

An exhausted but genuine smile crossed Colonel House's face as he straightened his shoulders, ready to face whatever was coming next with bravery. With a nod of his head to Ruby, he slowly pulled his hand away from hers. Once more, like with Griff, she watched for signs of his fate, but there were none to be seen. Where the feuding men ended up was entirely between the universe and their souls.

The Five Bloodiest Hours

The smoke of cannon fire obliterated the golden afternoon sun. In the haze, men hoped the soldiers at the other end of their guns were enemies. In truth, it was nearly impossible to tell. Eyes burned and watered as they blinked back the dust and stinging smoke. As the fighting intensified, darkness began to fall along with the bodies.

Soldiers converged on the trenches in front of the battered Carter House. Cannon fire blasted grapeshot and cannon balls at the troops racing down the hill, scattering them like dry leaves. Minie balls from the Confederates responding to the onslaught perforated the plantation's farm office. At the main house, windows shattered and furniture inside splintered. Cannons took aim from their positions further from the entrenchments. Some shots had gone too far and hit homes in town forcing the Confederate officers to order them pulled further back to keep the assault on the enemy instead of the citizenry. The Lotz House bore the brunt of the poor aim of the first shots that were supposed to take out the gunners at the Carter cotton gin. The entire south wall of the house collapsed leaving the home's interior exposed to the ravages of battle.

The structural collapses were lost to the background of the minds of the men that collided with each other between the plantation and the Lotz House. Control of Columbia Pike that split the properties was the main objective, but that didn't mean it was the only objective. Fighting stretched all the way to Carnton Plantation two miles away from ground zero at Carter House. As far as anyone could see, men rushed their enemies and fell back to reload and regroup. Surge after agonizing surge.

Night shrouded the combatants turning the flashes of the guns and cannons into eerie fireworks in the hazy darkness. Screams of the dying and wounded filled the spaces between the crack of rifle-muskets and pistols. Thundering of the big armament drowned out the cacophony until the echoes faded. Chilling shrieks of dying horses added to Death's dark symphony.

Men in gray climbed over spikes that shredded their clothes and skin to reach their foes only to be met with close range shots that dropped their lifeless bodies into the trenches below. One after another, the soldiers attacked. One after another, they fell on top of the ones before them. Men in blue fought for balance on the dead under their feet as they loaded and took aim again and again.

Even the entrenchments and spikes couldn't keep all of the Rebels from breaching the battlements. Ones that made it through the melee shot at anything that moved and stabbed bayonets at men who charged them hoping they were cutting down the enemy and not their own. Bodies continued to pile up as surge and repulse moved in lockstep. Horses fell dead with their riders, some already lifeless in the saddle. Other riders scrambled out from under the beasts with broken limbs slowing their retreat. Many were captured by Union soldiers and taken to the mill. Fewer of the men in blue were captured by the Confederates and taken back up the hillside out of the battle. Come morning, being a prisoner of war on either side would be seen as a saving grace.

Trenches dug to protect soldiers ran crimson with blood having quickly become mass graves. Uniform color didn't matter as Death stalked the lines hungry for more. It licked blood-stained teeth as its claws tore at any man in its path. Some wrenched free to continue the fight, while others succumbed to Death's icy grip. Between the Carter and Lotz houses, there was no room for the slaughtered to lay. Instead, Death began piling its spoils into greedy heaps. Corpses could not fall for the dead at their feet. Instead, they stood like bloodied and broken scarecrows, young faces still and gray with staring sightless eyes. Beneath the night sky, Cruelty and Terror walked beside the specter Death. And Death took no pity, gave no mercy as it reaped souls like a fall harvest under the November moon.

Thirty-Three

Onyx and Alabaster was bustling when Ruby walked in the door. A line stretched down the narrow space between the tables. Brentwood moms and tourists were making the most of the beautiful crisp day by stopping in for a coffee to warm their hands as they shopped. At least most of them weren't staying. There wouldn't have been tables for them if they'd wanted to. Ruby was in the mood for her London Fog since she was chilled after her walk over, but didn't have it in her to wait in that line. With a defeated and disappointed sigh, she made her way through the throngs to the gold sofa in the front hoping Mallory and Jake had managed to snag it. Luck was on their side and they waved Ruby over. Tilly was running around like a mad woman behind the coffee bar, but noticed Ruby as she slid into the booth. She gave Ruby a thumbs up and a wink. Sometimes it was good to have the right friends.

"Look at this place," Mallory said with a wave of her slender hand. "It's madness!"

"I guess word's gotten out that it's the best coffee shop in town," Ruby said scanning the crowd. "I'm going to have to throttle whoever is responsible for that." She forced a chuckle, but was actually quite irritated.

"Makes hiding in plain sight even easier, though," Jake, Mr. Logic, replied. "More conversations to drown out ours."

Ruby had to admit that as annoying as it was to not have their nice quiet coffee shop to themselves, Jake had a point. "I guess," she relented.

Mallory pushed her coffee cup back, like she always did when she had something important on her mind. "We've only got three mirrors left. Jasper's and two mystery ones."

"Well, since Bob hasn't told us we can put Jasper's back in Carnton, we'll have to go with what's behind door number two," said Ruby with a groan.

Jake rubbed at the whiskers on his face and thought for a moment. "We haven't talked to Bob in a while. He has to know more mirrors and ghosts have gone home. Maybe he's ready to cave, but won't be the one to bring it up. It's not like he's the type of guy to willingly admit he was wrong."

"Very true," Ruby conceded. "It might be worth another shot. Maybe somewhere other than the Bennett House. Somewhere neutral."

"Somewhere like a coffee shop?" Mallory asked.

"Somewhere like a coffee shop," Ruby agreed. "It will seem neutral enough to him, but it still gives us a little in the way of home court advantage."

Tilly managed to extricate herself from behind the counter and horde of caffeine addicts long enough to bring Ruby her drink. "One large cinnamon orange London Fog with skim," she said out of breath.

"Thanks Til," Ruby said. "You're the best. I'll pay you when the crowd thins."

"Sure thing. I know you're good for it, and where to find you if you aren't," Tilly said with her usual grin. "What are we scheming about over here?"

"A plot to overthrow Bob Lawrence," Jake answered dramatically.

"Sounds exciting," Tilly said, her eyes widening.

"It does, doesn't it?" asked Jake. "Sounds a lot better than 'asking Bob to coffee so we can beg him to take Jasper to Carnton.'"

"Oh, definitely," agreed Tilly. "Definitely go with plots to overthrow whenever possible." She glanced back at the other baristas who were struggling to keep up with orders. "Better go. Keep me posted!"

"Will do!" Jake said. "We ride at dawn!"

Mallory shook her head and laughed. "You're ridiculous. Funny, but ridiculous."

"Thank you. Don't forget to tip your waitress. I'll be here all week," Jake replied.

Ruby rolled her eyes. "And now you went one dad joke too far."

"Oh well," Jake sighed. "I suppose you have to be an actual dad to get the sweet spot just right."

"I'm not sure any dad in history has mastered that one," Ruby said with a laugh.

As the line began to dwindle, the trio in the gold sofa booth made a plan to get Bob to join them for coffee. Of course, the initial hurdle would be getting him to accept an invitation from people he condemned as heathens.

"There's one person who can convince him to come and listen to what we have to say," Ruby said tapping her fingers on the outside of her black cup.

Mallory's eyes lit up. "Miss Faye!"

"Yep, she's just the muscle we need." Ruby took a sip of her London Fog and felt the warmth go through her. Nerves about meeting Bob and a possible public explosion had given her chills. "If she can't do it, I'm afraid Jasper's cause is a lost one."

"Something tells me Miss Faye will get him there," Jake replied. "I don't think she'll take no for an answer, but she'll do it in the most genteel of ways."

"Gotta love the perfectly polished passive aggressiveness of southern women," Ruby said raising her tea in a toast to Miss Faye. "Bless their hearts."

Not only was Miss Faye successful in convincing Bob Lawrence to meet Ruby and the Winters, she escorted him to Onyx and Alabaster herself. "Not taking any chances that he'd chicken out," Miss Faye whispered in Ruby's ear.

Ruby stifled a laugh and thanked her. "Job well done, Miss Faye."

"Aye, aye, Cap'n." Miss Faye winked at the group and flashed a hot pink smile before she left them to their business.

An uncomfortable moment of silence hung over the four sitting in the sofa booth together. Bob was doing his level best to hide his discomfort and Mallory and Jake were waiting on Ruby to take the lead. Ruby, feeling a little sadistic, let Bob sweat for a couple of minutes. Deciding he'd had enough, more from the looks she was getting from Mallory and Jake than any actual pity, she got to the point.

"Bob, you know why we're here. We could beat a dead horse – sorry, bad choice of words – or we could get to what needs to be done. We need to get Jasper out of the Carnton mirror and we need to be at Carnton Plantation to do it. We'd rather do this the right way and let the house get a piece of its history back, but you're standing in our way. I don't have any problem going rogue if that's what it takes to do what's right by that poor soldier trapped in there, but I'd rather not." Ruby stopped, surprised at her own decisiveness. It seemed to surprise Bob, too.

Bob stared at Ruby for a moment at an unusual loss for words. "Someone has found their feet," he said finally. "About time, too."

"What?" Ruby asked, not trusting where he was going with that.

"You've always been smart, but you never took the responsibility that you could have. You let Mitch handle everything. You're just as good as your grandfather, but you don't see it. About time you realized what you're capable of." He paused and sneered at her. "Even if it *is* at my expense."

Ruby leveled her gaze at him. "I'm capable of a lot more than taking care of Pawpaw and running his business. But you don't seem to see the value in those capabilities since they fly in the face of your narrow beliefs. And yet, so many people in this town do see the value in them. Maybe you're the one that needs to take a good hard look at themselves."

Bob scoffed. "Maybe."

"Definitely," said Ruby. She paused and smirked at him. "And what better way to do that than with a mirror?"

"Witchcraft."

"Compassion."

Bob paused, surprised once again by Ruby's words. "Ghosts in mirrors. It's all either witchcraft or nonsense."

Jake leaned across the table. "Bob, I know how you feel. It's overwhelming and contradicts all logic. It goes against all you believe in. Happened to me, too. Once I realized that it was my own arrogance that kept me from seeing the world, no, the universe, as having more layers than I could imagine, I got to witness some incredible things. Scary sometimes, yes. But always incredible."

Ruby cocked her head to one side and took a good look at the older man across the booth from her. "You saw it, Bob. You can't deny that. What you *can* do is accept that there are things about the spiritual world that you don't know. Put your arrogance aside and see what's really at stake here. Don't think of Jasper as a ghost or a spirit. Jasper was a man once. A soldier. See him for what he was and still is because he's trapped in the Carnton mirror. He just wants to get back home to his family. Would you deny him that if he were flesh and blood standing in front of you?"

"No," Bob admitted softly.

Mallory put her hand on Ruby's and squeezed it. Tears were gathering on her eyelashes as Ruby fought for Jasper's soul.

"How can you deny the same man the chance to go home just because you don't understand what he's made of? How can you put your own prejudices and fears before a man's chance at eternal rest? You immortalize the Carter and McGavock families. Maybe they deserve it, maybe not. But you've completely ignored the people who gave their lives in that battle. People with no land, no plantation homes, no slaves to fight over. Just pride in their home towns. Towns that held family they would die to protect from invaders. Jasper didn't fight for politics. He fought to protect his family. And you," she spat, "sit here claiming to protect the soldiers' legacies but you won't even lift a finger to help one who needs it most. One right in front of you looking to you for help."

Mallory's hand had a death grip on Ruby's. Her knuckles were white as she poured whatever strength she had into the young woman who had forgotten her own insecurities and replaced them with fire and empathy. Jake smiled and mouthed, 'good job, kiddo,' at her. Bob sat motionless.

Ages seemed to pass before Bob finally spoke. Neither Ruby nor the Winters said another word while he turned things over in his mind. Ruby could only imagine the battle raging inside his head. How many times had he condemned her and to how many people? How could he go back and admit he was wrong? How did he balance what he knew about Jasper with his own faith?

The three others gave Bob space and time to wrestle with everything Ruby said and his own preconceived ideas. Ruby watched his expression changing with his thoughts. He was pained as he tried to reconcile everything that was strange and surreal with logic and faith. Ruby knew what that felt like. She didn't understand it at first, either. It was frightening. Not just the ghosts. No, the very idea that she could be responsible for their eternity was frightening. It was too much for her. At least, it had been.

Bob finally looked up from his coffee cup that he had been staring into as he thought. Ruby met his eyes with more softness than her earlier defiance. She needed to win him over, not make him feel stupid. She was already afraid she'd gone too far. "Alright," Bob said at last. The word was barely a whisper. Ruby wasn't even certain she'd heard him right.

"Alright?" she repeated.

"You can bring Jasper to Carnton. I'll put the mirror in the dining room where it belongs after he's made his way home. It's the right thing for the house, the McGavock's legacy, and for the young soldier."

Mallory beamed at Ruby and Jake patted Bob's shoulder. "You're doing the right thing."

"I sure as hell hope so," Bob said. "I don't understand any of this, but I know what I saw. I didn't stop to think about the reasons behind what you were trying to do. It's not about you and some secret dark power, is it, Ruby? It never was."

"No."

"If you can use this...gift, we'll call it, to help souls finally find their peace, I can't condemn that."

"You don't have to understand it all to do the right thing, Bob. I don't understand it all myself," Ruby said with a wry laugh. "I'm still figuring it out as I go along hoping I'm not sending these poor souls somewhere terrible."

Mallory smiled. "You know you aren't. They've shown you. Told you. Tod Carter said his family was waiting for him. The Lotz kids heard their parents calling. If they end up somewhere terrible, it's on their heads, not yours. All you can do is see them for the people they are and do your best to help them."

Ruby sighed and squeezed Mallory's hand. "There's something incredible about getting to talk to people who, before now, only existed to me on the pages of books or websites. For a historian, there's nothing more amazing than witnessing their own stories and talking to them about what matters most to them. And," she added, "you'd be surprised how different that is from what the history books think."

"Believe or don't believe," Jake said leaning back against the gold velvet. "Does it really matter if you believe or not? Ruby believes she is helping someone. Why stand in the way of that? Maybe she isn't doing anything at all as far as you believe. What harm is there in letting her do it in case she really is?"

The logic of Jake's argument seemed to resonate with Bob as he struggled to come to terms with what he'd agreed to. Nodding slowly, he said, "You're right. It doesn't matter. Maybe she's really sending them home. Maybe she's delusional. She could be doing worse things, I suppose."

"That's the spirit," Jake said. "She could be sacrificing chickens on the courthouse steps or something."

Ruby rolled her eyes. "Not helping, Jake."

"Bob knows what I mean, don't' you?"

"I do. At least she's using her powers for good."

Ruby steered the conversation away from her and back to the Carnton mirror. "When can we bring Jasper home? He's waited so long already."

Bob considered his options for a moment. "Let's meet at the plantation after closing on Monday. I'll arrange with the docents to let me lock up the main house. They can tend to the gift shop and head on home. The site closes at five. Shall we say five thirty?"

"Sounds good," Ruby replied. "One question, though, just out of curiosity."

"What's that?"

"How are you going to explain the mirror's appearance to the board and docents?"

Bob grinned. "Haven't you heard? We have a most generous donor who prefers to remain anonymous as the condition of his donation."

"Well, let's not upset the donor by giving them away," Mallory said.

Ruby couldn't resist a dig about the gaudy mirror. "I mean, if that weird thing was my mirror, I wouldn't want people to know I actually paid money for that, either."

Mallory gave Ruby a playful swat. "Not nice, Ruby," she said laughing.

Thirty-Four

As much as Ruby wanted to give Jasper the good news, she knew it would only make him more antsy to get out of the mirror if she did. So, instead, she focused on the last two mirrors in the house: a silver hand mirror, and a mantle clock with a beveled mirror on its base. It would be a couple of days until they met Bob at Carnton, which gave Ruby plenty of time to at least figure out where the mirrors needed to go.

She began with the mantle clock. The mirror itself was quite small in comparison to the others she had worked with. In fact, they almost hadn't noticed it was mirrored at all. Ruby and the Winters had been focused on more traditional places for mirrors to be. The clock was unexpected. Sitting at the kitchen table with Mallory and Jake on either side of her, Ruby leaned the clock back a little so she could see into the mirror better. Placing her fingers in the corner leaving enough glass to see the inhabitant, she waited to see who would appear.

Her reflection, what she could see of it, faded and was replaced with that of another Confederate soldier. The poor man looked haggard and dirty. Other than the disheveled state of his appearance, Ruby couldn't make out anything that might have killed him. No wounds she could see. Maybe it was sickness instead of the battle.

The soldier narrowed his eyes and his forehead wrinkled. "Who are you?" he asked. His tone held more suspicion than curiosity. "What am I doing here?"

"My name is Ruby Baxter. I'm here to help you get out of this mirror. You've been here quite a while it seems."

"Here? Where is here? I can't stay here anymore. I have a message for General Gist. If I don't get it to him now—"

"Slow down, soldier," Ruby said, holding her other hand up to stop him. "There's no one for you to give the message to. The battle has been over for one hundred and fifty years."

"What?" the man said as his confusion deepened. "That- that can't be. I-I have a message to deliver. I have to go. Please, let me go. So many have fallen. If I don't get this message to General Gist, more will die!"

General States Rights Gist was one of the many officers that fell during the bloody Battle of Franklin. He, along with others, had been laid out on the back porch of Carnton plantation. One by one, it was said, the injured men who had been brought to the house for medical care lined up and silently paid their respects to their fallen generals.

Ruby's heart broke as she tried to figure out the best way to break it to this poor soul that he was dead. Clearly, that point had been lost on him. "What's your name, soldier?"

"Captain Andrew Rutherford."

Ruby smiled at him. "Nice to know you, Captain." Her voice softened as she spoke again. "This might be hard for you to hear, but I need you to listen carefully. When you were fighting in the Battle of Franklin, you died along with so many others on both sides. It was a massacre."

The soldier's panic to deliver his message ceased as a new panic took its place. His face drained of color and his eyes blinked rapidly. "Died? I'm- I'm *dead*?"

Ruby nodded. "I'm so sorry."

Captain Rutherford shook his head violently. "No! No, this can't be right. I can't be dead. This can't be heaven."

"I wish I could tell you that it wasn't true, but you are indeed dead. And, no, you're right. This isn't heaven. Not by a long shot. This is Franklin."

"I don't understand."

"Let's go about this a different way. Can you tell me the last thing you remember from the battle?"

"I can show you," he offered.

Ruby smiled warmly. "Even better."

She placed the fingers of her other hand on the opposite corner of the small mirror. As she did, the usual transformation happened making her a ghost in the captain's reality. No matter how many times she had borne witness to the horrors of the night of November 30th, it never got easier to experience. Chaos and death reigned on the open field and in the trenches. The losses were catastrophic. Bodies of men and horses were piling up between Carter House and Lotz House. The trenches were slick with crimson and mud. Smoke hung in the air and shots rang out all around her.

Ruby turned to look for Captain Rutherford, but didn't see him immediately. After a moment, a horse came riding up the hill towards the commanding officers in the back. In the saddle was Captain Andrew Rutherford riding to beat the devil. He deftly steered his steed around fallen comrades and out of the line of fire from the cannons. He aimed the horses head at the top of the hill just behind where Ruby stood. As she watched him control the thundering horse with easy grace, his form was suddenly broken as his back arched and he screamed in pain. Ruby realized now why she couldn't see his mortal wound. He had been shot in the back, but the bullet had not passed through him. He tried, even through the searing pain, to get his horse to their destination. In seconds, though, the pain and blood loss were too much. Captain Rutherford lost consciousness and fell from the saddle onto the rutted ground.

The scene began to shift and Ruby found herself standing over the young captain as he lay on his side on a familiar front lawn. Clouston Hall. He had been taken to the field hospital and was awaiting his turn in the operating theater. His chest barely moved with his breath. His face was sunken and white. Sweat beaded on his forehead and rolled into his eyes. The only mercy Ruby could see was that he was unconscious and couldn't feel the agony as he waited for medical care. Care that wasn't to come.

Time seemed to slow to a crawl as Ruby waited alongside the

captain. The battle sounds echoed off the walls of the buildings in town. More men were carted to the house and laid on the ground. Nurses, some military and others women from town that stepped in to assist, treated what they could and sorted who would need the most urgent treatment. So many of them walked past Captain Rutherford and took no notice of his decline. The number of incoming casualties was overwhelming them. Likely, he simply looked to be asleep. Blood continued to soak through his clothes as the lodged bullet festered. Ruby could hear the soft chiming of a mantle clock from inside the house through the open widow. It was on the mantle in the operating theater on the other side of the wall where the captain lay.

After what must have been hours, the captain was still and pale. Deathly pale. One of the nurses finally stopped next to him with two men to carry him into surgery. However, as the nurse knelt beside him and felt for a pulse, she shook her head. Ruby wanted to scream at her that he was still alive, if only barely. He needed the surgery to save what little life was left in him. No one would have heard her even if she had been able to get the words out. Instead of carrying the captain to surgery, the two men lifted him and carried him around to the back of the house.

Ruby followed and remembered her history about the cellar. Men were dying more rapidly than the hospital could tend to the bodies. To make room for the incoming wounded, the dead were taken to the cellar and the bodies stacked. Captain Rutherford among them.

How many men were carried to that cellar who still had a spark of life left to save? How many men like Captain Rutherford met their death not on the battlefield but under the crushing weight of corpses in the cold darkness?

As Ruby watched in horror as the men came back up out of the cellar empty-handed, the vision began to fade and the soldier's reflection took its place. "'Not dead,'" Ruby said. "You're the one who whispered that in my ear, aren't you? You're the one who said that in Clouston Hall, too."

Captain Rutherford nodded slowly. "I needed them to know I wasn't dead. Needed them to know I had a message to deliver."

"You weren't conscious when you died. That's why you didn't

know." Ruby wondered if the battle would have ended differently if Captain Rutherford had been able to deliver his message. Given the carnage she saw as he was riding to his general, she very much doubted it. "Your soul stayed behind trying to deliver the message."

He nodded sadly.

"The battle is over and your job is done," Ruby said gently. "There are no more messages to deliver. It's time for you to rest."

"I don't know how."

"That's where I come in. You're lucky you stayed behind at Clouston Hall. I have friends there that will be more than willing to help. There's one catch, though. I can't send you to your rest if you aren't willing to go."

"The battle is done. There's nothing for me here."

Ruby nodded. "Let me get in touch with my friend. I'll have you out of that mirror soon. Very soon."

Captain Rutherford nodded. "Thank you, Ruby, for your kindness and your help."

With a warm smile, Ruby pulled her fingers away from the clock and let the captain fade away.

"Clouston Hall?" Mallory asked.

"Yep," Ruby replied. "I need to call Matt. At least this one is easy."

Jake chuckled. "About time you caught a break."

"I couldn't agree more." Ruby pulled her phone out of her back pocket and called the gallery in Clouston Hall. "Matt? Ruby. I've got another one for you."

———

As expected, Matt was more than happy to take the mirrored clock and help Ruby get its dedicated messenger home to his rest. He also was intrigued by the fact that this soldier was the one insisting he wasn't dead. "Now I feel bad about not going back down there to the cellar after my run in with him. Poor soul was just trying to get some help."

"That's what most of them want. Well, except Griff and Colonel House," Ruby had told him.

With Captain Rutherford easily sorted out, Ruby had time before meeting up with Bob at Carnton to tackle the last remaining mirror, other than Jasper's. Once more, Ruby and the Winters sat at the kitchen table with the hand mirror. Mallory had propped it up against a bag of sugar and held it in place with a couple of rolled up dish towels so Ruby could have both hands free to work with the mirror.

Once more using her fingertips because of the smallness of the glass, Ruby watched her own reflection be replaced by another. This time, it was a soldier in blue. Union. "I wondered when one of you would turn up," she said to the young man. "I'm Ruby."

"One of us?" the soldier asked.

Ruby smiled. "Sorry, so far all of the soldiers I've helped have been Confederate."

The man nodded slowly. "Makes sense. They were slaughtered. So many of them just charged to their deaths. I've never seen anything like it."

"Can I ask your name?"

"Apologies, miss. I'm William York. My friends called me Billy."

"Nice to meet you, Billy."

"Can I ask you a question, Ruby?"

"Of course."

"How long has it been? How long have I been stuck in this mirror?"

A wan smile crossed Ruby's face. "One hundred and fifty some odd years. My turn now. How did a man like you end up in a lady's hand mirror?"

The soldier chuckled and Ruby could swear she saw his eyes twinkle. "Well, now, that's a good question. And the answer is a good story."

"Mind sharing it?"

"See for yourself," Billy answered. He put his fingers on the glass and Ruby followed suit.

Rather than finding herself on the battlefield as she expected, she discovered she was inside a large open space. Long wooden benches filled half of it with men lying on them as many as could fit. Some benches had been moved away for the men to be placed on the floor. No, not benches. Pews. She was inside a church sanctuary. An oddly fitting place for an invading army to bring its wounded.

On one of the pews was Billy. His shoulder was dislocated and his neck had been grazed by a bullet leaving behind a nasty gash. He was lying on his back with cloth and bindings holding his neck in place to allow the fresh stitches to begin to heal. Behind him lay one of his friends. The two men exchanged a few words as best they could just to let the other know they were still hanging on. Soon, a young woman came to check Billy's bandages and stitches. As she approached, Billy's face lit up and the twinkle in his eyes that Ruby had seen reappeared. Clearly, Billy had a crush on his nurse.

The scene changed, but only slightly. The place was still the same and the two soldier friends remained in the same positions. However, their conditions were deteriorating. The friend was pale and had a rattling cough. From the look on his face, each cough brought with it excruciating pain. Billy looked worse for wear, too. The cut on his neck was angry and swollen. Infection had set in around the stitches. His shoulder was now bandaged and braced, but was protruding only slightly less than before. Ruby realized she had been mistaken about it being dislocated. It had been broken. Likely, she thought, he had fallen from his horse.

Even through his own pain and suffering, he continued to try to talk with his friend behind him. His words were met only by slight moans. The young nurse returned looking more tired and worn that before. She carried with her the small hand mirror. With tenderness, she put it in Billy's hand and helped him angle it so he could see his friend. As soon as Billy saw the face of the other young man, he winced and pulled his eyes tightly shut. After a moment, he opened them again, this time with tears gathering in them. Choking them back so his friend wouldn't hear the alarm in his voice, Billy began talking to him once more. It was as though as long as he could talk to him, the friend still had a chance.

After a few moments, Billy's own strength began to fail him. The young nurse took the mirror and held it for him for a while. Ruby could see that the nurse returned any feelings Billy had for her. Her kindness and ingenuity with the mirror spoke more than words could. Knowing what was coming for the girl made it heartbreaking for Ruby to watch.

Once more the scene changed slightly with only the passage of time. Both men were growing weaker. The nurse held the mirror for Billy as tears rolled down her cheeks. Billy's eyes were locked on the mirror watching his friend as tears ran out of the corners of his eyes and into his hair. His friend's breath had become a sickening rattle. He had only moments left and Billy was going to be there in the only way he could as his friend died. With a shudder, the friend passed away and left his suffering behind. The young nurse took the mirror and knelt beside Billy as he wept for the loss of his friend.

Again, the slightest of scene change. Billy's friend was gone, but he still held the mirror in his hand. He was dreadfully pale and the infection oozed from the stitches on his neck. Billy shivered underneath the quilt laid over him as fever set in. There was nothing more that could be done for him but to make him comfortable. Beside him as always was the young nurse. Her words were those of encouragement and strength but her eyes gave away her sorrow. The soldier she loved was not long for the world. Billy's breath became rapid and shallow as his hands clutched the mirror to his chest. The nurse laid her small hands over his and tried valiantly to control her sobbing. As Billy's body finally relented to the shadow of death, she laid her head on his chest and wept.

"You stayed for her, didn't you?" Ruby asked as the heart wrenching image faded.

Billy nodded. "I knew if I stayed in the mirror, I'd at least get to see her face even if she didn't know I was there."

"Love can make you do crazy things."

A slight smile turned the corners of Billy's mouth. "It sure can. It was enough to watch her over the years. Even in old age, she was beautiful. But then, she was gone and I was still here. When I chose to stay, I hadn't even considered that would happen. If I had gone, I might have been with her again. But now—"

"Now your wait is over. Now you can go to her again."

"Can you help me?"

Nodding, Ruby said, "I can. The church you were in isn't there anymore. It burned down, but there's a new church built in its place. Well, newer, anyway. If I can get your mirror inside the church, I can release you from it."

Billy's face darkened. "Something tells me a church might not be too excited about a haunted mirror."

"Likely not. But then again, they might surprise us. Even if I have to sneak it in, I'll make sure you see your young nurse again."

The darkness faded from Billy's expression and was replaced with hope. "Thank you, Ruby."

"You're welcome. Let me see what I can do and I'll let you know. With any luck, you'll be free tomorrow."

"Tomorrow?"

Ruby winked. "Well, tomorrow is Sunday. If you want to get into a church to save a soul, that's the day to do it."

The Five Bloodiest Hours

Smoke settled low over the battlefield as though it had surrendered with exhaustion. Moonlight shone down from a clear cold sky. The balminess of the day was gone. In its place was a night of plummeting temperatures that threatened to take more lives even as the guns stilled. Dark shadows formed a terrifying landscape as survivors surveyed mounds where flatness should have been. Knowing what those mounds were made of caused their blood to run colder than the night air.

It was dark, but far from silent. Deafening explosions and rifle cracks were no longer there to drown out the agonizing death throes of the fallen men. From beneath layers of dead bodies came forlorn moans of those who knew they would likely meet oblivion where they were. Those that could see shadows of men retreating one direction or the other cried out for help and water.

One such soldier cried out from the south side of the entrenchment. He was buried up to his shoulders in dead men with only one free arm and could do nothing on his own to extract himself. Sentenced to wait until someone from his side found him with an ambulance wagon, if they found him at all, he begged for water from Union soldiers who were nearby. His cries becoming more pitiful and desperate by the minute, eventually one of the enemy soldiers could stand it no longer and left his canteen with the soldier. The mercy was a small one on the surface given that the fallen man was not freed from what could likely be a grave of fallen flesh, but neither was he taken prisoner. With water, he was given time. Time to be rescued by his own.

Other soldiers wandered the field in stunned delirium with no direction or destination. Each horror illuminated by the moonlight brought fresh anguish. One soldier tried to make his way to join the Union line moving out of town, but as his feet could find no solid ground with the number of bodies in his path, he lost precious time and would be forced to catch up if the freezing night spared him.

Another stood dumbstruck behind one of the Ohio guns in an embrasure at the Carter cotton gin. On the other side of the cannon was a sickening visage in the dim starlight. Bodies of men who tried to breach the stronghold were blown to bits as the gun fired point blank. Over and over, they had rushed the embrasure. Over and over men fell, limbs were flung far and wide by the blasts.

Corpses filled the trenches with heads, arms, and legs sticking out in unnatural positions. A soldier staggered along the line searching for a canteen with even a drop of water in it to quench his agonizing thirst. Finding none and desperate, he fell to his knees and scooped a handful of water from a space in the trench mercifully free of the dead. Raising it to his parched lips, he immediately spat it out. In the darkness he hadn't seen that the water had been tainted with the blood of the dead and dying that also filled the trench. Exhausted, he collapsed where he was, hoping to stay awake long enough to cry out for help from a passing medic that was picking his way across the field.

Over the baleful cries, there was an occasional blast from a Confederate cannon as Hood nipped at the heels of the Federal soldiers to hurry them along on their retreat to Nashville. Often, the shots tore through a home in town just as those sheltered inside began to emerge from hiding sending them scrambling back into cellars as windows and walls splintered around them. Hood seemed to care nothing for the citizens as he sent his defiance over their heads toward the Harpeth River and the exiting Union troops.

In the darkness of the wee hours, the shadowy scene left behind after the massacre was terrifying. Only in the dawn light would the true hideousness be revealed.

Thirty-Five

Sunday dawned clear and crisp. It was one of those mornings where you can see your breath and be blinded by the sunshine at the same time. The trees along Main Street dressed in their fall colors were a wash of spectacular reds and yellows against the cloudless blue sky. Golden sunlight on one side of the street gave a promise of a warmer afternoon to come. Along Main and the numbered side streets, families made their way to the several churches that framed Five Points. A Methodist, Presbyterian, and Episcopal. Children skipped alongside their parents who held their little hands and cautioned against scuffing shoes and messing up neatly styled hair. Older couples walked arm-in-arm along the brick sidewalks smiling at the young people. It was picturesque. A Disney moment. A Hallmark movie in real life. Ruby wondered what the people in this pastoral scene would say if they knew the truth about the mirror in the bag on her shoulder.

Having made so much progress with Bob Lawrence, Ruby and the Winters decided not to make any more enemies for the time being and would keep the return of the mirror a clandestine mission. No reason to get the reverend in an uproar if they didn't have to. Ruby had dealt with too many homeless spirits to let the guilt of being sneaky this time get the better of her like it had with Tod Carter's mirror. Leaving a hand mirror tucked away somewhere in a large church would be much simpler than sneaking the gold gilt bubble mirror into Carnton. Getting Billy back to his young nurse was her only concern. That, and explaining why she decided to show up at a church for the first time in, well, ever.

Stopping at the corner to wait on the mechanical voice of the crossing light to give them the go-ahead, Ruby pulled her bag closer to her side. She could feel the hard outline of the mirror through the leather. It seemed to thrum the closer she got to the church corner as though Billy was getting more and more anxious to be home.

Once the light changed and they were given the 'walk sign is on' signal, Ruby, Mallory, and Jake trotted across the crosswalk to Franklin Presbyterian Church. Kids were tucking their little feet into cracks between stones trying to be sneaky about climbing on the wall that framed the front of the church as teenagers sat on the top of it chatting and waiting until the last minute to head into the sanctuary. Ruby looked at them and wondered how many of them knew of the soldiers not much older than them who sat on that same stone wall waiting for the bus that would take them off to World War II.

Ruby's heart began to beat a little harder in her chest as she saw Reverend Walker standing at the front doors welcoming his flock to the service. So much for sneaking in among the crowd. Jake saw her stiffen and put his hand on her shoulder. "It's ok, Ruby. He doesn't know anything about why you're here. Just play along." If anyone asked what brought them to the church, the plan was to say that Mallory and Jake were looking for a new church home and asked Ruby to come along to introduce them around. It was a flimsy plan, but all they had.

Reverend Walker's eyebrows went up as he spied Ruby in the line of incoming pious. As young as he was, no more than forty, he seemed wizened and stately in his liturgical vestments. "Ruby Baxter, as I live and breathe. Never thought I'd see you here. Welcome!" Ruby shrugged and managed a smile until the pastor added, "Here to send some spirits home?"

"I-I, um," Ruby stammered, thrown by the mention of the truth in her visit.

Mercifully, Jake jumped in. "She's here to introduce us to folks as we look for a church. We're new in town. Jake and Mallory Winters," Jake said extending his hand to Reverend Walker.

"Ah, yes!" the pastor said shaking Jake's hand. "Good to meet you both. Make yourselves welcome! And, Ruby, if you feel the need to send any spirits away, can we keep the Holy one here, please?" he said with a teasing grin.

"Of course, Reverend," Ruby said recovered from her initial surprise enough to resume the charade. "I haven't had much use for that one myself. You can keep it."

With a chuckle, the pastor motioned them inside the church as more of the faithful filed in. Once inside the main sanctuary, Ruby's jaw dropped at the stunning wash of color from the stained-glass windows as the brilliant autumn sunshine poured through them. "I can see how people could be inspired to find faith here."

"It's definitely beautiful," Mallory said running her eyes across the sanctuary. "I'm not a fan of the trend of modern sleek churches. There's just something about an old church that brings on the nostalgia for me."

Ruby didn't share the nostalgia but could appreciate the beauty in the place and the peace that came with that. With a haunted mirror in her bag, she didn't actually feel that peace herself. As the pipe organ played gathering hymns in strong rich tones, Ruby and the Winters found seats in the back row of pews giving Ruby an easy path for sneaking out during the service to release Billy and hide the hand mirror.

As the worship service began, Ruby's face began to flush and a glistening of sweat appeared on her brow. Nervousness about being discovered in her real purpose for being there stemmed more from being interrupted in releasing Billy and having something go horribly wrong than what the reverend would say about her task. Opening hymns were sung and prayers recited. Ruby played along, even though she didn't really know any of them. Jake and Mallory had a bit more familiarity and guided her quietly through the motions.

After a lot of singing and standing, Jake whispered in Ruby's ear, "They're going to have everyone greet the people around them in a minute. Greet a couple of people, then sneak out while everyone is standing and moving around a bit."

Ruby nodded and gripped her bag a little tighter. As Jake said, at the end of a hymn, Reverend Walker instructed the congregation to greet one another. Ruby shook the withered hand of an elderly blue-haired lady in a salmon polyester skirt suit and then turned to the lady's husband who had kind eyes and wore a little too much cologne. Once she had done that, Ruby picked up her bag and slipped out into the aisle. As she reached the back doors of the sanctuary, she turned back to see if she had been noticed. At the head of the center aisle, Reverend Winters was looking right at her. Their eyes met and the reverend's eyebrows raised before giving her a slight nod. He knew, and he wasn't going to stop her.

Knowing the reverend was in on the task at hand allowed the pounding in Ruby's chest to subside some as she wandered the halls searching for an empty room. Most of the rooms were being used for Sunday school for the younger kids. Other rooms had tables set up for adult classes. With the adults occupied at the moment, Ruby snuck inside one of them and into a corner where she wouldn't be easily seen through the small rectangle of glass in the wooden door.

Settled on the floor, she sat still and quiet for a moment letting her anxious breathing return to normal. She reached into the bag and pulled out the small silver hand mirror. Energy seemed to flow from it through her hand as though Billy was as anxious as Ruby was. Pulling her legs in crisscrossed, she laid the mirror in her lap and placed her fingers on the edge. The expectant face of the young Union soldier replaced hers.

"Ruby? Is this the church?" he asked looking around at the room that seemed more like a modern office than a historic church.

"Yes. We're in one of the classrooms. The service is keeping the prying eyes of the congregation occupied."

Billy nodded and relaxed a little bit. "What do I need to do?"

Ruby smiled at him. "You just think about your young nurse and seeing her again. Let me and the church be your bridge for getting back to her."

Billy closed his eyes tightly at first. After a moment, his expression softened as a slight smile curved his mouth. He was ready.

Ruby gently placed the fingers of her other hand on the mirror. Billy's eyes flew open as he felt the energy shift around him.

"I feel it," he whispered. "I can feel it pulling me home."

"Can you feel her? Hear her?"

Once more, Billy closed his eyes, searching for his love with his heart and soul. A tear eased out from between his lashes and ran slowly down his cheek. For a moment, Ruby thought it wasn't working, but soon Billy smiled and opened his eyes. "I can hear her. She's calling for me."

Ruby nodded. "Go to her. Let go of the mirror and find your lady love."

"Thank you, Ruby. Thank you for not turning your back on a Yankee soldier."

Ruby chuckled. "That war is long gone. I've known a lot of good Yankees in my life." Smiling warmly at him, she added, "And now I have one more to add to that list."

Billy nodded humbly and smiled back at her. "Goodbye, Ruby."

"Goodbye, Billy."

The soldier pulled his fingers away from Ruby's on the glass and shimmered into the ether.

Ruby took a deep breath and sat with the mirror on her lap for a while. The task was half-done. Step two was hiding the mirror in the church. That would have been a lot simpler had she been familiar with the building. The classrooms were sparsely furnished and likely had things moved around a lot to accommodate different groups and activities. She needed a place that wouldn't be disturbed often. A place that the mirror could be hidden for a long time. In a moment, she had it. Reverend Walker's office.

Making her way down another hallway, she managed to find the church offices. There were several in various states of order and late 80s decorating, but one was different from the others. Reverend Walker's office had large mahogany bookcases along one wall filled with books and various items brought back from past mission trips. His matching wooden desk, like she expected from the young clergyman, was covered in papers and books, some closed and precariously stacked, others laying open on top of each other. Scrawled notes were laying on the very top of the heap that contained various verses and candid thoughts. Sermon notes. Ruby made her way around the upholstered guest chairs and to the worn leather chair behind the desk. Pulling desk drawers open,

Ruby looked for one that she could stash the mirror in. Outside the office in the hallway, she heard footsteps approaching. Considering her options of running away or hiding behind the desk, she opted for hiding. For a moment, feeling completely ridiculous sitting on the floor under the desk, she waited and listened. As the footsteps passed the office door, she released the breath she had been holding.

"Time to get this thing hidden and get out of here." The bottom drawer of the desk was deeper than the two above it and crammed full of papers that were turning yellow with age. The paper itself had to be older than Reverend Walker, which meant this was an unused drawer full of documents from his predecessor. "Perfect," Ruby said as she pulled the mirror out of her bag. She reached to the far back of the drawer and wriggled her hand enough to make a space for the slim mirror. With some difficulty, she swapped her hand wedged in amongst the papers for the mirror.

From the sanctuary, the pipe organ began to play a triumphant hymn signaling the worship service coming to an end. "Time to go," Ruby said putting her bag on her shoulder and pulling herself off the floor. Looking both ways down the hallway to check that no more passersby were aware of her presence, she made her way back to the sanctuary.

Ruby peeked through a crack in the doors to make sure she wasn't going to make a spectacular grand entrance before pushing a door open enough for her to slip through. The congregation was on its feet singing the closing hymn with their backs to her. Even though she knew Reverend Walker had seen her leave, she hoped no one else had noticed her absence. Church folks were some of the best at being nosey behind the guise of questions of concern for one's well-being.

Mercifully, the pious had been focused on worship and not the odd exit of a newcomer. Jake and Mallory gave her expectant looks as she took her spot beside them in the row. Giving them a nod, she put her bag on the floor and opened a hymnal to a random page. Looking past the music minister who was directing the hymn from the pulpit, she saw Reverend Walker meet her gaze again with a quick knowing grin before he looked away.

Ruby's plan had been to be quick out of the sanctuary at the end of the service so she wouldn't have to cross paths with the reverend again, but was foiled when the reverend and altar attendants walked up the aisle to be in position to bid farewell to the congregation as they went back out into the world for the week. Reverend Walker stopped Jake and Mallory as they exited the building and asked how they enjoyed the service.

"It was very nice, Reverend. And the church is just beautiful," Mallory said with sweet diplomacy knowing full-well it was unlikely they would return, not being religious types.

"Thanks for having us, Reverend," Jake added shaking Reverend Walker's hand.

"You're always welcome," he replied before turning to Ruby. "So," he said quietly, "was the service that bad that you had to escape, or was there a more pressing spiritual matter?"

"Does one soul count more than another? Is it any difference if the church saved mine or another's today?"

Reverend Walker paused, looking down at Ruby's passive defiance of his faith. After a moment, his face broke into a grin. "I'll take whatever soul saving I can get. As long as you left us with—"

"The Holy Spirit. Yes, you still have that one." Ruby said. "At least, I assume you do. That one's out of my control. More your department, I think." With a wink, she trotted down the steps to catch up with the Winters who were waiting for her on the brick paved sidewalk. As she walked away, she glanced back to see the reverend chuckling and smiling at her. Apparently, he had decided to coexist with Ruby and her spirits if he believed in them at all. With a deep sigh of relief, Ruby focused on the final mirror that needed to make its way home. Jasper's.

Thirty-Six

The Winters and Ruby waited in the parking lot outside the Carnton visitors center as the sun sank in brilliant oranges across the streaks of feathery fall clouds in a deep blue sky. By the time the docents closed up the shop, the early evening of fall had settled into night. With the mirror wrapped safely, the three stepped out of the white pools of parking lot lights into the darkness of the quiet plantation.

From the visitors' center, a path stretched through a white picket fence and up to the back porch steps of the stately home. Soft warm lights shone through the antique wavy glass windows. In the shadow of the balcony above him, Bob Lawrence stood at the wooden door waiting. Even though they were the only ones on the property, a reverent silence for what the place meant to the soldier they carried with them settled over the group. Without a word, Bob held the door open and motioned them into the first room on their left.

The dining room was decorated to represent the style and feel of the antebellum era, though only a few broken pieces of China remained. Those pieces were encased in glass while a full set of a similar pattern dressed the long wooden dining table. Built in shelves painted in the same greenish slate color of the walls contained larger serving pieces and table linens. Large pocket doors opened the space to the equally large study. On either side of the main hall that stretched from the front door to the back door were two rooms. The dining room and study on one side, and the best parlor that was seldom used and another sitting room on the other. A staircase in the main hall led to the family bedrooms upstairs. Large blood stains still tarnished the polished wood one hundred and fifty years after the rooms were used as operating theaters. Downstairs, the horrors were covered by carpeting, or painted floorboards in the case of the dining room, so the war could be put momentarily in the back of the visitors' minds as they learned the family and home history.

The dining room bore no evidence of the battle, except for the remnants of China that were the only pieces to survive the battle and aftermath as the soldiers occupied the house turned hospital. The space was spared from being used as an operating room because it was used instead as the only living space for the family during that time. Ruby, however, had seen the room through the window as she watched Jasper die. For her, there was no separating the space in its splendor from the tragedy it bore witness to.

Bob gently cleared his throat, breaking the reverent silence. "How can I help, Ruby?"

Ruby looked around the room and thought about how she wanted to go about things. "There's no reason to move any of the place settings and use the table. I'm just fine sitting on the floor for this, but I'll need help keeping the mirror propped up. Being round on the bottom, leaning it against the wall or a chair isn't going to be stable."

"We'll hold the mirror, Ruby," Mallory offered. "That way Bob can see you work your magic."

"Might not have been the best choice of words, Mal," Jake said with a chuckle.

Mallory blushed realizing referring to Ruby's abilities as magic might have been a bad idea given Bob's earlier objections. Seeing her embarrassment, Bob smiled. "It's alright, Mallory."

Mallory decided finding a task to do would be the best way to hide her lingering embarrassment so she set about making a place for Ruby to work. She pulled out a chair and set the back of it against the wall. "If we lean the mirror on the floor against the front of the chair, Jake and I can sit on either side against the wall and balance it."

"Works for me," Jake said. "Ruby?"

"Same here."

Bob and Jake carefully unwrapped the mirror from the quilt that was protecting the bubble of glass and the candlesticks on either side of the circular frame. Ruby stood back and looked at the mirror. Somehow in the opulence of the large dining room, it didn't seem quite as garish as it had in Mallory's powder room. The Winter's took their places on the floor on either side of the chair sitting cross-legged. Each tucked one of their feet under the rounded edge of the mirror's frame to support it and keep it from rolling as Ruby worked with it. Then, each put a hand on the outside edge of the frame to keep it from tipping forward. Being older and less enthused about the prospect of getting himself down on the floor much less up from it, Bob pulled one of the dining chairs out and turned it to face the mirror.

Ruby let the others get settled before she tucked herself between them directly in front of the mirror. As she did, the temperature around her dropped. Chill bumps sprang up on Mallory's arms and Ruby knew Bob must have felt it to. Of course, he could easily attribute it to a draft in the old windows. Ruby and the Winters knew better.

Ruby's reflection was sheer and distorted in the curve of the glass. From behind her, she heard Bob utter a 'hmm' which told her he could see the difference in her reflection, too. Ruby knew he wouldn't be able to see anything once her fingers touched the mirror, so she let the moment linger. Deciding she'd waited long enough, Ruby took a deep breath and placed her hand on the glass. A moment later, Jasper shimmered into place.

His eyes searched the space around her. "Where are we?"

"Carnton," she answered. "In the dining room."

His eyes widened and he looked around again. "It's beautiful. How did you manage getting us in here?"

"Well, it turns out that Bob back there," she said pointing to the older man with her free hand, "finally came around and invited us in."

In the mirror she could see Bob smile as she talked about him even though he couldn't see or hear anything else.

"You're actually in the room where the mirror was when you died," Ruby explained. "I saw the mirror glint through the window when you chose to stay behind."

"I remember now," he said softly. "It was different then."

"I imagine so. Now that you're in the house, are you ready to go home?"

Jasper pulled his gaze away from the beautiful room around them and focused his eyes on her. Tears made them shine in the warm yellow lamplight. "Yes," he whispered. "I want to go home." Pausing, his forehead furrowed. "Will they be there? Will they know me?"

Ruby smiled at him and placed her other hand on the glass. "See if you can reach them now."

Jasper put his other hand on the mirror to meet hers and closed his eyes. A smile played on the corners of his mouth. "Yes," he said as his eyes opened. Tears that were gathered on his lashes escaped and rolled down his cheeks. "They're waiting for me. They've been waiting for so long."

Ruby could feel her eyes sting with tears. She couldn't release the mirror to wipe them away, so she just let them fall. "I'm so sorry all of you had to wait. Let's not make them wait any longer. It's time to go home."

A sob rocked the soldier as her words washed over him. "Home," he whispered. "I'm going home."

Ruby nodded. "Yes. There's nothing keeping you here now. You can go as soon as you're ready to let go of the mirror. The house and I will be your bridge."

For a moment, Jasper struggled to control the sobs of relief and gratitude. Ruby couldn't help but sob herself. She longed to reach through the mirror and hug the soldier who had been so lonely and lost, but couldn't. Instead, she leaned forward and let her forehead rest on the top of the glass bubble. Sensing it was Ruby's way of comforting him, Jasper did the same.

Moments passed as both struggled to calm the flood of tears. As she pushed them back, Ruby realized that it wasn't just Jasper she was crying for. His was the last mirror. His was the last soul she would help. With him went her purpose. A purpose that she had only recently embraced as she began to see herself as others did. One that gave her an anchor at a time when she'd felt so adrift. Without it, who was she? Ruby couldn't focus on that now. Jasper needed her. Taking a slow breath, Jasper regained his composure. He and Ruby pulled away from the mirror and met each other's gaze. Her voice thick with tears, she whispered, "It's time, Jasper."

"Thank you, Ruby," he whispered back.

"You're welcome, soldier."

As much as she knew he needed to go, she wanted to hold on to the moment as long as she could. Each time she became the bridge for homebound souls, she was both drained of energy and filled with purpose. Ruby desperately wanted to remember the feeling. Maybe Jasper sensed that. He hesitated a long moment before he nodded and pulled his hands slowly away from hers. Seconds later, Jasper was gone and the mirror reflected Ruby's tear-stained face. The full force of the final soul finding freedom and what that meant for her came crashing down. Emptiness consumed her and another wave of sobs came hard and fast. Burying her face in her hands and folding into her own lap, Ruby felt Bob's hand come to rest on her shoulder.

Thirty-Seven

Onyx and Alabaster's usual coffee shop sounds tumbled over each other in a pleasant cacophony as the three people in the gold horseshoe booth sat in silence staring at their cups. Ruby didn't notice her London Fog going cold in her hands. Her thoughts were far away and all over the place. When she lost Pawpaw, she had felt unmoored in a town she knew like the back of her hand and yet, not at all. She had sought anchorage more than purpose, but purpose had found her. She had tasted it, even learned to savor it, and now that it was gone, anchorage wasn't enough anymore.

Jake and Mallory sat beside her lost in their own thoughts. So much of the time they thought they would be spending getting to know their new town and setting up their offices had been spent in a strange combination of nightmare and revelation. Instead of learning things like where the grocery stores were or how to navigate Southern over-politeness at four-way stops, they knew more about the bloody and tragic past of the perfectly pristine little town.

So lost in their own heads, none of them noticed the young man walking up the center aisle towards them. When he spoke, all three of them nearly jumped out of their skins.

"I thought I'd find you here," James Cavanaugh said with a grin.

Ruby nearly knocked her cup over in her startling, but just managed to keep from making a mess. "James. What are you doing here?"

"Aside from getting coffee like everyone else?" James said with an easy laugh. "Looking for you."

Ruby stared at him. "Why?"

James cleared his throat as his confidence wavered slightly. "Well, I was hoping to talk to you about something."

Jake grinned and went to get up. "We'll leave you two to talk. Mal, you ready?"

James held up a hand to stop him. "Actually, I was hoping you'd stay. I might need back up."

Jake settled back into his spot and said, "I'm intrigued. By all means, have a seat."

Ruby scooted closer to Mallory so James could slide into the round booth. She had a sneaking suspicion about what James was there to talk about, but since nothing in her life had been predictable as of late, she held her objections for the time being. 'Something I can do for you, James?"

"I hope so. I heard you managed to get the last mirror into Carnton."

"That's right. And?"

"And I'm impressed that you were able to convince Bob Lawrence to admit there might just be something to your particular talent. But—" James paused as though he'd forgotten a well-rehearsed speech. Giving up on whatever he had planned to say, he went on. "Look, Ruby, I know that was the last mirror in the Bennett House that needed you. I also know that you're more than just a great tour guide. Franklin needs you to be more than that. This is a great town, but there is so much more to it than anyone sees, hell, *wants* to see. But you see it. Even if it's through the experiences of ghosts of the past. You know this town like no one else." James paused again.

"I'm flattered, but I'm not sure what that has to do with anything," Ruby said.

James glanced at Mallory and Jake who were looking at him with pleasant smiles rather than giving him any encouragement in finding his words. "What I'm trying to say is that I really want you to take the job with my company."

Ruby rolled her eyes. "James, that's nice of you, but you don't have to do that just because of Pawpaw being a friend of yours."

James looked hurt. "Because of— no, Ruby. I'm not asking you because of him. I'm asking you because of *you*. With your knowledge of history and your ability to connect with it in such a special way, I could really use your help with the historical restorations of the buildings here. They have stories to tell and people should know them if they own them."

Ruby had all sorts of prepared objections for this very instance, but she suddenly couldn't think of a single one. As James had done, Ruby looked to Jake and Mallory. "Well, don't just sit there with those goofy grins on your faces," she snapped more than she meant to in her frustration. "Help me remember why I'm not the right person for the job."

Mallory laughed. "Ruby, whatever your original objections were don't hold any water now. If you don't want to do it, that's fine. Just say so, but if you're just trying to wriggle out of it because it's new and frightening, then, I'm sorry, we can't help you with that. We believe in you. And by now, you should, too."

Ruby stared back at her dumbstruck. Jake wasn't helping. He just nodded and grinned at her. Turning back to James, she tried to recover her composure. "James, I really appreciate it, but I just don't think I can."

"It's your choice, and I'll honor that, but at least tell me why not," he said gently.

There wasn't a reason. There really wasn't. Ruby had objected to it from the moment Tilly mentioned it to her and objecting had become habit. She hated to admit it, but Mallory was right. She wasn't the same person Tilly mentioned the job to. She was more connected to the town than anyone else and in a truly special way. Maybe this job was Pawpaw's way of telling her not to lose that connection. To use it instead.

"Are you sure you're not doing this for Pawpaw's sake?" she asked James.

"Positive. Look, I liked Mitch Baxter, but I certainly wouldn't hire someone I didn't think was right for a job just because I liked the guy. No, Ruby. I'm offering because you're the only one who can do it."

Ruby stared at James for a long moment, unsure what to say. Instead of answering, she looked at the Winters. They looked back at her with their eyebrows raised expectantly awaiting her answer. "You two look just like a couple of parents with a belligerent teenager."

Jake looked at Mallory. "Feels that way to me. You?"

"Oh, absolutely," Mallory agreed.

Ruby shook her head and stuck her tongue out at them. "You two are no help at all," she said petulantly which only made them look even more dramatic. "Okay, okay, will you two stop that? Fine," she said turning back to James. "I don't have a reason to give you. I used to, but like Mallory said, those don't apply anymore. This is all uncharted water for me. From the haunted mirrors to this job. The only reason I have against it is that I don't know that I can do it. I don't know that I can connect with anything other than mirrors. And I don't know if I can connect with any others of those than the ones I already have."

"Ruby," James said softly, "your gift is a bonus. You're still the best person for this job without it. I trust your expertise. I know you'll be honest with me if I'm doing something that isn't historically correct. You aren't afraid to speak your mind. I just need you to see yourself like I do. You're amazing." James blushed as he spoke the last words realizing he'd said more than he meant to.

Color rose in Ruby's cheeks. Unaccustomed to the feeling, she fought against it and was more serious in her response than she intended. "I accept the job, then."

Mallory and Jake rolled their eyes at Ruby for missing the chance to take a compliment from James, but said nothing. Instead, they congratulated her on making a good choice.

"Great," James said with a relieved smile. "Meet me here tomorrow morning at 10? We can go over details then."

"It's a date," Ruby said before realizing how that sounded. "I—I mean, yes, that works for me."

James said his goodbyes and left with a glance back over his shoulder at Ruby. Jake cleared his throat and grinned across the table at her. "I don't want to make you run from this job, but I think your new boss likes you. *Likes* you likes you."

Ruby rolled her eyes. "What are you, twelve? He's my boss and he's glad he got the employee he wanted. That's all."

"If you say so," Mallory said with a chuckle. "Come on, Jake. We should be getting back to the house. I want to change and head out to some of the antique shops. I have spaces on some walls to fill."

"No mirrors!" Ruby exclaimed.

"No mirrors," Jake and Mallory replied in unison, then slid out of the booth and left her pondering her new situation.

Once more, she had purpose. It might be different than the one she had yesterday, but it was still purpose. Would she be able to connect with things other than the mirrors? Was it psychokinesis that she had, or was it some connection to only active spirits who needed help? There was only one way to find out—get to work.

Sunlight shone on the stones of Rest Haven Cemetery. Ruby couldn't help but wander over to Tod Carter's headstone and sit with him a while. It seemed so long since he showed her what her purpose was and how to do it. Even now, she still felt the tears stinging her eyes as she thought of his face as he found his way to his eternal rest. In her mind, she knew he was at peace. In her heart, it was like missing an old friend.

Wiping tears away with her fingertips, she stood up and brushed dirt from her jeans. The grass crunched under her feet as she made her way towards the center of the cemetery where her grandfather was laid to rest. As she walked, she thought again how strange it was that his was the one spirit she had truly wanted to hear from, yet his was silent. Each of the spirits she met were tortured by their past. Grudges, messages, lost loved ones. Pawpaw had none of those things binding him to the earth. Just Ruby. But he hadn't stayed for her, either. Standing in front of the dirt mound that had settled some since she last visited, Ruby finally understood why.

He was at peace with the fact that Ruby would be just fine on her own.

The Five Bloodiest Hours

With the dead gray light of dawn came a chill wind that bit into the flesh of the wounded that clung desperately to life. Cries for water blended with fevered ramblings and convulsive gurgling. Death walked gingerly among the men, gathering the souls of those that could fight for life or liberty no longer. Gone was the wild ravaging of Death's gaping bloody maw. Instead, there was a quiet pity for the broken men. Gone were Cruelty and Terror at Death's side. Instead, Compassion and Sorrow trailed behind in Death's long shadow.

Weary soldiers carried litters laden with the dying to ambulances, walking over corpses that lay too deep for their feet to find the earth. Creeping cautiously out of their homes, citizens carried water, cloth for bandages, and wine to the battlefield. As they searched for brothers, fathers, and sons, some paused to provide relief to strangers hoping silently that someone would do the same if they came across their own loved ones. As more people emerged, the strangled cries of the dying men were joined in chorus with the grief-stricken wails of broken mothers and new widows.

Young boys, too young to fight but old enough to resent that fact, walked along the entrenchments. On one side of the berms, Union dead lay several men deep. Almost all to a man had a bullet hole in their forehead put there by the Confederates who managed to breach the fortification. Beyond those men lay the soldiers whose guns took down the Union men and forged into the enemy lines. A variety of fates more gruesome than the mercifully quick bullets to the head had met the Rebels. Some were blown to bits by muskets, some had skulls bashed in by rifle or pistol butts, and some bore the savage gouging of bayonets. As the boys walked on, the scenes of battle were on horrific display as they began to piece together the events from the positions of the fallen. Union and Confederate soldiers fell opposite one another, guns in hand, each the victim of the other. Two enemies lay in a heap, joined together in death by their bayonets still wedged in each other's chests. What had once seemed a battle of fearsome glory in the imaginations of the young boys became a tragic waste. There was no one left behind to gather the bodies of the Union dead, so the boys began to push the dirt of the berms over the stacks of bodies in the trenches creating mass graves.

Families carried their own dead home if they could, but most of the fallen were travelers through this land. No one searched for their bodies. No one mourned them on the field. Instead, shallow graves only two and a half feet deep were dug in the frozen battlefield ground by the town citizens. If they could be identified, a small wooden plank was carved with the soldier's name and regiment, then placed on the forehead of the deceased before they were covered in earth. There were too many to bury to dig proper graves of a proper depth, and the cold ground made digging even shallow ones a grueling task. The make-shift graves were well intended and would protect many until they could be found and given a proper burial, but rain was coming. Torrential rain. In a few days, much of the work would be washed away leaving limbs and faces terrifyingly exposed to the elements.

Men that had not succumbed to their injuries were either treated on the field, made comfortable in their last moments, or brought to one of the hospitals in town. As the morning gave way to afternoon, many hospitals filled to more than their capacity to help. Wagonloads of amputated limbs gave evidence of the tireless work of the surgeons who continued to serve even though exhaustion plagued them. Carnton Plantation's expansive grounds soon became the only available repository for the wounded. Even so, the bodies soon began to fill the lawn. Corpses were stacked and covered until the coverings were needed for bandages. Carnage ravaged the once stately home and grounds. Even the young mistress of the house bore the stains of blood on the hems of her skirts as she walked among the suffering giving what relief she could.

The armies had moved on. The damage done. The cause tarnished. Pride replaced with pity. Glory replaced by grief. Blood-shot tear-filled eyes opened wide, the town saw the war for the horror it really was. Pulling together to find food and supplies for the wounded, sacrificing their own for others, the people saw each other not as rivals divided by politics and ideals, but as humans. Suffering differently, but all suffering.

For a brief time, sides didn't matter. In the days following The Five Bloodiest Hours, Franklin wept.

THE END

Afterword

Growing up in the deep south of Louisiana, I heard the legends of mirrors needing to be covered when someone died or during a wake to prevent the soul from being caught in them. Mirrors are often seen as portals in the magical and metaphysical worlds. I can still remember the first time I saw a mirror that supposedly had a soul trapped inside. It was hanging in The Myrtles Plantation in St. Francisville, Louisiana. In the spots where the silvering had deteriorated, there was what could clearly be interpreted as a hand print. The legend said that no matter how many times the mirror had been re-silvered, the hand print would always reappear.

While this is the basis for the hauntings in House of Mirrors, the idea actually began with a story told about a mirror not staying on a wall at Shuff's Music in Franklin. The tour guides tell the story as if the spirit that haunts the house didn't want the mirror, causing it to fall and slide across the room over and over. My thought was, what if it was the mirror that didn't want the house? And so, a story was born.

The tale and the metaphor of the mirrors goes much deeper. Often, it is the mirrors who are the only ones who see us for who we truly are. When we look at our reflection, we interpret what we see with our own baggage and insecurities. Others may look at our reflection and not see the flaws that are glaring to us. Instead, they see what is meaningful to them. A child might look at his mother's reflection and see only the kindness in her eyes, eyes that she only sees dark circles underneath. It's all about who is looking in the mirror.

It works for places too, only here the mirror is figurative. Groups of people often won't see what they don't want to see. A sordid past behind a pristine façade, for example. However, when those in that place are made to look their past in the eyes and see it for what it truly reflects, there can be growth and understanding. We can't change the past, but we can always learn from mistakes and be inspired by successes. The trick is actually looking for them rather than turning a blind eye.

It was important for me to show the past, not from the perspective of a history textbook that highlights the military strategy of the leaders, but instead from the perspective of the people that the decisions of those leaders affected. Those with no voice to share with the people who came after them. No voice to share their struggles, heartaches, or pride. Whether they were servants, citizens, or soldiers, each played a crucial part in the battle and deserves to be recognized for their sacrifices. It's not about sides. Like Ruby says, the war is long gone and the sides are irrelevant now. It's about the humanity, for better or worse. The past is more than dates and events. It is people. All the people involved or affected, not just the leaders who have monuments, plaques, and photos in the textbooks. There is humanity in the history if we allow ourselves to look for it.

Another key to this story is the idea of finding anchorage in life. Ruby, like so many, has suffered great loss. Like many, she dedicated her life in service to those she loved. Once they are gone, a large part of her identity and self-worth are gone with them. When we lose our mooring, we can find ourselves adrift. For Ruby, she needs to take a closer look at her own reflection to help her find anchorage. Until she sees herself as capable of more than caring for the loved ones she's lost, she will continue to be adrift. We don't have to lose loved ones to feel like Ruby. Other major life events can have a similar effect: divorce, becoming an empty-nester, and so on. When these things happen, it's even more important to take a closer look at our reflections and see how the change has impacted what we see versus what is truly there.

    This book was a personal one for me to write. Having experienced significant change and loss, I can relate to Ruby's struggles to know who she is as a result of those things. I know many others will find themselves on such a journey. It was interesting to write someone else's story while also looking at myself introspectively. Within the reflection of this book, I was able to see myself differently. To see that I am not just the mess left over from a difficult journey, but someone whose past scars add to the beauty of the soul that survived what gave those scars to me. It is my hope that Ruby's story and the stories of those in the mirrors touch your soul as well.

~ Nola Nash

Acknowledgments

This was a special book to write and involved some special people. Besides my family who are always so supportive, I'd like to thank some individuals who made this book what it is.

Rebekah Stephens for meeting me every week at Onyx and Alabaster and listening to me babble on about the new fascinating facts I learned in my research and for giving me the courage to ask for a tour of the Bennett House from one of the employees there. Love ya!

Katie Brenner, the manager of Onyx and Alabaster Coffee Lounge, for her continued support and friendship as I worked for hours and sipped my slowly cooling tea. There are many staff members who make my time there a pleasure, but she's been with me the entire time and I'm happy to count this joyful young woman among my friends.

Alicia King Marshall, owner of Franklin Walking Tours, for letting me tag along on many a tour and joining me in my potty-mouthed enthusiasm for all things historic and haunted in Franklin. Go take her tour. You won't regret it.

All of the tour guides at Carter House, Carnton, and Lotz for sharing their knowledge and working so hard to preserve the stories of those on both sides of the worst time in our nation's history.

Laura Kemp, my writing partner in crime and dear friend, for all her encouragement and venting sessions as we navigate the wonderful and wacky world of publishing. I couldn't do it without her.

Pam Stack, my sistah I feel like I've always known, for her unbridled enthusiasm, support, faith, and heart-felt understanding of shared personal events. We all need people like Pam who give us strength and let us cuss and rail when we need a safe outlet. I hope you find your Pam, too.

Terry Shepherd, author, podcaster, and friend, who has lent his support in my work as well as giving some 'dad advice' now that my own daddy has passed and can't do that for me. It's an honor to be your 'Rock Star!'

My amazing therapist, who shall remain nameless for obvious reasons, who helped me see myself in the journey of this book and talked with me about what different elements brought to my own experience with life, Franklin, and most importantly, myself. I'm grateful every day for her compassion and guidance.

There are so many more who have encouraged me and made this all possible. You know who you are and how much you mean to me. None of what I have achieved would be possible without the army of support from far and wide. Much, much love to you all!

About the Author

Originally from south Louisiana, Nola Nash now makes her home in Brentwood Tennessee, and spends most of her time in Franklin. Growing up in Baton Rouge, she spent long hours onstage or backstage in the local community theaters. Her biggest writing inspiration was the city of New Orleans that gave her at an early age a love of the magic, mystery, and history.

When she isn't writing, Nola is an online high school instructional coach or interviewing authors on Dead Folks Tales and BYOB on Authors on the Air Global Radio Network. She also considers tacos and coffee major food groups.

Location Reference

Carter House
1140 Columbia Ave. Franklin, TN 37064
https://boft.org/carter-house

Carnton Plantation
1345 Eastern Flank Circle Franklin, TN 37064
https://boft.org/classic-tour-carnton

Lotz House Museum
1111 Columbia Ave. Franklin, TN 37064
https://www.lotzhouse.com/

Bennett House
134 4th Ave. N Franklin, TN 37064
https://visitfranklin.com/see-and-do/bennett-house-bagbey-house-antiques

Rest Haven Cemetery
324 4th Ave. N Franklin, TN 37064

Onyx and Alabaster
234 Public Square Franklin, TN 37064
https://onyxandalabaster.com/

Gallery 202 (Clouston Hall)
202 2nd Ave. S Franklin, TN 37064
https://gallery202art.com/

The Heirloom Shop
404 Main Street Franklin, TN 37064
https://theheirloomshoptn.com/

Mellow Mushroom
317 Main Street Franklin, TN 37064
https://mellowmushroom.com/location/tn-franklin-317-main-st-ste-100-37064/?utm_source=gmb&utm_medium=organic&utm_campaign=Franklin-TN&utm_content=4

Savory Spice Shop
324 Main Street Franklin, TN 37064
https://www.savoryspiceshop.com/

Rock Paper Scissors
317 Main Street Franklin, TN 37064
https://www.rockpaperscissor.com/

Historic Franklin Presbyterian Church
435 Main Street Franklin, TN 37064
https://www.historicfranklinpc.org/

Pope-Moran House
120 3rd Ave. S Franklin, TN 37064
https://visitfranklin.com/see-and-do/the-moran-house-office-building

Gray's on Main restaurant and bar

LOCATION REFERENCE

332 Main Street Franklin, TN 37064
https://graysonmain.com/

Landmark Booksellers
114 E. Main Street Franklin, TN 37064
https://www.landmarkbooksellers.com/

Winstead Hill Park
4023 Columbia Ave. Franklin, TN 37064
https://www.franklintn.gov/government/departments-k-z/parks/park-locations/winstead-hill

For more about the charming town of Franklin, TN visit the following:
Franklin Walking Tours: https://franklinwalkingtours.com/
Lovely Franklin: https://lovelyfranklin.com/
Visit Franklin: https://visitfranklin.com/

Also by Nola Nash

Crescent City Moon

Crescent City Sin

Traveler

Made in the USA
Middletown, DE
08 January 2023

20637333R00168